The Last Genet

THE LAST GENET

A Writer in Revolt

HADRIEN LAROCHE

Translated by David Homel

Arsenal Pulp Press

Vancouver

Originally published in France as *Le dernier Genet*, Copyright © 1997 by Éditions du Seuil

THE LAST GENET
by Hadrien Laroche
Translation copyright © 2010 by David Homel

ARSENAL PULP PRESS
#101 – 211 East Georgia Street
Vancouver, BC V6A 1Z6
Canada
arsenalpulp.com

This book was published with the support of the French Ministry of Culture—National Center of the Book. Ouvrage publié avec le concours du Ministère français de la Culture—Centre national du livre.

The publisher also gratefully acknowledges the support of the Government of Canada (through the Canada Book Fund) and the Government of British Columbia (through the Book Publishing Tax Credit Program) for its publishing activities.

Translator's note: Where previously existing translations of foreign-language works are available, every effort has been made to use and credit them. The spelling of certain proper nouns has been standardized for easier reading. This translation was done by Enrico Caouette, Jacob Homel, and David Homel, under the direction of David Homel.

Cover photo © 2010 The Richard Avedon Foundation

Printed and bound in Canada

Library and Archives Canada Cataloguing in Publication:

Laroche, Hadrien, 1963-
    The last Genet : a writer in revolt / Hadrien Laroche ; translated by David Homel.

Translation of: Le dernier Genet: histoire des hommes infâmes.
Includes bibliographical references and index.
ISBN 978-1-55152-365-1

    1. Genet, Jean, 1910-1986--Last years. 2. Genet, Jean, 1910-1986--Political and social views. 3. Authors, French--20th century--Biography. I. Homel, David II. Title.

PQ2613.E53Z76313 2010   842'.912   C2010-904251-4

CONTENTS

Introduction: Narrow Straits

In 1968, Jean Genet crossed the Strait of Gibraltar, reached Paris, and strode into the courtyard of the Sorbonne. There he saw, next to the red booth of the Maoists, the Palestinians' set-up. What color was it? He signed the first of a series of interventions, tracts, prefaces, stories, and political writings. Seventeen years later, in 1986, *Prisoner of Love*, his last book, was published posthumously. The writer is buried in Larache, in Morocco.

Between these two crossings of the Strait, Genet "hopped everywhere things were hopping in the world."[1] He was seen in Chicago and Jordan, he traveled to Strasbourg and Chartres, in France. He met parties and movements and the men who made them: the Black Panthers in the United States, the Red Army Faction in Germany, the Palestinians in the Middle East. Everywhere he went, he saw the disinherited. It was in Vienna, in 1983, where he expressed his understanding of the past and the future translation of an experience whose rules he would set down. He spent fifteen years on the side of men from everywhere, and began writing his last book. "When I finished with writing, I was thirty-four, thirty-five years old. But that was a dream. It was in any case a daydream, a reverie. I wrote in prison. Once I became free, I was lost. And I didn't find myself again in reality, in the real world, until I was with two revolutionary movements, the Black Panthers and the Palestinians. So then I submitted myself to the real world. I was acting in relation to the real world and no longer to the grammatical world [...]."[2] The first act—submission to a real world—led to another. It wasn't by looking at the Palestinians or the Black Panthers, but by remembering the change of attitude of the Algerians in Paris after the independence of their country that he could say, "to explode forth out of shame is easy."[3] In reality, it is a single gesture, with both hands, moving from one world to the next, a movement out of unhappy captivity: getting out, as you might get out of prison, or yourself, or leave some port. To speak of that gesture is to open yourself to the possibility of a story wanting, in itself, to be liberated.

This book is not a monograph about Genet. The limits I've imposed on myself—the period from 1968 to 1986—are not definitive. The period involves a series of actions: those of the writer's, those of the movements'. Before that, there was Genet's unwillingness to sign the "Manifeste des 121" demanding the right to refuse a draft notice for the war in Algeria in 1960; that is another beginning to this story. His judgment of the occupation of Lebanon, which he witnessed in 1982, must be understood in relation to two others he experienced: the German occupation of Paris (1940) and the French occupation of Syria (1930). We'll go further: if he decided to choose as his father a member of the Black Panthers whom he met in the United States, and his mother a Palestinian woman of Ajloun in whose house he spent the night, in Jordan, if this choice has political consequences, then we have to return to his experience at a public school in 1920, the day Genet, an abandoned child, could not describe the house in which he lived. Later on, this story will echo in what remains as the writer's legacy.

In 1977, at the turning point of this period, Michel Foucault undertook a project: he wanted to speak of the "Lives of Infamous Men."[4] This historical project was concerned with the seventeenth century in France, most particularly the prison archives of the years between

1660 and 1760 in that country, though he added that it could be applied to other times and other places. Foucault wanted to describe the political life of these monstrous abominations—the madman, the sodomite, the atheist; men filled with violence—from the tiny traces they left behind, "the discourses that in misfortune and rage they carried out with power." Whereas Foucault gave up the project, Genet took it at face value. Or, rather, the infamy that haunted the writer found, in those years, a way of speaking its name and living its experience. Yet Foucault said some time later, in 1984, that "the misfortune of men must never remain a mute vestige of politics."[5] Genet, who at that time had just met Foucault the philosopher, would be faithful to that thought.

In this perspective, the last incarnation of Genet means *the one at the end*, the echo of the writer's last period, when the man attempted political action by the means the poet uses: language. But the *last* also signifies the *lowest*, the way we speak of the lowest of the low, if the black and Palestinian experiences of Genet do not exclude war, the incitement to murder, and the hatred of the enemy.

Men of infamy, the last Genet among them, are not men lacking in dignity, but rather those who struggle against the shame of being silenced.

"When a traveler comes from abroad, from Morocco, for example, he may read an article in *L'Humanité* on Cohn-Bendit [...]."[6] This sentence begins Genet's first political article. "When I hear the word 'man,' I run to him at once..."[7] Thus spake Erasmus in a text written in 1517 entitled *Querela Pacis*. To a nearly perfect degree, Genet's political writing expresses the same concern as Erasmus does. Both may exclaim, "The man of whom I speak is struggling against himself." My hypothesis is that Genet's political project embraces the movement of this hurried impulse; it makes Genet come running in the name of man, concerned. An explanation of the name of man—that's the political will of the last Genet's incarnation, the direction of his intent.

Meetings with movements, dialogues with youth and an old man, friendships, and politics all involve a certain relationship with ancestors, with tradition and history. These exchanges help us understand Genet's metamorphosis, and this is the objective of Part One of the book. Investigations into brutality, terrorism, and war—the issues of the concept of violence—aim to preserve the possibility of revolt without giving in to terror. This way of looking at fascism is also a way of checking the state of poetry in the world: Part Two of the book is concerned with these issues. Genet's research into the fables, often religious in nature, used by movements and his reflection on fictions, at the origin of his adventure, will constitute the final part of our study, for they will move Genet to attack evangelism in politics.

Chronologically, but not only and not really, these are three *circles of matter*—the critique of friendship, of violence, and of history—that each time recreate a genealogical line. These chapters seek to establish a path that is not the only, nor the final, one. I wanted to find the means of seeing the grain of sand, yes, but also the sea in which the writer drowns.

Endnotes

1. Jacques Derrida, *Glas* (1974) (Paris: Denoël/Gonthier, 1981), 50.
2. "Une rencontre avec Jean Genet," *Revue d'études palestiniennes*, Fall 1986; republished in *The Declared Enemy* (*DE*), translated by Jeff Fort (Stanford: Stanford University Press, 2004), 239–40.
3. "Four Hours in Shatila," *Revue d'études palestiniennes* 6 (January 1, 1983); *DE*, 225.
4. Michel Foucault, "The Lives of Infamous Men," in *The Essential Works of Foucault 1954–1984* (New York: The New Press, 2000), 3:157–175.
5. *Libération*, June 30, 1984.
6. "Les Maîtresses de Lénine," *Le Nouvel Observateur*, May 30, 1968; *DE*, 18.
7. Erasmus, *Collected Works of Erasmus: Literary and Educational Writings* (*ER*), (Toronto: University of Toronto Press, 1989), 5:296.

Part One

The End of Youth

1 | The End of Youth

First, the dance, by which all begins. It's joyful, and Genet speaks of his happiness: "Even naked, without any frills, my ten fingers have a life, a dance, that's already independent of me."[1] We don't see the writer dancing. Yet he's part of the dance of the times. The end of youth is also the childhood of an experience; it is prolonged in *Prisoner of Love* where its rules are discovered. To refuse to feel the rhythm of the dancer's fingers is to miss the happiness of the writer's emergence into the world. Dancing is the way of coming out of oneself. Shot through with eroticism, a "funereal chant," the dance expresses joy and mourning. It doesn't exhaust the meaning of the last book; the psychedelic, in those days, determines it. It's just a way of beginning anew. Why psychedelic? Because in full light, it is invisible.

THE DANCE

In 1968 in Paris, Daniel Cohn-Bendit launched the dance, a wave of colors and rhythms that traveled the world. It would upset things even in Egypt, when Gamal Abdel Nasser died. Cohn-Bendit's dance, at the origin of the movement, will run until the dance of death, September 28, 1970. From Cohn-Bendit, for his first political intervention, to Nasser, in 1970, with whom his last book opens, a shock that Genet witnessed shook the world. It will last on this planet until at least 1977.

Street demonstrations, the murder of a boy, the death of a chief of state; the dance is political.

The students in Paris dance. Genet arrives in Paris, he's returning from Morocco. Later, he wrote, "The nocturnal games in the streets [in May '68] have more in common with dance than with combat."[2] The demonstrators dance in Chicago. During the Democratic Convention in August 1968, during Genet's first trip to America, he sees this: "At about ten o'clock Saturday evening, the young people have lit a sort of bonfire in Lincoln Park. Nearby, hardly visible in the darkness, a fairly dense crowd has gathered under the trees to listen to a group of black musicians—flutes and bongos."[3] The following Tuesday night, at the Chicago Coliseum to celebrate Lyndon Johnson's Unbirthday—an event Genet attended—3,000 people danced in front of the stage where two guitarists and a drummer with a ten-piece drum kit played. The musicians, with their hair down to their chests, looked like women, and they were loud.[4] During the same period, Jalal Mansur Nuriddin created the Last Poets: "We were living out the end of the era of poems and essays, the word was without weapons, so we were the last poets." Between the two movements, the exchange took place, from words to weapons, from weapons to words, through the writer.

A man dances near the camp at Baqa, in Jordan. Genet stayed with the Palestinians for the first time in 1970. Sitting beside a Toyota with a tape player, to the sound of the Rolling Stones, he watched his friend: "Mubarak, barefoot and wearing only his trousers, was dancing. He needn't have been ashamed, either, for he danced very well, mixing rock style with Sudanese [...]."[5] Dance circulated throughout the world. In America, hippies danced to music played by blacks. In Jordan, Mubarak danced to a Rolling Stones tape. The Rolling Stones, as his friend Mohammed Choukri reminded Genet in 1969 when the latter visited him in Tangiers, traveled to Morocco to record. Brian Jones went into the Moroccan Rif to listen to, then record, in the little village of Jahjouka, *The Pipes of Pan at Jahjouka*.[6]

Fazia danced on the edge. Fazia Ben Ali was the sister of Djelali, a boy murdered in the Goutte-d'Or district, the Arab quarter of Paris, in 1972. Fazia, the daughter of immigrants, was young, a dancer, a writer, and much more. Genet met her with Catherine von Bülow. Both accompanied Genet in those years. In a café in the nineteenth *arrondissement*, Catherine watched Fazia: "As I was talking, I looked toward the room at the back where Fazia was dancing like crazy. She was glowing and she seemed happy. She looked like a kid set free among adults."[7] Fazia Ben Ali, born in 1958, was fourteen years old at the time, a kid "very sure of herself, a kind of mockingbird, a little bit of a tease, but in a nice way, naïve." And Cohn-Bendit, a "kid, a friendly pain in the ass," wrote Genet, was at the origin of the movement. The girl and the kid danced together at the time.

In the desert, the dance is illuminated. "The Bedouin dance is chaste because it takes place between men, mostly holding one another by the elbow or forefinger. But it's also erotic because it takes place between men, and because it's performed before the ladies."[8] Erotic and chaste, the dance speaks of an encounter that will never be. Ten years later, because it is more like rock'n'roll than combat, Genet will mock the events of May 1968. If singing is closer to dance, then dance can help lose the war in America. He declared, "You are losing this war because you don't listen to the singing of the hippies."[9] In Jordan, the dance of the Bedouins that he witnessed seemed to have power over the Hashemite army and, beyond it, America and, before it, the Palestinians: "If this severe and simple dance had continued it would have put the Palestinians to rout."[10] Both gentle and violent, the dance triumphs over war by miming it. Its joy is obvious. In Paris, Fazia Ben Ali dances her dead brother. In Chicago, the demonstrators, to the sound of the bongos, throw a party for a dead man. He's the "boy who disappeared," seventeen years old. Indian or Black, murdered by the police, I could not find out his name. On the cover of *Esquire*, the issue with Genet's article about the Democratic Convention, we see him standing by the feet of the boy's body played by a student. Young people aren't dancing because they're happy. Mubarak isn't young, Nasser is a dead man.

The dance surrounds him, young and old, and Genet the writer is born anew. It is movement, it travels through men, from the hippies to the Sudanese, and he recognizes it as his own. Genet didn't like youth *for itself*. It wasn't fixed or frozen as something eternal; change transforms it. A running dance, not only it and not only youth, that's what interests him. Dance is a force that disturbs order; it moves the world.

"To put it simply: the Guarani sing and dance and tears fill my eyes," wrote Genet in a 1972 article published in a provincial magazine.[11] If it wasn't political at the beginning of this experience, would he take the trouble to write this article on dance, and in particular on one performed by this Indian group from South America, decimated after the Spanish Conquest of Paraguay, a group on tour in France at the time of his writing?

The Guarani speak of a "disordered era," of "misery," and of man "bent to the earth." Dance is both the consequence of this era without orientation—as the situation of these Indians and of a certain current of thought displays—but it is also what can disorient the era in another meaning. Orienting toward the action that it already is, for example. And so, breaking the thread of time. Then, logically, it speaks of a misfortune. The dance that girds the world first girds the misfortune of the world. The way the Guarani have of dancing displays a people. The Indian people are in a state of misery. "They show us that any man can dance and sing," wrote Genet. Misery travels the world. People, by dancing, display the misery from which they arise, alone. The people have the power; the expression belongs to the liturgy of the times. Intellectuals no longer speak for or in the place of others, or so it is noisily expounded. Whereas here, the reiteration of an era is not at stake. No one is talking for the Guarani. Much better: they are speaking of themselves, without words. They are alone, dancing, pounding the earth. Humus is humble, as is dance, definitively. The contact with the earth is a lesson, like a practice of humility. Of a conversation with Palestinian students in Paris in 1973, Genet wrote, "The artist is humble, and artistic work increasingly becomes an experience of humility. I'm not saying stupidity, but humility."[12] Youth is not fool-ish, but humble. Between youth and adults, who remember the past, there is transmission through dance. After having seen what he saw, Genet returns, tears in his eyes. The humility of dance is not opposed to stupidity, but to power, as strength is to weakness. Humble means the earth, the desert that becomes the ground of experience. Between the era (disoriented), the world (misfortune) and the Indians and the young (humble), Genet captures a movement at the beginning of what is, for him, a rebirth. His act encounters dance, and he is isolated from his contemporaries. Before the grace of the Guarani, the syntax of he who describes it: therein he finds the *new*. It must be obvious that the praise of dance is not the circumstantial cult of youth, but an invita-tion, for all eras, to dance. Time must be experienced differently, in the here and now.

In the Arab world such as it appears in *Prisoner of Love*, the death of Nasser in 1970 sets things in motion. Returning to the event later in the book, Genet wrote, "No one watching the television program I mentioned at the beginning of this book actually saw Nasser's funeral, though they may have agreed to say they did."[13] Why this complic-ity? Genet's eye goes for unseen realities. Better still, he chooses to highlight this event over another: the death of Charles de Gaulle, in November of the same year.

Genet's last book begins with this dance of death in Egypt, a cor-tege that haunts Genet to the point that he felt "swept into a mael-strom, swirled around and yet soothed by strong yet gentle arms."[14] The memory of dance may come from the first pages of Gérard de Nerval's work, *Voyage en Orient* (1851), one of the last books that Leila Shahid brought to Genet's room.[15] Nerval is half asleep; he thinks that "someone is carrying him to the grave in a manner both ceremonial and burlesque [...] a sort of patriarchal gaiety and mythological sad-ness combining into a strange concert, wherein lamentable religious chants form the basis of a clownish tune that might set down the rhythm for a Corybantic dance." He wakes up and concludes, "It was a wedding, there can be no mistake."[16] For the traveler who crossed the Strait, nothing separates the wake from the wedding: birth and death, the changing of the child to an old man, that's what mattered to Genet. The opening of his book captures both the moment and the impossible covenant with history, belonging as much to the times as to memory.

But the collusion of poetic and political memories possesses a clear historical meaning: "The cradle, the football, you could call it the coffin [Nasser's], pitched and tossed in the air [...]." And later: "Despite the guard, two or three thousand feet, relieved of their load, danced on the grave till morning."[17] Dancing on Nasser's casket means the end of unity; it begins a process of mourning, launches "the era of nations." Nasser's great laughter echoes one final time after his death, opening a new era and the book that relates it. Let's remember what was called the Suez Crisis. Shortly before this story begins, in 1956, Nasser announced, "'We shall take back our rights, for the canal is the property of Egyptian[s] ...' And, to the ovations of the crowd, Nasser ended his speech with a loud burst of laughter."[18] His laughter would be transmitted via La Voix des Arabes, a radio station the CIA gave to Egypt; it would travel to North Africa, then echo further, all the way to Paris, then London, where it would generate an angry response. And then war. His laughter must still be echoing in his casket and in the book that tells the story, trampled by the dancers.

The first burial and the last book: a new era begins. The child grown old falls with Nasser's cradle, the kids stumble with the Raïs' casket; the end of (Arab) unity, the end of youth, enter history!

At the time, for Genet and a certain stratum of youth in Goutte d'Or and Cairo, historically the dance meant this: not only do men turn away from the Western model, not only do they assert their national vocation, but they show—by dancing in the streets, in a park, or on a casket—that a society can secrete a story that belongs to them.

OUTRAGEOUS HAIR

The life and times of Genet coincide for a moment with the experience of the haircut. The attention paid to hair, as to dance, provides a rule for his last book; it thickens, it pushes back borders. Through hair, the Black movement meets the Palestinians, and together the book and the movements push back limits.

The culture of hair is most obvious in the United States. It had something of an outrageous aspect in that country. Genet's work was to transfer attention from the most visible—white hippies with their long hair—to the invisible: the blacks and their Afros. And this, without separating the expressions of young people that could be described, but only temporarily, as provocation. In a section of *Prisoner of Love* about the Black Panthers, he points out that, "I believe it was in the sixties that the fashion started, timidly at first and then boldly, for young men to wear their hair down to their shoulders. Any style would do, apparently: long; medium length; with a fringe; straight, black and greasy; flowing; all over the place, brown and frizzy; blonde and curly [...]. This fashion, carried to extremes and even beyond in England, was born in California and grew out of the American army's reverses in Vietnam."[19] The first determination of the times—the 1960s—took on the aspect of fashion. The writer's work is to extract, as for the dancer, what belongs to the times. Immediately, politics, here in the form of the war, shows the work of extraction. Hippie hair is a legacy, forbidden and inverted, but a legacy all the same of the crew cut, the GI style that soldiers wear everywhere. Hippies and blacks wanted to transform this legacy. The latter wanted to become visible. Genet asks the hair question early on, in 1971, returning from the United States: "The condition of blacks in the USA? One title sums it up. *Invisible Man*, the name of Ralph Ellison's book. The black is nonexistent, society doesn't want to see him, he must not be seen. In the US, you can see a lot of blacks with extravagant hair [...]."[20] Ralph Ellison, born in 1914—*Invisible Man* came out in 1952—passed into the world of the invisible on April 16, 1994. He fought invisibility. As a black man, he wanted to appear in the world; as an intellectual, he wanted to enter the ghetto. He failed on both accounts. Later, he wrote another book, *Shadow and Act* (1964). In the shadow of Ellison, the writer, and in this shadow the common concern of all the disinherited: to become visible. Visibility and ridicule, and so despair: these were the features of Genet's research at the time. What is futile, or rather what is fragile, returns in the form of what is serious, without losing any of its humor. The slogan of the times expresses the issue of hair: *Black is beautiful*. From those years on, men who had been hidden now became visible. In other words, provocation by hair is the visible manifestation of a political inversion of values. If it were nothing more, it would remain a simple provocation, but the writer will not let that happen. Simple provocation does not belong to the last Genet or the movements at issue. It is a new way for blacks to be seen.

What form does the attitude toward hair take among the fedayeen in Jordan? In 1983, Genet declared to those who came to talk to him about the Palestinians, "You know, Arafat is bald, he has no hair. And there are fringes on a kaffiyeh. And I remember he always did this, as if the fringes were like hair. I'm talking about this with you now. But it wouldn't occur to me to write a piece on Arafat's handling of the fringes of his kaffiyeh."[21]

Around the same time he wrote about Arafat's kaffiyeh in his last book, in a description of the head of the Palestine Liberation Organization (PLO).[22] Before that episode, he recalled, "The lengthy ceremony had begun. [...] They took turns to be shaved. The whole thing usually lasted from eight o'clock to ten, and took place three times a week."[23] Even beneath the trees, where the fedayeen waited their turn, the scene in Jordan did not have the visible vegetal quality it had in the United States; instead, it followed a schedule, an order, and a ranking. Different spaces and times were at stake here. The street in America alongside the Black Panthers did not follow the same rhythm as the desert bases of the fedayeen in Jordan. The discipline of the latter group is simply military, not religious, and typical of an armed camp.

Hamza is the Palestinian son described in Genet's last book. He—a fedayee encountered in Irbid, Jordan, in 1970—and his mother form a couple, more like a pietà that will become the North Star for the Palestinians. Genet slept one night in the boy's room while he was away. Subjective, political, and religious, the couple, "Hamza-His Mother," would return.[24] Hamza would not break the rules: his hair is cut regularly. Speaking of his mother, Genet would write about the use of henna: "Arab fiancées and brides use a lot of henna. It fades from the skin more quickly than from the hair."[25] Traces of henna in the woman's dandruff was a subject of interest for him. Genet saw her again in 1984, after fourteen years; for one night, she would be his mother.

Hair fashions speak for the differences in time and place—loose in America, ordered in the Middle East—and can express a conflict in manners. Nothing in common between these universes and their two separate movements: black madness and fedayeen order. Genet's point of view, at first amused by this arborescence, turns critical when contemplating this sculpted mass. We might recall his hardening attitude toward youth and his tendency toward discipline. At first, the students of May '68 were a model, then they were left behind in favor of workers and then the Panthers; finally his praise was reserved for the severe austerity of the fedayee soldier. This radicalization, linear in time and obvious, of the meanings attributed to youth, is quite harsh. Life is not a continuum. Youth is made up of differences and transformations. The various forms of youth, like the hairstyles of its members, are not determined by a forward progress, but need to be constantly redefined, with all their variations and directions. Between the movements and between them and Genet, there are gazes, exchanges, and transmissions, and his writing works to assemble all of that to speak for the era at large.

Everything changed, and this is why: "The laughing Panthers wore a dense furry sex on their heads."[26] At the end of the second passage on the Black Panthers in *Prisoner of Love*, we find Genet's last word on the subject, and it is akin to panic. The paragraph ends this way: "Nothing can be as it was before. Up to 1793 the king = the king. After January 21, the king = the guillotine, and the princess de Lamballe = a head on a pike, sovereignty = tyranny, and so on. Letters, words, a whole dictionary changed."[27] In his time, Georges Bataille gave the political translation of this value inversion; Genet provides the hair version. I don't know if Genet read Bataille. If we think he did, we might understand a completely new political meaning. *L'Anus solaire* was written in 1927, and was reprinted in 1970. In it, Bataille wrote, "This eruptive force accumulates in those who are necessarily situated below. Communist workers appear to the bourgeois to be as ugly and dirty as hairy sexual organs, or lower parts; sooner or later there will be a scandalous eruption in the course of which the asexual noble heads of the bourgeois will be chopped off."[28] Nothing less than that. The similarity of thought is striking: the same premises, the hairy parts, by the same movement, inversion, reaching the same ends, the heads of the powerful chopped off. We might want to give Genet a similar tendency: idealism turned into materialism, and the lofty cast down, with severed heads providing the way. One difference? Bataille's Communist workers become Genet's Black Panthers. The change-around means that the hierarchical structure that supports it lives on: top/bottom in the physical order; governing/governed in the political order. This method leaves the form of the world unchanged, and idealizes those on the bottom. Georges Bataille remains in provocation through hair; Genet's Afro period doesn't escape the simple recourse to infamy.

Next to the Black Panthers and the fedayeen—but also a Palestinian mother and two Gypsy girls—the writer, who has been swept into the dance of the movements participates in an experience whose result is panic. It's based on brute facts and realities: the Black Panthers, in Genet's eyes, but not only his, invented hair panic that, since the 1970s, hasn't stopped growing. It has become a fabulous means of becoming visible. Panic isn't inversion; from all sides it propagates itself, fertile, gaining ground. Through panic, what was only provocation becomes a movement. The dictionary is corrected. Then a second way appears, along with dance, for what we could call a slight movement toward black, the color and rhythm of metamorphosis: Europe is no longer the center. The hair experience is a form of youth; it doesn't belong to it, Genet contemplates it, a curious sway moves it through the world. If provocation (hair-based or not) seems to be an oblique progress, actually a head-on revision, panic (Afro or not) is a dance that leaves nothing after its passage. In joy, provocation brings laughter to life, while panic is a necessary translation of survival, the condition of people under the gun.

Through hair, Genet experiences a ritual passage, and enters into the world of young men. He himself was twice the subject of a hair-cutting scene: once in the United States with the Panthers, the other time with the fedayeen in Jordan—all space and time expressed in *Prisoner of Love* is influenced by the experience.

Hair I: "David and Geronimo took me to a barber in the ghetto for a shave, and the barber was a black woman of about fifty with mauve hair. She's never shaved a White before. The men—black, of course—who were waiting their turn talked to me about Bobby Seale, whom they'd watched on TV the night before."[29] David Hilliard was Genet's friend; Elmer Pratt, alias Geronimo, appears in this passage only, but in a manner that leaves nothing to chance. Genet defended Bobby Seale, who was in prison at the time. All were members of the Black Panther Party. The scene took place in the spring of 1970 in New York. The energy, intelligence, and fireworks of Bobby Seale's speeches from prison inspired a generation of radicals, as Hilliard points out.[30] In this context of hair politics, the scene at the barbershop is a way of entering the ghetto.

    Genet participated in a public occupation. In a single movement, the scene displays belonging and exclusion. He's the only white man ever shaved by this woman. It is a moment of community, not communion. More than that: the men discuss what they saw the previous evening, the Bobby Seale speech on TV. Genet saw Nasser's burial on the small screen as well. Later, but at this time, he is already part of the war. In the section before the haircutting scene, he described the speech and his surprise. At first, he didn't understand what Seale was saying, as the TV was in the kitchen. "Suddenly, and it was suddenly, I understood: Seale was talking not to me but to the ghetto." Now Genet is in the ghetto, with people he sees and is listening to. The following comments are heard in the barbershop: "Did you come from France to listen to him or to help him?—It's up to the blacks to get him out.—It mustn't be the whites who do it. That would be another victory for them over us."[31] The writer can't make the decision to liberate Seale and the witness. By recognizing his incomprehension (he doesn't belong to the ghetto), by writing it, he becomes witness to the ghetto. *Nothing can be as it was before* means that Genet is the only witness to the ghetto. The political translation of the haircutting scene—to become a witness—spills over onto its political meaning: the witness's humble position established by the barber.

Geronimo ji-jaga Elmer Pratt, arrested December 8, 1970, was released from prison on June 10, 1997. He and his comrade Mumia Abu Jamal lived in solitary confinement. They refused to cut their hair.[32] Sentenced to death on August 17, 1995, Mumia Abu Jamal had the sentence suspended indefinitely. His meeting with Genet lives on today: "The fact that I write at all reveals the utter failure of their intimidation tactics—as does the fact that you read."[33]

Hair II: "What role was there for me under those golden leaves? My only importance, but it was a great importance, was this: because of me the fedayeen used to gather together, tired but cheerful, usually in the evening. I think the first assembly was organized by Ferraj: I'd mentioned that my white hair was too long. 'A fedayee can turn his hand to anything. Sit down on this stone and I'll turn you into a hippie.' He said it very ingeniously, the French words for 'hair' and 'stone' entwined with others in English and classical Arabic. [...] [Genet answers in the same language:] 'Why did you say you're going to turn me into a hippie?' I asked him, used the same language he had. 'Because now your hair will be down on your shoulders every month.' They all laughed. And not only my shoulders but my knees as well were covered with snippets of white hair. The first stars came out, timidly at first, then in droves all over the still purple sky. It was more beautiful than I can say. And Jordan is only the Middle East! By now my hair was coming down to my feet."[34] Ferraj was a fedayee in the Baqa camp. Here is a situation that will occur again—the opportunity, the evening, an assembly—but this was Genet's first night spent with the fedayeen.

One little joke, and Genet is turned into a hippie. All he could get was a little trim! In one of the articles that describe his stay in the United States, there is a photo that shows him next to Jerry Rubin, the apostle of LSD and one of the leaders of the anti-Vietnam War movement, who died on November 28, 1994. The caption reads: "The French poet (bald) and Jerry Rubin (hairy)." Just that quickly, Genet is transformed into an ancestor, with hair reaching down to his shoes. Taking his place in the shaving chair, he enters the community of the young. Humble, his importance is measured by his aptitude for metamorphosis. The assembly, the exchange between the young and the old man, and the dialogue that ensues, makes the writer a witness.

At the beginning of this story, Genet wonders: what will be my role? A reflection on paternity surrounds the haircutting scene in Jordan. Four pages earlier in the same book: "What did it mean, my pink and white presence among them? This: for two months I was to be David [Hilliard]'s son. I had a black father thirty years younger than myself."[35] A few pages further on, his questioning of "the relationship between Hamza and his mother"[36] provides the link. Bringing the two hair-cutting scenes together, he attempts an answer: "But what did they mean to do with this grey head, with its grey skin, grey unshaven beard—this grey, pink, round head forever in their midst? Use it as a witness?"[37] An old man gets his white hair cut by a group of young people beneath Jordan's purple sky, as purple as the barber's hair in New York. One moment he's a hippie, the next, an *ancestor.*

Genet is gently dubbed twice. Shaved, his hair cut, Genet is made witness. His godfathers are the Panthers and the Palestinians, the young who surround him. Here is a scene of transmission, but in reverse. The father is younger than the son, knighted by one younger than he is; he could be the father of his forbears. These are exchanges: from the young to Genet, witness to the movements, from the old man to the young. Young again. Who? The old man. They are grateful. Who? The young. Between the first and the latter, the legacy travels. His beard has already grown back. A moment of life fled.

NEMBUTAL

"Americans, are you asleep?"[38] Genet asked the question in August 1968 after attending the Democratic National Convention in Chicago, and the question brings us to the issue of drugs. LSD, heroin, and Nembutal belong to the times. The drugs aren't an object of the times but a way of measuring them, a purple-colored way of sensing temporality. The movements develop a critique of the drug experience, especially the Panthers. Yet Genet moved through that period of youth and the world in general going up or coming down, like the psychedelic young man's experience, in a state of otherness. The body has limits of its own.

The witness experiences the times; what's important is to take the trip. Genet boasts that no policeman is aware of "the natural but invisible route—like the one for drugs—that led me, through an underground or celestial pathway, into the United States."[39] Traveling in those days meant a trip, but Genet changed the meaning of moving. As early as 1970 he wrote, "It's not the police who put an end to drugs in the black ghettos, it's the Black Panther Party itself."[40] In *Prisoner of Love,* the point is made this way: "Young Blacks ... replaced marijuana with outrageous hair-styles."[41] Another critique ran this way: "Police were therefore able to hide the true meaning of their intentions behind unqualified pretexts; trials based on drug, murder, and conspiracy charges. The fact of the matter is that they were trying to massacre those responsible for the Black Panther Party."[42] For these young people, it's important to break through the confusion and separate the sedative (a way of slowing rebellion) from the psychedelic (an attempt to promote it by all means). After all, you can recognize a cop by "his enormous thighs [...] high on LSD."[43]

Continuously, from 1968 to 1986, Genet moved in a cloud of Nembutal. After a filmed appeal for the liberation of Angela Davis, a member of the Panthers and a friend, Genet met a journalist from the French daily *Le Monde*. On October 17, 1970, Genet admitted to his state of mind: "Of course I'm not quite here. I never am. I'm somewhere else most of the time. First because I'm old and emotional, and I'm full of Nembutal. I'm stoned. I told them so."[44] To confuse the drug state with sleeping, to call that "not being all here," to conclude that the syntax of the last incarnation of Genet is structured like a dream—that means nothing; the charge is as vague as the dream we're accusing him of. Is he over the hill? This book begins in an atmosphere of confidence I've granted to the writer's intelligence. Old age, the poetry of it, that's what we want to discover. What does memory remember? The end of youth is a step in this questioning.

From the other side of the voyage, in Beirut, on September 13, 1982, Genet finds himself with another woman to whom he remained a faithful friend. Leila Shahid of the Palestinian Authority in France described the moment: "He showed up half-stoned from Nembutal, his pants hanging off him, unshaven, his hair standing on end, he didn't say a thing, he looked at me and then he said, I love them. I asked, Who?"[45] The answer did not come. An unquiet love, a form of relentless emotion, the simple exhaustion of a writer always on the alert—the stupor of T.E. Lawrence in the Hejaz Desert is close to this

state. Ill with dysentery, lying in his tent, the British officer wrote of
his campaign with the Arabs against the Turks in 1918: "My brain
became sick of unsupported thinking and had to be dragged to its
work by an effort of will, and went off into a doze whenever that effort
was relaxed."[46] Around these two women under threat—Angela Davis
and Leila Shahid—grew an emotion lasting twenty years that took the
form of a dual disposition that lengthens it rather than being its effect:
"old and emotional." Frail, it described an immense tension. In one
case, Genet called for the liberation of Angela Davis; in the other, he
offered an attentive prayer: September 13, 1982, war in Lebanon, the
Israeli Army enters Beirut, killings at the Sabra and Shatila Palestinian
refugee camps by Phalangist militia. His appeal came from a state of
deepest torpor. His old age and endless travels formed this emotion as
none other. Genet took Nembutal for eighteen years. He admitted to
it without shame. The continuity of Nembutal in Genet's life stood in
opposition to the young blacks who replaced marijuana with "outrageous" hair. For him, the psychedelic halo added to the radioactivity
of illness: during the writing of his last book, Genet was in treatment
for throat cancer. Sickness and death are not things you show, the way
you display a wound. But the writer can sing them and their distress.
Old and emotional: the brevity of the description lengthens and still
endures. The *haggard witness* is the portrait, in sleep, standing.

From emotional old age to haggard witness—the last book rounds this
cape. Two spaces now familiar, near and distinct, come together: in
Jordan in a tent, in the United States in a car. As he drove with Black
Panther member David Hilliard in 1970, Genet wrote, "As a privi-
leged witness to a mystery, I was no longer fair skinned, no longer one
of the Whites. When David Hilliard held out his hand to pass the
hash joint and smiled at me for the first time in the car—it was being followed by a police car—I was quite happy to descend into the
world of darkness."[47] David Hilliard was twenty-nine years old; the
writer was off to the barbershop. The police were watching, and from

the depths of fatigue, Genet watched back. The police were never far behind them, following the Panthers' car. The tail is political. The Panthers' goal was to "patrol the patrol," watching the cops watching them in the ghetto. Drugs have a social significance. They're not the escape routes offered by the hippies. By smoking hash in a car tailed by a police cruiser, the two men weren't trying to escape power but provoke it. The economic aspect of hash was part of it too. For smaller budgets, like Hilliard's and Genet's, the drug was a way to increase their ability to fight for their existence.

In the tent in Ajloun, a short time later, still in 1970, Genet remembered the burlesque way he entered the United States. He traveled an invisible pathway, as drugs do. He found his presence with the fedayeen even more laughable: "Just before I lay down on the blankets spread for me in the shelter, the fifteen or twenty terrorists peered in amazement at my medicine bottle, at the eight Nembutal capsules I took, and at the tranquil expression on my face. As I gulped the poison down they gazed at my Adam's apple with amazement and perhaps admiration. They must have been thinking, 'To put away a dose like that without showing any fear—that must be French courage. We have a hero among us tonight.'"[48] The figure of the comical assembly, the writer's apparent function, returns one last time. On both sides of the Jordan, Israelis and Palestinians keep a watchful eye: the formation is that of astonishment. Once again, the armed nature of the entourage means it can't be the subject of a drug experience. Yet the soldiers still do play. As the men in the tent look on, Genet quickly transforms himself into a hippie again, not by his hair, but by swallowing pills. Hero is a joke. But this self-mockery goes with significant presence in the tent. The witness is in the tent, itself pitched in a shelter dug deep into the ground. He is sitting on a stone for his haircut. Depth, both earthly and heavenly, dominates the writer's night. He descends, keeps watch, the world surrounds him, and he realizes that more than anyone else.

Genet went back over this page in the manuscript. He added the lines that speak ironically of his heroism. The scene of the eight pills was there from the beginning, and it's important because it offers a modest answer to the old question: does the witness have a witness? For the moment, in the tent, the answer is yes. The fedayeen, terrorists, stars, or monsters are the writer's amazed witnesses. For a moment, between the generations, there is exchange. Only eyes, but it does take place.

In *Only Lovers Left Alive*, a book by Dave Wallis (1964) whose rights were purchased by the Rolling Stones to make a movie (a project later abandoned), the young run the world after the adults all commit suicide. Political movements, the Panthers and the Palestinians in particular, Genet among them, have something else in mind. Dance, outrageous hair, and drugs all measure the tensions and the limits between the public and the private, solitary and collective experience, violence and non-violence—with oneself and with self-forgetting. Movements of witnessing: only the magic virtues of language can carry out the experiments thrown together here. At each step, Genet transforms what belongs to fashion and what really is the essence of the times. "Time had undergone a curious transformation since I arrived in Ajloun. Every moment had become 'precious,' so bright you felt you ought to be able to pick it up in pieces. The time of harvest had been followed by the harvest of time. But I managed to surprise them by swallowing eight capsules of Nembutal."[49] Nowadays, crystals of crack have made way for crystals of time. Juxtaposition of the highest state of vigilance and abandoning oneself to what will be. Definition of the haggard witness: he who harvests precious time. He stands in the antechamber of the king; there's nothing to do, but every moment counts. What mystery is he witnessing?

The end of unity, experience of a truly political separation, entry into a story without style. With the end of youth, the work of *legacy* begins.

ENDNOTES

1. *Prisoner of Love* (*PL*) (1986), translated by Barbara Bray (New York: New York Review of Books, 2003), 351.
2. "Violence et brutalité," *Le Monde*, September 2, 1977; *DE*, 174.
3. "The Members of the Assembly," *Esquire*, November 1968; *DE*, 267.
4. FBI files: Hampton, *The National Observer*, September 2, 1968.
5. *PL*, 245.
6. M. Choukri, *Jean Genet et Tennessee Williams à Tanger* (Paris: Quai Voltaire, 1993), 73.
7. C. von Bülow and F. Ben Ali, *La Goutte d'Or ou le Mal des racines* (Paris: Grasset, 1979), 306.
8. *PL*, 78.
9. "A Salute to a Hundred Thousand Stars," *Evergreen Review*, December 1968; *DE*, 278.
10. "Près d'Ajloun," in *Per un Palestinese, Dediche a più voci a Waël Zouaiter* (Milan: G. Mazzotta, 1979), *DE*, 157.
11. "Faites connaissance avec les Guaranis," *Le Démocrate vernonnais*, June 2, 1972; *DE*, 98.
12. "Les Palestiniens" (II), *Shoun Falestine* (1973), in *Genet à Shatila* (*GC*) (1992), new edition (Arles: Actes Sud, Babel, 1994), 147.
13. *PL*, 217.
14. Ibid., 12.
15. E. White, *Genet: A Biography* (New York: Knopf, 1993), 600.
16. G. de Nerval, *Voyage en Orient*, 1, in *Oeuvres complètes* (Paris: Gallimard, Pléiade edition, 1984, t. II), 263.
17. *PL*, 8, 9.
18. M. Ferro, *Colonization: a Global History*, trans. K.D. Prithipaul (London: Routledge, 1997), 323.
19. *PL*, 182.
20. "Jean Genet témoigne pour les Soledad Brothers," *La Nouvelle Critique* 45 (June 1971): 57.
21. "Une rencontre avec Jean Genet," *Revue d'études palestiniennes*, Fall 1986; *DE*, 242.
22. *PL*, 140.
23. Ibid., 34.
24. Ibid., 192–193 and 201–204; chapter 7.
25. Ibid., 406.

26. Ibid., 252.

27. Ibid., 247.

28. G. Bataille, *Visions of Excess: Selected Writings 1927–1939*, trans. A. Stoekl, C.R. Lovitt and D.M. Leslie Jr. (Manchester: Manchester University Press ND, 1985), 8.

29. *PL*, 250.

30. D. Hilliard and L. Cole, *This Side of Glory* (Boston: Back Bay Books, 1993), 302.

31. *PL*, 249–250.

32. H. Kleffner, "The Black Panthers: Interviews with Geronimo...," *Race and Class* 35, no. 1 (July–September 1993): 14, 24.

33. As quoted in T. Latner, *The Quotable Rebel: Political Quotations for Dangerous Times* (Monroe: Common Courage Press, 2005), 148.

34. *PL*, 303.

35. Ibid., 300.

36. Ibid., 304.

37. Ibid., 96.

38. *DE*, 276.

39. Ibid., 275.

40. "Letter to American Intellectuals," speech given at the University of Connecticut (March 18, 1970); *DE*, 31.

41. *PL*, 50.

42. "Bobby Seale, the Black Panthers and Us (White People)," *Black Panther Newspaper*, March 28, 1970.

43. *DE*, 270.

44. "Jean Genet chez les Panthères noires," interview with F.-M. Banier, *Le Monde*, October 23, 1970.

45. L. Shahid, in *Genet à Shatila*, 35–36.

46. T. E. Lawrence, *The Seven Pillars of Wisdom* (Fordingbridge: J. and N. Wilson, 1992), 199.

47. *PL*, 248.

48. Ibid., 118.

49. Ibid.

2 | The Genealogy of Movements

Genet declared in 1970, "Immigrant workers never asked anything from me."[1] And in 1983: "Very quickly, I will answer by saying that I went immediately toward the people who asked me to intervene. The Black Panthers came to Paris and asked me to go to the United States. It was Klaus Croissant who came to ask me to intervene in support of Baader. It was the Palestinians who asked me to go to Jordan ten years ago. Leila Shahid asked me to go to Beirut a year ago."[2] The writer was solicited by various political factions. Genet's disposition—"naturally I put myself at her disposal"[3]—was located somewhat above history, which it fractured, and a little behind politics, which it limited; it placed personal mutation and collective agency in relation; it was random circumstance turned into event. There is always more than one movement; these movements are heterogeneous, and in the fabulous partition of becoming and transforming, Genet positioned himself at times as the sum of their relations, other times as the zero point from which they became organized, other times still as a link in the chain of their effects. Politics remained as a sore point: how to speak of those people who asked nothing from you?

BLACK PANTHERS

"On reflection I have to say this: from its foundation in October 1966 right up to the end of 1970, the Black Panther Party kept on surpassing itself with an almost uninterrupted stream of images."[4] In his last book, Genet introduces the movement he knew. He first went to America for a week in August 1968 for the Democratic National Convention, then from March to May 1970 to be with the Black Panthers. A *Newsweek* journalist gave a Wild West version of this tumultuous story: "They started in 1966, two men, two guns and a lawbook, shadowing cops through the tacky black slums of Oakland."[5] According to the method governing bodies use to mock the genealogy of the disinherited, that's the way it is. In reality, the Black Panthers can't be understood without understanding American history and the failure of the civil rights movement to create an orderly transition between the North and the South. The *Civil Rights Act* made segregation illegal in the US in 1964, but illegality did not stop segregation. Blacks constituted what a historian at the time called an internal colony within the motherland.[6] For the Panthers, it was time to cross the border between protest and politics.

In December 1955, Rosa Parks, a black woman in Montgomery, Alabama, refused to give up her seat in the part of the bus reserved for white people. Soon after, 42,000 blacks started boycotting the public transit system, a situation that continued for a year. In 1977, Genet recognized and drew attention to Parks, this "tired black housewife" and her "swollen legs."[7] The title of his essay—"The Tenacity of American Blacks"—could also be applied to him: he continued to talk about the Panthers, whose origins were of great significance, according to one commentator: "The black man had stood up—and walked—in a sort of incandescent beauty that men seldom attain in the mass except on their quest for themselves."[8] In November 1963, Eldridge Cleaver, in prison at San Quentin, organized meetings under the name "The African-American History and Culture Group." It fell under strict surveillance once a federal directive was circulated, asking prison officials to root out the children of Malcolm X (X being the letter that stood for his slave name) and destroy them.[9] Cleaver escaped the shock treatments. Huey Newton, nineteen years old, the son of a carpenter, created the "Soul Student Group" at Merritt College with Bobby Seale. The two friends met Cleaver in 1966. The Black Panthers' founders—Cleaver, Newton, and Seale—were young college dropouts; some of them received their education in jail. The Black Panther Party was born in 1966 in the ghetto of Oakland, California. In the meantime, Malcolm X (in 1965) and Martin Luther King (in 1968) were assassinated. With these murders, committed in the belly of white America, a panther was born.

On that April day in 1968, a raging witness, Black Panther member Bobby Seale, was lying low in his house when he heard the news. "I had just turned on the TV and walked out of the room. It didn't dawn on me that Martin Luther King had been assassinated, because here I was, hiding out in this room until we finished our investigation."[10] He was one of the few free men left in the movement for another two days. Huey Newton and George Jackson were in jail; Eldridge Cleaver was about to go into exile.

What did the Black Panthers want? Their "Ten Points" are serious and practical. "To say that the Party had no ideology because its 'Ten Points' were either vague or inconsistent and its Marxist-Leninism was unorthodox is neither here nor there. The main object of a revolution is the liberation of man."[11] Genet's statement is not an incitement to forget about the Panthers' platform—anything but that. It was written in an atmosphere of friendship. In the offices of the Poverty Center, two friends, Newton and Seale, decided to write what they wanted and what they believed in two columns: on one side, practical, specific things, on the other, their concrete philosophical expression. A third friend, Melvin Newton, corrected the spelling mistakes. The origin of the Panthers' platform—these two columns—involved these three men, and it was an act of friendship meant to toll the death knell for the contempt to which they were subject.

OCTOBER 1966

BLACK PANTHER PARTY

PROGRAM AND PLATFORM

We want freedom. We want power to determine the destiny of our Black Community.

We want full employment for our people.

We want an end to the robbery by the white man of our Black Community.

We want decent housing, fit for shelter of human beings.

We want education for our people that exposes the true nature of this decadent American society. We want education that teaches us our true history and our role in the present-day society.

We want all black men to be exempt from military service.

We want an immediate end to POLICE BRUTALITY and MURDER of black people.

We want freedom for all black men held in federal, state, county and city prisons and jails.

We want all black people when brought to trial to be tried in court by a jury of their peer group or people from the black communities, as defined by the Constitution of the United States.

We want land, bread, housing, education, clothing, justice, and peace. And as our major political objective, a United Nations-supervised plebiscite to be held throughout the black colony in which only black colonial subjects will be allowed to participate, for the purpose of determining the will of black people as to their national destiny.[12]

The Black Panthers had their work cut out for them. The goal of this book is not to analyze its platform point by point, but to point out that the Panthers' activities found their origins there. The movement started by tracking police patrols in Oakland and San Francisco, then moved on to offer free breakfasts for children from the community, and ended with threatening death to Richard Nixon. It fought against oppression, which pleased Genet, and its perspective was not only racial.

The alliance with whites was an important moment for the movement; it allowed Genet to get involved and be present on American university campuses. It remained strong as the Vietnam War continued. On November 5, 1969, in Washington, DC, with white radical movements—the Student Non-Violent Coordinating Committee (SNCC) and the Peace and Freedom Party—and the Panthers too, the biggest demonstration ever was organized against the War: a half-million Americans. A variety of speakers stepped before the microphone. Only one speech was not read by its author, and it began this way: "This is Bobby Seale, from the San Francisco County prison…" The alliance was soon to be broken. We can understand Genet's position in America and elsewhere, through understanding the alliance's downfall: at the breaking point, at the unhealed limit between two eras, when everything is still possible and when there is no further reason to hope. "The Panthers and I," he wrote, "were to give a couple of lectures there, one for the students and the other for the professors. The idea was to talk about Bobby Seale and his imprisonment, and the real risk that he might be sentenced to death. We were also going to discuss Nixon's determination to wipe out the Black Panther Party, and the black problem in general."[13] The quick description in *Prisoner of Love* doesn't hide what's most important; it prepares the terrain for it.

In 1964, Malcolm X told American students, "One of the first things I think young people, especially nowadays, should learn how to do is see for yourself and listen for yourself and think for yourself. Then you can come to an intelligent decision for yourself."[14] Thinking for oneself involved a delicate choice: violence or not.

Coming to America to lend his aid to the Panthers six years later, Genet also spoke to students. On April 27, 1970, at the University of

California, Los Angeles, he took the stage. "Now you must—and you have the physical, material, and intellectual means for this—now you must confront life directly and no longer in comfortable aquariums, I mean in American universities, where people raise goldfish capable of nothing more than blowing bubbles."[15] The comparison was well thought out and based on local reality: the California university was close to the Pacific Ocean and the sunny coastal beaches. The students don't exist; they are like fish in America, or dancers in France: in each situation, they have to find a new way out. But the will is the same: "desert the university." In this desire to help the Panthers free their imprisoned members, we find Genet's future relationship with the Palestinians. You must travel into the desert. In the desert, there are no more goldfish. Genet isn't saying the same thing here as Mao, who defined the revolutionary group as the sea where fish swim. He wasn't telling the students to leave the aquarium to join the sea, but to go into the desert of politics and language. The inseparable delicate nature of language and action—that's what he was asking them to reflect on.

Is that a joke? Genet wasn't giving any advice. He was simply exhorting the hippies to turn into yippies, the political fringe of their movement. That day, the students were expecting a talk about literature. They left the room feeling disappointed.

Expressing goals doesn't mean neglecting means. On May 1, 1970, in New Haven, Connecticut, at a major demonstration supporting the Panthers, Genet gave his idea about the alliance. "Now I'm coming to the point that seems very important to me: the kinds of relations that exist between leftist organizations and the Black Panther Party. Here I believe that whites need to bring a new dimension into politics: a delicacy of heart. But be careful: it's not a question of sentimentalism, but of a delicacy in relations with people who do not have the same rights as we do."[16] This new attitude, this beginning of sensitivity, found an echo: in 1991 in Paris, Angela Davis took up the theme. "In California, Genet spoke of a delicacy of heart. That is a serious lesson. Genet knew how to express emotions that were not pity, and people could immediately recognize them. Blacks have been silently observing Whites for centuries. But Whites don't know how to observe us. Today, Whites have to learn the history of Blacks."[17] That day, Angela Davis spoke of the memory and the political meaning of a necessary delicacy, and not her attachment to the writer. In his case, from emotion to politics, from politics to delicacy, in the end into the desert, a politics of sensitivity is at issue. Well understood, it is a political quarrel, even a *frisson* of fraternity.

In New York City quite a while ago, there was an art installation by Adrian Piper entitled "Out of the Corner." On a video screen, a close-up of a young woman, apparently white, in a self-assured, calm voice, is telling us, "I'm black…" After her short speech, men and women begin to chant: "Some of my female ancestors were so-called 'house niggers' who were raped by their white slavemasters. If you're an American, some of yours probably were too."[18] In Paris in 1964, one could see Andy Warhol's *Pink Race Riot* (1963) at the Gallery Ileana Sonnabend. Genet told a German journalist who came to interview him on December 21, 1975, "Perhaps I'm a Black whose color is white or pink, but a Black."[19] In this non-racial context, his comment creates a number of reactions.

In his own way, Genet was developing his version of "Black is Beautiful." We can also understand his comment as an attempt at appropriating the title of Frantz Fanon's book, the breviary of black struggle, *Black Skin, White Masks* (1952). He appropriates the famous title known to revolutionaries everywhere, including the Panthers, and turns it into a signed poetic statement, a challenge, whereas before it was a slogan without a subject, without any temporal markers. The poetic operation aims to make it completely natural for a black to be white. The exaggeration works. Freed from its period, the statement seems new and surprising, symbolically important, like a reversal of values. Genet is simply a poet turning multitude into solitude. Alexander Pushkin, Arthur Rimbaud: the black writer has his traditions.

Pier Paolo Pasolini wrote, *"In fondo assomiglio molto a un negro,"*[20]—but then he scratched it out. Declaring yourself to be black has a political value that conjures up revolt. For the black universe, from Malcolm X to Genet, it signifies independence, separation, a new sharing. The Panthers chose Genet because he was white. His role in the movement was expressed at the time in the pages of a New York journal: "The only white the Panthers have really taken up is Genet."[21]

In his autobiography, David Hilliard, his friend and a Black Panther member, called Genet "a comrade in arms."[22] Between friendship and war, the hesitation persists. If Genet states that he was accepted by the Panthers "immediately," Hilliard remembers that he was accepted by him "completely and simply." Friendship, a secret space where each admits to his hidden desire for recognition?

HAWKS AND YOUNG LIONS

"But in 1970 an old word that had disappeared from political vocabularies was heard again; the word Palestinian."[23] Genet isn't interested in the nationalist organization or its leader, but in the men of the movement.

The first time he discovered the Palestinian resistance, he was on a train. In 1972, in a piece of writing that hadn't yet been published at the time, he remembered it this way: "In 1968, right after the Israeli-Arab War, I was in Tunis. It was Ben Salah's golden age. I learned by accident that detachments of Algerian and Moroccan troops were traveling north and south, on the road to Cairo, to join the Palestinian resistance. I was in the train between Gabès and Sfax when I heard that for the first time."[24] The scene is replayed at the beginning of *Prisoner of Love*: "In the train from Sousse to Sfax I met a group of six young men, laughing and eating cheese and sardines. They were in high spirits because the recruiting board had found them unfit for military service. From what they said I gathered they had pretended to be mentally defective or mad, or deaf from self-abuse. They must have been about twenty."[25] A chaste scene, or at least with its eroticism veiled, becomes immediately erotic. The last incarnation of Genet doesn't draw the line between masturbators and combatants, the poetic and the political encounter. The birth of revolutionary movements has a special love for train travel: borders are crossed, and there is magnetism and affinity.

The time that Genet spent in Jordan and Libya is well documented. In 1982, in his final intervention of the Palestinians before *Prisoner of Love*, the book on the Palestinian revolution, he writes, "For me, if the word 'Palestinians' occurs in a title, in the text of an article or a tract, it immediately evokes the fedayeen of a specific place—Jordan—at a time that can easily be dated: October, November, December 1970, January, February, March and April 1971."[26] In a laconic manner—one of the traits of his last book—he writes, "We left Salt for Ajloun, and I stayed there from October 1970 until May 1971."[27] Genet first traveled to Damascus in Syria for his military service in the 1930s. In 1981, after another extended stay in Jordan—thirty days of Ramadan and 180 of encounters—he tried to return the following year, but was expelled. He left for Lebanon, where he stayed from September 13 to 18, 1982. In July 1984, finishing his cycle of travels, he returned to where he had been in April 1971: in the Irbid camp in Jordan, at the house of a Palestinian mother whose son was called Hamza. Genet recognized the life and will of the Palestinians who left for Lebanon and Jordan.

Once again, he asked himself the question, "The source of the revolt may be hidden as dark and as deep as that of the Amazon. Where is it? What geographer will go in search of it? But the water that flows from it is new, and may be fruitful."[28] The history of the Palestinian movement has to be understood as an invention of a particular space and time. The return to Palestine cannot be a simple return, nor a return to a Palestine of the past. In January 1919, the Paris Peace Conference received a telegram in which the Palestinians were worried about "a certain promise the Zionist might have received according to which our country would become a national homeland for them ... Whereas we constitute a genuine Arab nation, as living as the other small nations the Allies have liberated."[29] Around the same time, in

1923, in front of a group of British parliamentarians who had traveled to that part of the world, Vladimir Ze'ev Jabotinsky, a political writer and Zionist, said, "There has never been a single case in which indigenous people gave their agreement to their country being colonized."[30] At the beginning, there was a three-sided game: the Arabs, the Jews, and the British. There was also the double antagonism between the circumcised nations (i.e., Arabs and Jews) on one side, and their collective antagonism toward the West on the other—the quarrel of peace. Before, during, and after the Balfour Declaration that gave this part of the world to the Jews, during the creation of the state of Israel on May 15, 1948, the 1967 War that increased that nation's size against the belligerent pressure of the Arabs, and the 1973 War that saw the country's size grow again, this time under the nationalist pressure of the Israeli right—the West Bank, Gaza, Golan, East Jerusalem, southern Lebanon—the Palestinians left in droves: in all, some 726,000 of them left for neighboring countries.

They went to Jordan, Lebanon, and Tunisia. But between September 1 and 9, 1970, aided by Israel, whose air force protected the Jordanian army, and US President Nixon, who supported the action, Jordan's King Hussein expelled the Palestinians; 3,400 of them died.[31] Genet wrote, "During the bloody week of September 1970 in Amman, between twelve and fifteen thousand Palestinian men and women were burned alive or incinerated."[32] The Americans took advantage of the Palestinians' disarray to massively arm the Jordanian government, thanks to an airlift from Cyprus to Amman. The gift came with a single condition: the Jordanian army must never use it against Israel. "Hussein is a petty bourgeois defending the propertied classes of today, just as Thiers defended those of yesterday."[33] Black September, as it became known, marked the end of the relationship between Palestinians and Amman. Genet arrived there the following month. In 1971, Beirut became the effective capital of Palestine and the PLO's political seat.

From September 13 to 18, the Israeli army, which had occupied

Lebanon since its invasion in June, took over Beirut. According to the Kahan Commission, the Phalangist Christian Lebanese militia entered the camps: a little less than 1,000 people died.[34] That was the event at Shatila and the departure from Beirut. Genet was there: "They must have been between two and three thousand, the Palestinian and Lebanese dead, together with a few Syrians and some Jewish women married to Lebanese, all killed in the camps at Sabra, Shatila and Bourj Barajneh."[35] As a result, Tunis became the official capital of the PLO.

The uprising in the occupied territories began in December 1987 and continues to this day. According to Betselem, the major Israeli human rights organization, at the time 1,104 Palestinians were killed.[36] That was the intifada. On the first pages of his last book, Genet wrote, "When Leila [Shahid] advised me to go to the West Bank, I refused, because the occupied territories were only a play acted out second by second by occupied and occupier."[37] Now we can see what he did not see: on September 13, 1993, crouching in the two entwined palms of Yasser Arafat and Itzhak Rabin, shaking hands in Washington; all these victims, and others still, or peace.

Birth, departure, and displacement measure out the time and space of the Palestinians. In all, today the population is estimated to be around 11 million people, more than half of whom are in exile. Genet had a lot of friends! The Palestinians call this period the *nakbah*, or disaster.

Hawks, fedayeen, young lions, women, girls, and Palestinian mothers—all are refugees. The refugee had his normal place of residence in Palestine until at least two years before the 1948 conflict. He lost his home and his livelihood and found refuge in one of the countries where the United Nations Relief Works Agency (UNRWA) lends its help.[38] Genet returned to the definition provided by the international organization that was created in 1948, but he did add quotation marks around one word: "The 'refugees' were not even the subject of dreams, but seen merely in terms of aid allocated annually and distributed by UNRRA (United Nations Relief and Rehabilitation Administration) in some camps somewhere to an undifferentiated mass in which no one had a name."[39] During the period that concerned him, in Lebanon and Jordan, there were more than a million of them.

"There were ten or twelve camps in Jordan. Jebel Hussein, Wahadat, Baqa, Gaza Camp and Irbid were the ones I knew best."[40] He remembers exactly where he had been, though the description of life in the camps and, within that routine, the differences between the camps and the bases are, for him, a simple matter of methodology. Take this camp near Amman, Jordan: "The fact that the tents were of many colors, because of the patches, made them pleasing to look at, especially to a Western observer. If they looked at them from far enough away and on a misty day, people thought the camps must be happy places because of the way the colors of the patches seemed to match: those who lived beneath such harmony must be happy, or they wouldn't have taken the trouble to make their camps such a joy to the eye."[41] With this description at the beginning of the book, Genet announces his colors. Right from the start, the gaze in the mist ironically mimics the vision of final beatitude. Yet he finds it difficult to veil the cliché: the final clause of the sentence displays through word play ("a joy to the eye") what the entire paragraph denies. Yet there are two realities based on the cliché of the camps, revealing joy where the Western eye sees only despair. The rhetorical fable takes on a political value. By the act of setting them against each other, Genet refuses the misery-loving description of things that pleases Western eyes and serves Palestinian propaganda; the idealist description may please him, but it would disregard the reality of camp life.

Rachid Boudjedra, the Algerian author of the 1992 French-language book *FIS de la haine*, was in Jordan in March of 1972, a short time after Genet. In his *Journal palestinien*, published in French ten years after it came out in Algiers, Boudjedra wrote about the Bekaa camp: "The camp, that holds 31,000 refugees, is the poorest I have seen during my stay. Located in the middle of the desert far from major cities, it is made entirely of cone-shaped tents that flap in the wind at the slightest breeze. The sight of this installation, when the sandstorms whip it, is terrible."[42] Later on, he writes that the Shatila camp in Lebanon is "nothing but a slum construction, a miserable agglomerate of zinc, sheet metal, string, tents, a few concrete walls and rutted roads, flooded with stagnant water."[43] The comparison between Boudjedra's and Genet's text increases the difference already present between the camps and bases. It is not the result of the length of time the two men spent in Jordan—a month for the latter, much longer for the former—and it cannot be reduced to unequal qualities of style between a greater and lesser writer; it is a difference of method. Between Boudjedra's *Journal* and Genet's last book, we see what separates the definitive repetition of the cliché from a descriptive movement fashioned by distinction, the will to break down confusion and point out differences. Semantic distinction, historical archeology, reflection of the writer's gaze in the eye of refugees—this is a method that shares nothing with the description of a person who is convinced by the cause he thinks he's defending. *Prisoner of Love* is not a Palestinian journal. Elsewhere in his book, in the same camp, Boudjedra asks some girls to draw him pictures. He describes the one made by Yusra Malik, age nine, who arrived in Amman in 1968: "The flowers are very large and look like guns, the birds have terrifying beaks and, at all times, a staring red eye."[44]

Genet is obviously not out to deny the fact that the Palestinian camps and others like it on the planet are, according to his way of putting it, "the discarded refuse of 'settled' nations."[45] But in the end, he comes back to the disappearance of the refugee camps. Their metamorphosis should split into camps of citizens or military bases, or even autonomous cities, though he has not seen them yet. This would signify the emergence of the Palestinians from their status as refugees and international aid recipients. Already, Genet is hoping to transform a humanitarian situation into a *political reality*.

The camp population is made up of students, or at least young people of school age, who have come from all sorts of places. But once there, at the beginning, Genet wonders, "How then is a fedayee different from any other boy his age? It must first be said that the Palestinian fighters are very young. In the mountains near Jerash, Salt, and Ajloun, their activities are limited and are no different from those of any other soldier on a campaign."[46] This piece, written in 1971, comes from a collection published in Italy in 1979, then in England in 1984. Genet does not wish to blend all Palestinians into the anonymity of the fedayeen, but for this book and against it, he decided to dedicate the piece "To the memory of all the fedayeen."

After several months spent on the bases, the words "Palestinian revolution" don't mean anything more to him. In 1973, he remembered instead, "a multitude of faces."[47] In *Prisoner of Love*, he supplies the names of friends who were part of the population: Nabila, Alfredo, Ferraj, Hamza, Dr Mahjoub, Abu Omar, Mubarak. The names of these different friends are all matched to the acts that Genet witnessed, the many actions that would be impossible to name or attempt to describe one by one: a departure by night, hands forming a fan, smiles, songs, happy quarrels, laughter most of all, marches, burials, card games, suspicious glances, making fun, women squatting around the fire, the fedayeen posing for the camera, a man bent over his cane, smoke, etc. The ancestral history of these people, the politics of their leaders, the acts of a single fedayee could never speak adequately of the writer's desire at the dawn of this new life in a new country.

To do justice to the branch of the movements he encountered does not mean presenting a program or a charter, but rather supplying a schedule. Here is the daily schedule of a fedayee in a camp situated northwest of Irbid. He shared in it though he did not write it:

5 a.m.	Reveille. Half an hour's run. Half an hour's gymnastics.
6–8 a.m.	Breakfast. Wash. Tidy up the camp.

8–12 noon	Commando training. Close-combat training.
12–2 p.m.	Lunch. Free time.
2–5 p.m.	Weapons training. Target practice.
5–8 p.m.	Political course. Discussions.
8 p.m.	Supper.
9 p.m.	Lights out, or, sometimes, night expeditions.[48]

The watch that ends the schedule must not have been unpleasant, for the experience was that of an openness to what may come, a vigilance, on alert: the weight of a body in the desert. The space and time created by the last Genet can be described by the expression "everyday fraternity."[49] It seeks to sum up the entire tone of *Prisoner of Love* and asks the only worthwhile question, which is, "How is the party going to end?"[50] The actions, the words, the nights of those who inhabit the country of fraternity—this is the forest where Genet loses himself.

A first questioning about the nature of the enemy helps us understand Genet's changing role within a story that is, in itself, in flux. In 1971, in a first article about the Palestinians, he writes, "We must be clear; the Palestinians' enemy, though it may be merged into one, has two faces: Israeli colonialism and the reactionary regimes of the Arab world."[51] Today the language seems dated. In 1986, he is told by a Palestinian leader, Abu Omar, "But we had the good fortune to discover our three enemies: the reactionary Arab régimes, America, and Israel, in that order."[52] The change in name and order of the enemies, if we wish to read more closely, is part of the critical attitude of *Prisoner of Love*: the attack against oneself; the analysis of one's own complicity; the impossibility, once you know that everything under the moon has at least two sides, to see which one is the good one—this is the writer's basic disquiet.

In this last book, he wrote, "For the Palestinians, the misery of being driven out of their country in 1948 with few belongings and many children was followed by the cool reception given them by the Lebanese, the Syrians and the Jordanians, and the reluctance of the Arab countries to use enough force to make Israel withdraw, or at least to bring about a fairer partition than that drawn up by the UN in 1947."[53] The hyperbaton—that is, adding another clause to the sentence when the latter appears to be finished—must not be missed. Genet does not insist on the need to eliminate Israel; he draws our attention to the need for a fair solution. Perhaps that is his wish. The sentence is critical of the Arab countries, either lightly or more severely. Yet in this list of enemies there is one missing, and that is Yasser Arafat—the obvious idea that is trumpeted from every position, that the enemy is oneself. Arafat won't be spared, either.

The question remains: why did Genet need the head of the PLO? Genet wanted to define himself in relation to Arafat, the prince and protector of the poet, to whom he entrusted a letter so he could move freely from camp to camp, among the bases and factions. No doubt Genet wanted to go to extremes, to the very head of the movement. We can't give all the reasons for this need, nor can we supply the exact date of their meeting in Jordan, at the Whahadat camp, some time in November 1970, or whether it led to the drawing of the portrait at a later date: the reflection of the political leader in the writer's eye.

In the last book, Hitler's mustache and Churchill's cigar create a tenuous link with the kaffiyeh: the cloth that hides Arafat's shaven head. To the act—the gift of the kaffiyeh—the word is joined: "Do this in *remembrance* of me."[54] We don't know whether Genet was asked to put on the kaffiyeh or whether he was encouraged to write the book of the Palestinian revolution. Memory, the only word in italics in the portrait, points to continued transmission, an act to carry out, and Genet won't hesitate; he gets down to work. Another echo: Luke in the New Testament: "This do in remembrance of me" (22:19), the Last Supper, the Passover meal, when the body of Christ enters the mouth of the believer who expresses a circle in time: creation, birth, and death—then eternity. A new figure decorates the kaffiyeh, that of the Son. Christ's words, repeated by Luke, placed in Arafat's mouth, turn this scene in the Virgin's house into an appeal to a son.

The encounter draws another circle of fire, a limit between the worlds of action and writing. In the past, another writer met another leader, which the former tried to explain. Ezra Pound met Benito Mussolini on January 30, 1933. Pound, his poetry, his affection for "Mus," his captivity, his end, the alliance between poetry and politics—all can help to illuminate this story. At the time, Pound was mourning two disappearances: on a personal level, there was Henri Gaudier-Brzeska, his sculptor friend who died during World War I, and on an artistic level, there was Francis Picabia, the painter who was no longer himself. When they met, Pound gave Mussolini an eighteen-paragraph document about Social Credit, the monetary theory he embraced. In incendiary fashion, speaking of Mussolini, Pound defended himself, asking: "Put it this way: AS A MIND, who the hell else is there left for me to take an interest IN??"[55] That is a question. The end of youth, friends who are gone, the terrible necessity of having to rekindle the ashes of the domestic hearth with the flame of politics, a death to mourn (Abdallah, Genet's tightrope-walking lover, killed himself with Nembutal on March 12, 1964)—these were the events in Genet's memory as he went to meet Arafat. Genet wants to be judged from the heights of political ideas, which is what burns him.

In fact, without giving any explanation, the lines of his last book reveal his transformation after having met the Palestinians: "The various hazards that have allowed me to survive in the world don't allow me to change it, so all I shall do is observe, decipher and describe it. And every phase of my life will consist in the undemanding labor of writing down each episode [...] I've only spoken of my life in order to tell a story."[56] On the manuscript, he added, "a story of the Palestinians." His addition flows from a sense of generosity and a recognition of the facts. Genet transforms the mythological declaration that refuses to change the world into a Herculean affirmation of just that impossibility. The slight difference between the verbs "speak" and "tell," the movement in his own life toward another's story, the turning point that moves him to tell his story in the eye of others, in front of no one's personal gaze—is that enough to believe that his political coming out took place?

An old man arrives and does what he can to help a young nation in revolt, which is not much.

YOUNG THRUSHES

More than anything else, Genet remained faithful to his preoccupation with the foreigner, the newcomer, the immigrant, the man who has deserted his army or his country, who takes to the road. In the 1970 interview in which he expressed his view of the differences between the demands of the Panthers and the fedayeen and his silence regarding immigrants, he stated, "It's very easy to cross the border."[57] He was alluding to his trip to America in 1968 for the Democratic National Convention, a journey vexed with difficulties, since he did not obtain a visa and had to cross the border from Canada at night. The clandestine nature of the trip is important. In one of Genet's letters, dated November 9, 1961, concerning just this issue, he asks for a visa for a third party. Genet's act has deep roots. To read this letter is to shed light on the first action he ever took regarding immigrants. Compared to the Black Panthers he tried to spring from prison and the men in Jordan he tried to free from camps, the actions he undertook over and over again on behalf of an immigrant friend subsumes all else. The idea was to allow a man to cross borders freely.

Before and after the pages where this letter could have appeared, his biographer points out that Genet encouraged Abdallah, the tightrope walker who was still his companion at the time, to desert the army, as he did with Jacques Maglia, which he did not mention. Both men refused to be called up, which led Genet, Abdallah, and Jacques to leave France.[58] Genet wrote to Bernard Frechtman, his agent at the time, "Jacques Maglia deserted at the end of December. I'd like him to be judged in absentia, and rather quickly. Could you ask Roland Dumas to look after it? You know he deserted the Army in Algeria because of the objectives of that war and the methods of war in general." Here is the letter that followed the first request, which concerns Jacques' brother, Robert Maglia:[59]

> Dear Sir,
>
> Bernard Frechtman believes, and I agree, that you might be able to do me a favor on this case. Here it is: the son (married and with a three-year-old child) of one of our friends wishes to immigrate to the USA. His goal, of course, is to work, and he has established himself in two professions, as a plumber and a locksmith. [...] He has already done his military service, he's twenty-two years old. [...] I don't wish to influence your decision, but if I do insist, it's only because they are young and dream of living in America. [...] They have enough money for the crossing and to live on for three months. They should not pose any problems because they have not been involved in any political activities or any other reprehensible actions. They have no intention of assassinating Kennedy or MacMillan. They are very nice people. The portrait I am drawing of them will undoubtedly convince you that they are boring. It's always that way when you're trying to recommend someone. You praise the person to the skies, and they barely seem human. But these people are very real, quality people, and they would certainly add to the glory of the USA if they were given a chance. His name is Robert Maglia; his wife Paulette Maglia. Their address: Montée des Oliviers, Rocheville (A-M), France. [...] Please accept my warm affection, etc.
>
> J. G.

Jacques and Robert Maglia were brothers; they seemed unsullied by any political activity, as long as desertion was not considered a political act. This letter is part of Genet's poetic work: the attention paid to what we are writing at the time we are writing it, the irony about the absence of criminal motives, the toying with military service. It's as if the favor requested is premised on an enormous joke. Jacques did not fulfill the demands of military service, and Robert, who has not deserted, wants to go into exile. The game about military service illustrates the method of substituting one word for another, of slipping one meaning under another, and wearing down the meaning of an expression that might be too direct. This use of language opposes military service, the way poetic method opposes torture. The favor is a political one. With the little favors he often asks for, Genet wants to gently corrupt the armies of nations. He is working to extract one man from the military corps, then another, then another still. In this way, he tries to wear down the base on which the French Ministry of War is built.

According to Article 6 of the Order dated November 2, 1945, an immigrant in France is considered to be a foreigner who has established himself in the territory of the nation for a duration greater than three months, on a continuous basis and for an indeterminate length of time.[60] Genet provided a definition of the word "immigration" in 1974: "Provoked especially by the looting of natural resources in Third World countries, by the impoverishment of the land and its minerals, by the wastefulness of the colonial and neocolonial system, immigration is now nothing but the recruitment, for France and the rest of Europe, of an underpaid labor force that has almost no hope of surviving."[61] In France, it all began in 1947 with the granting of citizenship to Algerians. In 1962, after the country won its independence, and an agreement gave citizens of both countries the right to freedom of movement, 300,000 Algerians arrived in France. In 1966, the FASTI (Fédération des Associations de Solidarité avec les Travailleurs Immigrés or Federation of Associations for the Support of Immigrant Workers) was created, bringing together 156 different pro-immigrant associations. From 1968 onward, thanks to the work of far-left organizations at first and unions thereafter, issues pertaining to immigrants' living and working conditions became both public and political. FASTI's work has continued, including with governments that have questioned these agreements. The immigrant's status in France is the legacy of a fairly recent period, when the country's map was entirely pink, the color of the French colonial empire.

In 1972, Genet found himself in the Goutte d'Or neighborhood in Paris, for the creation of the Djilali Ben Ali committee, named for a boy who was murdered by the superintendent of his apartment block. In one snapshot, we can see Genet wearing a winter coat, separated from Jean-Paul Sartre by an (unknown) woman, seen from the back. Lesser known is the "Intellectuals Appeal to Arab Workers" that was republished in Catherine von Bülow and Fazia Ben Ali's book, *La Goutte d'Or ou le Mal des racines* (1979). The two women often accompanied Genet to committee meetings and cafés in the eighteenth *arrondissement* of Paris: "I have a meeting with Genet in a café in the Barbès neighborhood. Our Arab friends offered to show us around, the point being to let Genet talk with the Arabs in the district. [...] Genet started up a conversation with some Arabs playing cards. There was an enormous amount of smoke. No alcohol anywhere. Genet understood a little Arabic. I am the only woman in the café and feeling very much out of place."[62] The sense of discomfort, which is part of the times, is obvious in the appeal:

INTELLECTUALS APPEAL TO ARAB WORKERS

The pride and noble spirit that we, your friends, see proof of every day, though we never needed proof in order to understand and love you, your nobility and pride are being abused on a constant basis here in Goutte d'Or, and in many other neighborhoods, and cities in France, by the police and part of the population. These insults to human dignity are more and more often joined by physical attacks that go as far as murder. A certain number of Frenchmen—an increasing number, or so we hope—have judged that it is time to put a stop to this injustice, these crimes and the silence with which the press has systematically greeted these events. To the population of this neighborhood and others in Paris (where no one knows what's going on in Goutte d'Or), workers and intellectuals, we announce that several weeks ago we formed the Djilali Committee, named for the young Algerian who was murdered in conditions we all know about, in racist circumstances. This Committee will soon have a full-time office in the neighborhood, where all who have been mistreated, or in any way have suffered racist threats or attacks, can come and explain their cases. They will find friends and brothers there. More than that: they can make use of moral and legal support. Now, the police will not be able to allow criminal actions to take place, for they will have been informed, because not only will anonymous inhabitants of the neighborhoods be telling them and asking them to step in while there is still time, but also professors and journalists whose names are not unknown to the public and to power. We intend to work in a focused, efficient manner. This is why, since we cannot be everywhere at once, we have decided to limit our action to Goutte d'Or. Obviously, it would be ideal if such committees could be formed in the neighborhoods of Paris and other French cities where the need is felt. We will be happy to help the organizers of such committees by offering our experience in this work.

The Djilali Committee, December 7, 1971, consisting of [names of celebrities]. Office currently open every Sunday, 9 rue St-Bruno.[63]

Genet worked in the committee's office for a number of Sundays. Except for Foucault's signature, and the political creation of moral and legal support for immigrants that no doubt helped slow down police brutality, this appeal reeks of the clichés of the times. It reminds us of the Panthers' Ten Points. The Djilali case crossed a border, not only because a death was involved, but because the struggle was undertaken by intellectuals. Soon Genet would be slamming a process that can only be called demagogy.

A little later, he declared, "I need a transformation of the lot of disenfranchised workers."[64] He didn't say, I love workers; because if he did, as Valéry Giscard d'Estaing was talking the same way at about the same time, the response would be, "We Arabs have had it up to here with your love."[65] Genet wasn't writing to defend immigrants. *The last incarnation of Genet was concerned with (need) the movement (transformation) of men subjected to a violent legacy (disenfranchisement)*—impoverished, forgotten, invisible.

In an interview he gave to Tahar Ben Jalloun in *Le Monde* when, in 1979, the government was imposing a new law on immigrants' rights to live and work in France, Genet recalled a contemporary image: "When he invited a Malian garbage collector to the Élysée—one New Year's Day, with cameras there to capture the event—that is probably what the president wanted to show: the hands of the invited worker are rather cumbersome in the midst of a receiving room. They are more suited to holding a balaclava. And there are no jackhammer operators under the chandeliers of the Élysée Palace."[66] The juxtaposition of the tool and the light is insufficient; it is a poke in the eye. The reality of the scene has been so perverted by the French president that for Genet it is indescribable. He could not accept this way of dealing with immigrants, from the committee's appeal to the president's invitation. Today, quite the opposite is true: the more something is visible, the more intellectuals talk about it. To discover a political way of seeing things underlies the issues over immigration. Djilali's death occulted the living conditions of immigrants. At the time, some people went looking for immigrants in the factories, but Genet found them in books.

He spoke of them in a speech called "On Two or Three Books No One Has Ever Talked About" from 1974: "The books I am speaking of—and this time I will mention them by name—*Harrouda* by Tahar Ben Jalloun, *Une vie d'Algérien* by Ahmed, *Le Cheval dans la ville* by Pélégri, *Le champ des oliviers* by Nabile Farès—these are books that

you will read in order to know the poverty of immigrants, their solitude, and their miseries that are also our own."[67] The book by Ahmed,
whose full title is *Une vie d'Algérien, est-ce que cela fait un livre que les
gens vont lire? (Does an Algerian's Life Make a Book People Will Want to
Read?)*, may have influenced the title of the article that is partly about
this work. Ahmed is a pseudonym. His book is oral, unsigned, and
organized into numbered sequences of memory. Nabile Farès' work is
a narration, written according to a telegraphic style made up of quick
sentences, sometimes without punctuation. Ben Jalloun's book cap-
tured the imagination through its magical transitions. The first chapter of *Harrouda* closes with an ejaculation that fills a hand, then a vial,
then a jar, while the following chapter opens with a garden: "The jar
gave birth to a garden."[68] The sentences of each of these books weave
a portrait of Genet: the different styles each open onto paragraphs
of *Prisoner of Love*. Oral style for the dialogues, separate memories,
chance transitions, each time a new juxtaposition to consider.

Ahmed—not the generic name given by the bosses to immigrants,
but the pseudonym chosen by this laborer—belongs to the men known
as *harkis*, the 200,000 Muslims who fought in the French army in Algeria, of whom half were killed. After the war, French Minister for
Algerian Affairs Louis Joxe outlawed their repatriation. Only some
20,000 made it to France, and they were dumped in camps in the forest around Manosque in northern Provence and elsewhere. When it
comes to his joining the French army, Ahmed says he was "screwed
over": "I was seventeen, I didn't know where I was, I didn't know where
I was going."[69] Historians tell us that the peasants were moved most
by fear, family solidarities, and the need to find work. Speaking of his
journey to France in 1962 to find a job, Ahmed says this: "They had
us pretty much like little white mice. They showed us off at the fair
(I saw that in Marseille), white mice that they send up in a plane, they
make us run treadmills ... it's like those mice have been to school [...].
That's how they take us on, Tunisia, Algeria, Morocco, they take us
like mice."[70] Why choose Ahmed? Because, in Genet's way of seeing,

and in a completely coherent fashion, the misery of misery is reflected, the exclusion from exclusion: absolute misfortune. Ahmed is an Algerian *harki* immigrant, thus doubly an outsider, estranged from his place of birth and from the place where he lives and works. All the others, and the writer with them, can say, as Ahmed does, "I was born miserable like a weed."[71] *The last incarnation of Genet wants to express trash, misery, absolute misfortune.*

Confronting these works doesn't just shed light on the life of immigrants or, by contrast, the way that reality was understood at the time, but on the writer's position when faced with misery. This time, the issue is the self in the outsider's eye. In *Harrouda*, Genet intervenes directly: he is named, criticized, and held up as an example. In the fourth section of his book called "Tanger la trahison" ("Tangiers Betrayed"), Ben Jalloun writes, "Genet, will you still speak of the prestige of this city that's no more than a den for the traitors you love? No one else would dare betray those young men who loiter in the *socco chico* in search of some kind of seduction believing they are betraying order believing they are betraying power believing they are betraying the family. They come from America and Europe at the very moment our continent is losing its difference."[72] Then this: "The homosexual (often rich) with all his travels who journeys to Tangiers [...] doesn't know—cannot know—even if he is exploiting this incredible situation where bodies are given for so little, how he is considered by those bodies: complicity scarcely exists, shame falls upon the other, [...] in fact there is only the illusion of exchange, nothing flows or passes between them (except for sperm)."[73] A terrible juxtaposition between two sexual miseries: the immigrant worker whose body is broken by work, and the Moroccan (the same person) who gives his body to the traveler. Here, Ben Jelloun is touching on the point of maximum tension, the limit where Genet's relationship with the movements disintegrates.

Two symmetrical Western attitudes toward the immigrant, the other, appear: the employment of anonymous men, emptied of their desire but full of the ability to work, and the use of men, still anonymous, but full of desire and emptied of their identity. My hypothesis? The impact of the sexual body submitting to the foreigner, in a foreign country, and the body as workforce, submitting to France (or any other country), here indicates the breaking point from which Genet can no longer speak and write in the same manner about immigrants. Because the writer is a participant in the misery of this relation with immigrants, since he recognizes himself, at least partially, in this Western practice of using the disinherited—practice both private and public, sexual and economic, in a word, political—he must make his own relationship with these men, and transform it.

Genet wanted to meet Ben Jelloun, and they did indeed meet. Their meeting, which represented the willingness to accept the criticism, would have had no impact if it weren't expressed in poetic terms. The meeting would have remained in vain if it hadn't created a vision of oneself as a foreigner, the sense of oneself as a Frenchman in the eyes of the immigrant. Genet's adventure was chaste, and more desolate for that. This borderline situation forces him less into a change of point of view or a revolution in his personality—not yet—and more into the concern and the necessity to feel the lover's truth.

The immigrant question, the third branch of Genet's movements, is the last and yet, in a certain way, brings together all the men and women encountered to this point. If only, for example, as a displacement. While Genet's last book speaks most of all of the Black Panthers and the Palestinians, to maintain that it ignores immigrants would be an empty and wrong statement. Not only did he never abandon the issue, a page written about it constitutes his last public act of writing, if we set aside the final interviews: a piece entitled "Registration No. 1155." The file he describes dates back to 1940; it is that of a man considered by the French state to be a soldier and Moroccan worker. This file, rediscovered in 1982 among others kept in a filing cabinet, and chosen and commented on by Genet in 1983, speaks of immigration in general, and the army, labor, and misery in particular. But first, Genet points out the color: "As we can see, the file and the card are pink. The same pink as the one that used to color the map of the globe, indicating the French Colonial Empire."[74] Salman Rushdie expressed himself in a manner very close to Genet's when he wrote, "After all, surely the one thing one can confidently say about that roseate age of England's precedence, when the map of half the world blushed with pleasure as it squirmed beneath the Pax Britannica, is that it's over, isn't it?"[75] Rushdie could have read Genet, since another of the latter's articles on immigration was translated into English and entitled "Genet on Immigrants" in the *Guardian Weekly* on April 6, 1980. Already he had used the expression "the symbolic pink of the empire."[76] Rushdie and Genet are not setting down a new border; they are asserting a truly political separation, and questioning an identity.

The pink file Genet chose belonged to a Moroccan worker named Salah Ahmed Salah. His father's name is not given in the file, but Genet noticed the son's date of birth: "Card no. 1155 concerns a Moroccan worker named Salah, born in Morocco the same year I was born in Paris, 1910." He goes on to write, "The word 'skeleton' comes immediately to mind."[77] In the other book Genet wanted us to read, Farès sang of the immigrant he became: "Young thrushes. The days we were among the olive trees. Young thrushes." Winged animals with the gift of song. And we acknowledge the initials of Jean Genet in Young Thrushes (*Jeunes Grives*): J.G. The sphere of private life is now part of public space, and the indecency of the subjective self—"it seems indecent of me to speak of myself"[78]—and the political project are no longer in contradiction, the ashes of the domestic hearth are mixed in with the charges from France and elsewhere.

After "Registration No. 1155," the writing of *Prisoner of Love* can begin. With the description of the pink identity file, Genet wrote the smallest possible page on another one. In a way, the last book seems to be the enlargement of this page, or identity card, as big as the universe. To emerge from one's limits is a labor that lasts some twenty years. In other words, every sentence Genet wrote is an attempt at coming out.

ENDNOTES

1. "Jean Genet chez les Panthères noires," interview with Michèle Manceaux, *Le Nouvel Observateur*, May 25, 1970; *DE*, 42.
2. "Une rencontre avec Jean Genet," *Revue d'études palestiniennes*, Fall 1986; *DE*, 235.
3. Ibid., *DE*, 242.
4. *PL*, 55.
5. "The Panthers and the Law," *Newsweek*, February 23, 1970.
6. T. Milstein, "A Perspective on the Panthers," *Commentary*, September 1970.
7. "La ténacité des Noirs américains," *L'Humanité*, April 16, 1977; *DE*, 159.
8. A. Sivanandan, "Black Power: The Politics of Existence," *Politics and Society* 1, no. 2 (January 1971): 226.
9. K. Cleaver, "On Eldridge Cleaver," *Ramparts*, June 1969.
10. B. Seale, *Seize the Time* (New York: Random House, 1970), 230.
11. *PL*, 49.
12. B. Seale, *Seize the Time*, 66–68.
13. *PL*, 54.
14. Malcolm X, December 1964, in *Malcolm X Speaks: Selected Speeches and Statements*, ed. G. Breitman (New York: Grove Press, 1994), 137.
15. Same speech as the "May Day Speech" (New Haven, CT, May 1, 1970); *DE*, 39.
16. Ibid., *DE*, 35.
17. A. Davis, "Journées Jean Genet," Paris, Théâtre de l'Odéon, May 1991.
18. A. Piper, *Out of the Corner* (installation at the Whitney Museum of American Art, New York, October 1990).
19. "Interview with Hubert Fichte," *Die Zeit*, February 13, 1976; *DE*, 126.
20. P.P. Pasolini, *Qui je suis* (1966) (Paris: Arléa, 1994), 12.
21. W.J. Weatherby, "After the Panthers – What Next?" *New Society*, August 1970.
22. D. Hilliard and L. Cole, *This Side of Glory*, 260.
23. *PL*, 148–149.
24. "Les Palestiniens" (II), *Shoun Falestine*, 1973; *GC*, 112.
25. *PL*, 18.
26. "Four Hours in Shatila," *Revue d'études palestiniennes* 6 (January 1, 1983); *DE*, 209.
27. *PL*, 279.

28. Ibid., 237.

29. Israel State Archives, quoted in O. Carré, "Arafat vingt ans après: 'Cent ans de solitude...,'" *Maghreb-Machrek* 104 (June 1984): 52.

30. Bella, M., *The World of Jabotinsky* (Jerusalem, 1984), 313.

31. A. Perlmutter, "The Crisis of the PLO: Dilemmas of an Absolutist Movement," *Encounter*, February 1988, 27.

32. *DE*, 72.

33. "Les Palestiniens" (I), *Zoom* 4 (August 1971); *DE*, 73.

34. M. Naïm, "Les massacres de Sabra et Shatila," *Le Monde*, September 13–14, 1992, section entitled "Il y a dix ans."

35. *PL*, 377.

36. *Le Monde*, June 30, 1993.

37. *PL*, 6.

38. "Point: L'UNRWA," *Le Monde*, January 14, 1994.

39. *PL*, 148.

40. *PL*, 101.

41. *PL*, 15.

42. R. Boudjedra, *Journal palestinien* (1972) (French translation, Paris, 1982), 11.

43. Ibid., 131.

44. Ibid., 140.

45. *PL*, 15.

46. "Près d'Ajloun," in *Per un Palestinese, Dediche a più voci a Waël Zouaiter* (Milan: G. Mazzotta, 1979); *DE*, 155.

47. "Les Palestiniens" (II); *GC*, 101.

48. G. Chaliand, *The Palestinian Resistance*, trans. M. Perl (New York: Penguin, 1972), 110.

49. "Les Palestiniens" (I); *DE*, 73.

50. *PL*, 285.

51. *DE*, 73

52. *PL*, 315.

53. Ibid., 236.

54. Ibid., 141.

55. H. Carpenter, *A Serious Character: The Life of Ezra Pound* (Boston: Houghton Mifflin, 1988), 492.

56. *PL*, 237.

57. *DE*, 42.

58. E. White, *Genet: A Biography* (New York: Knopf, 1993).

59. Frechtman file, the Moraly Collection.

60. P. Weil, *La France et ses étrangers* (Paris: Gallimard, 1991), 62.

61. "Sur deux ou trois livres dont personne n'a jamais parlé," France Culture, "Réflexion faite" (radio show), May 2, 1974; *DE*, 102.

62. C. von Bülow and F. Ben Ali, *La Goutte d'Or*, 108–109.

63. Ibid., 139.

64. "Quand le pire est toujours sûr," written for *L'Humanité*, May 7, 1974, then lost; *DE*, 106.

65. "Mourir sous Giscard d'Estaing," *L'Humanité*, May 13, 1974; *DE*, 108.

66. "Entretien avec Jean Genet," *Le Monde du dimanche*, November 11, 1979; *DE*, 180.

67. "Sur deux ou trois livres..."; *DE*, 102.

68. T. Ben Jelloun, *Harrouda* (Paris: Seuil, 1973), 18–19.

69. Ahmed, *Une vie d'Algérien...* (Paris: Seuil, 1973), 29.

70. Ibid., 29.

71. Ibid., 174.

72. T. Ben Jelloun, *Harrouda*, 145.

73. Ibid., 154.

74. *No. Matricule 1155*, exhibit catalogue, "La Rupture," Le Creusot, March 1, 1983; *DE*, 231.

75. S. Rushdie, *Imaginary Homelands* (London: Granta Books, 1991), 129.

76. "Entretien avec Jean Genet,"; *DE*, 178.

77. *No. Matricule 1155*; *DE*, 229–230.

78. "Letter to American Intellectuals," speech given March 18, 1970 at the University of Connecticut; *DE*, 28.

3 | The Luxury and Misery of the Revolution

"Are you happy? Always the same answer: why not?" The revolution, Genet asserts, just might be "the opposite of sadness."[1] In the case of the Algerian revolt and the black and Palestinian revolutions, the *metamorphosis* of Genet takes place. These movements, and the writer too, share the same need, which is to invent a maturity for oneself—in other words, to see what's coming. The same myth, the same maturity of these men from all over the world is no dream. The governing classes see in their children rightful heirs, while the disinherited see liberators in their ancestors. Discovery, creation, invention: this is the revolutionary principle of the movements.

THE MANIFESTO

To travel backward, upstream in the chronology of the last incarnation of Jean Genet does not mean deserting his story. Upstream means further up the shallow stream of experience, closer to its very source. Making the journey implies an attempt to speak of the archeology of his political coming out, though it may be impossible to identify its origins.

Genet wrote this letter in September 1960; it is addressed to his

translator and lawyer Bernard Frechtman. In it he discusses a request
to get involved, and his refusal to put his name to a petition. The letter
reveals his first overtly political action:

> My dear Frechtman,
>
> I don't have much to say, maybe because I'm bored out of my
> mind. I'm correcting *The Balcony* a little. I read it over again.
> It's very bad, very badly written. Pretentious. But what can
> I do? If I tried to have a more neutral style, less twisted, it
> would carry my thoughts toward myths and themes that
> are too careful and too conventional. Inventing doesn't
> mean telling a story. To invent, I have to get myself into a
> state that will call forth fables, and these fables themselves
> impose a caricature style on me [illegible]. With *The Screens*,
> I think I arrived at another kind of style. But the fable
> is more rational. So the play will be flattened out. More
> morose. Stuck to the ground. Crawling.
>
> I have to start *Le Bagne* again. I made some wrong decisions.
> At the beginning, I took a tone that was too dignified.
> My fable-making faculties drove me toward predictable
> prolongations, almost caricatures, banally social. I think I've
> found the right tone now. But I don't have the courage to
> start back in on the play. I'll have to redo everything. From
> start to finish. Before that, I'd like to get rid of two or three
> thousand pages of *La Mort*. I'm writing badly. Boringly.
>
> If it works, *Le Bagne* will be my best play. I'll spend ten years
> without writing.
>
> You should have told me the impression you got from *The
> Screens*. A few lines would have helped me. Not "very good"
> or "admirable," but more like what I gained and what I lost.
>
> I didn't sign the manifesto for the show despite [Dionys]
> Mascolo's letter, very pressing, and despite my own desire.
> I sent a letter giving my agreement to [Jacques] Vergès, but
> that's because [?] called me and said Vergès wanted it. It
> wasn't read, and besides I was weak. It's pretty hard to be
> like that, without being able to say a word that makes sense.

Expressing myself always through fables, and necessarily
the most ambiguous kind, is a disaster, first because I have
to keep this complex and difficult ambiguity in me—always
at a moral risk to myself—and also because of the opinion
my friends—that I'm a coward—will have of me. You see,
Florence Malraux called to tell me how surprised she was
that I didn't sign. I explained. She understood, but she was
still sorry that my name wasn't among the 121. But I have no
regrets. I'm telling you this so you'll see that my situation
is not too comfortable. Because I support the rebels, I
support everything they do. And I can't say it. And I'm the
only writer in France who can't say it. [Louis-Ferdinand]
Céline—if he felt like it—could support the rebels, because
his revolt and even his mistakes were "noble."

Talk to me about *The Screens*. Theatrically speaking. Are
the scenes with the Soldiers strong enough? Do we see the
Soldiers? The Three Old Women? Saïd? The style? Can it
be said that way?

That worries me too. And preoccupies me. I think it's
finished, or will be soon enough, padded theater [?], divided
into boxes, bathtubs, balconies. I would like to write for
a 20,000-seat theater. For that I'd need a style that would
be hushed, but screamed. And situations that would justify
this screaming. Writing for those boxes—theaters the way
they are now—will kill me. I think the day will come when
people will go to the theater—ten or twelve times a year,
no more—the way they'd go to a carnival—preferably in
the open air, but all the [?] from the film world, theater,
etc., that's bullshit! To see and hear what? There are only
two modern plays that could safely be staged at Epidaurus:
The Blacks and *Waiting for Godot*. *Godot*'s language is simple,
but the meaning is in the silences and the gesticulation
(indicated by Beckett). At Epidaurus, if we were seated in
the back row, we'd get the feeling we were watching a fine
play through the wrong end of the opera glasses. *The Blacks*
with its mish-mash language would be at home. Not *The
Balcony*. But *The Screens*. I don't know. When it's printed I'll
be able to [?] it once and for all.

All this bugs me.

Jean Genet.

My hotel is historic: the 1925 conference with [?] took place here. There's a marble plaque in the lobby that says so.[2]

I will leave the theater analysis aspect of this letter to other readers; the theater of the letter. Florence Malraux, Jacques Vergès, Dyonis Mascolo, Bernard Frechtman ask him to get involved politically. Genet begins by considering the problem of his image: remain true to himself or be recognized by his "friends"? Pride, doubt, putting on airs, critical admiration (Beckett), trust, awareness of his genius (if I succeed...), egotism, projects (*Le Bagne*, *La Mort*) and requests, fears, politeness, contempt are all poses the writer strikes in this letter. The reflection on the future—or rather the end—of theater (Epidaurus) itself is theatrical. But Genet, in the letter, abandons his own theater. The reference to his three plays is like a farewell. A successful dramatic trilogy (*The Blacks*, *The Balcony*, and *The Screens*—the last work published while the author was alive) is dismissed, and accounts are settled with a certain image he has of himself. In the letter, Genet very clearly differentiates between the old style and the new: "Inventing doesn't mean telling a story." Fable versus story. A temporary distinction, a tactic, false but necessary for the writer who is preparing an action that is already present, waiting its time. Woven from fables, *Prisoner of Love* is absolutely political. The order of legend, therefore, of history—is the writer's old obsession. But for now, he must think that theater is only theater, the novel only fiction, and faculties only fable-makers. In other words, he must believe that these genres distance him from reality. Submitting to a real world—that will mean finding something new, that will seal the break. Here, he is already considering a new way of reflecting on the relation between these two worlds. To come out of the grammatical world doesn't mean leaving behind language. To embark on that journey means abandoning the rules of fable, doing it not to free himself from all grammar, but in order to obey other rules no less real since they belong to the world. This letter begins to prepare Genet's passage. One kind of work is ending; another is beginning. One period is wrapping up, another begins, creative but completely new. Who can deny it? The serpent sloughs off its skin.

Genet did not sign the Manifeste des 121 (September 6, 1960) calling (among other things) for the right of French citizens to refuse military service in Algeria; a call for desertion. If the separation had been where people thought it was, everything would have been simpler: writing for the theater is sent to the trash heap of history, and the historic Manifesto is signed. But things didn't happen that way; quite the opposite. Genet didn't sign. There was a theatrical reason for his refusal: he's still talking about revising his plays, so he wishes to put the signature off till later. The era is at work here too: he is so surprised at being on the right side (in other words, among people whom one asks for their signature) that he thinks his name can only cause harm. It's better to withdraw and keep silent, be circumspect, aloof, strike a reflective attitude, so rarely accomplished. There is a historical reason, as well: the Manifesto comes late, and victory in Algeria is near; Genet can feel it. A letter written around the same time to the same friends confirms this hypothesis. When the lawyer Jacques Vergès asks him a little later to testify at the trial of the Jeanson network (a group of French militants who helped Algerian National Front agents during the war), Genet answers, "Dear Sir, you are asking me to be a character witness. But do you really think that for a military judge I have any character at all? [...] Why am I on the side of the FLN? Easy: I'm always on the side of the winner. Have you noticed the new sense of joy in the world since this revolution broke out, since these attacks took place?"[3] There was no need to sign up on the side of the losers.

The appearance of Céline's name gives another meaning to this letter. We should not forget that Jacques Vergès, the man for whom that particular allusion was made, was the lawyer who specialized in "difficult" cases: Klaus Barbie's, for example. Even in the atmosphere of the war in Algeria, Genet was a master manipulator of quotation marks. The ambiguous praise of Céline's rebellion involves a certain amount of provocation, no doubt, striking poses and image-making, but all that is quickly swept aside.

Céline is there to point to the dangers of political action. To understand what the allusion to him means, let's go back to Ezra Pound. Céline, Pound, and Genet create a constellation of their own. Pound always began his broadcasts on Italian fascist radio during World War II with these words: "Europe calling! Pound speaking! Ezra Pound speaking! [...] Ezra Pound speakin' from Europe for the American heritage." On May 16, 1942, he discusses Céline, calling his program "To Be Late." This is how it goes, in part: "Ah hear one of mah ex-editors has bin sayin', oh yeah, Pound talks are all right but they *arrrre*—what was that? Belated. No, he said, uh, they're retarded. [...] If yew hadn't bin such *mutts*, you woulda *heerd* me, and Céline for that matter, long before now!" And he launches into a long quotation from Céline before continuing: "The Yew-Nited States may take twenty years or more t' get t' where Céline was ten years ago. Ah be late? Ah be belated? [...] Céline denies that there is any fundamental and i*rrrrr*emediable hate between the F*rrrrr*ench and the Ge*rrrr*mans. [...] Mebbe in time the Amurrican cawledge boys will git roun' t' readin' me, or Céline, or some of the livin' authors... Time t' read Céline for the simple truths... You may be a bit late in startin'... Ezra Pound speakin.'"[4] Céline makes it possible for Pound, and for Genet as well, I believe, to consider a certain delay in political action. In Genet's terrible refusal to sign the Manifesto, "three ideas" contained in political action stand and wait. It is impetuous—without reflection but after the fact. It is impossible—you must act and you may be mistaken. It is necessary. The risk of being wrong, the particular urgency and the impossible necessity create the nobility and danger of this action.

A new configuration begins to develop: on the side of the temporarily victorious and Céline, that is, on the side of German national socialism during World War II, on the side of the Nazis. This is what

Genet cannot say, though he will later, albeit too late.

Genet's refusal to sign is a first manifestation of the unhealed scar between two eras. Negation, solitude, and powerlessness character- ize the experiences of the last incarnation of Genet. In the letter, he writes, "Without being able to say a word that makes sense. [...] And I can't say it. And I'm the only writer in France who can't say it." The refusal is simple. He is waiting for the final one, the only one. He has not yet made up his mind about political action, yet it is already there. Coming out requires another vocabulary, another way of seeing, in order to sign his action. Refusal and will, desire and waiting, urgency and collapse are all brought together a first and last time in the letter that delivers the meaning of this unbelievable, impossible act. Infi- nitely simple as well, as is the breaking free into this world, possible at every second we live. Not always legible, it is always present, when he finally reaches that point. In the letter there are simple truths: the choice political, as a submitting to the real world, and legal, as an im- perative we grant ourselves and obey. With the first manifestation of his act, the last incarnation of Genet is there in its entirety, preparing the coming out, if it is not already present. The writer's first political intervention was his refusal to intervene. In this refusal we see the impossibility of making a *decision* and the concern for his *responsibility*. The writer and his political act would take on their legitimate mean- ing here, if we can still find one for him.

LUXURY OF THE EYE

How to write about the Palestinian resistance or the black movement without being terribly mistaken? How is the revolution to be seen so that we may do it justice? What changes in our way of seeing are necessary to write the book of metamorphosis? Under the same label, we have to make sure not to confuse the will to be a non-conformist (which may or may not have intrinsic value), which powers a certain kind of artistic creation, with systematic action that seeks to trans- form the world and implies changing its very real foundations. For the writer, there are two difficulties: revolutions both political and poetic. Genet begins humbly by admitting what is impossible: poetry will not change the world. The humble future of the artist is a refrain of that period. Political stance-taking is a new reflection on poetic means. The difficulty of political revolution doesn't win out, nor the impossibility of a poetic revolution; Genet is interested in the difficult—impossible—relation between poetry and revolution.

In September 1972, in an apartment in Paris, seven Palestinian students and Genet held a conversation. "The Palestinians" (another article with the same title appeared the previous year in a magazine called *Zoom*) was not published in French, though it did come out the following year in an Arabic magazine *Shoun Falestine*, and later in English. The decision not to publish the piece in French was typical of the last Genet: he is seeking a way of seeing, and not of being seen. Militant activity is best shared that way, whether it involves organizing committees, defending minorities, or through established channels. In that apartment, Genet imagines the subjects about which he will be writing. Munich, for example—he begins writing shortly after the September 6, 1972 attack against Israeli athletes at the Munich Olympic Games, an attack organized by the fedayeen of Black September. There are other subjects besides Black September: Islam, Zionism, and French Jews, the failure of the resistance in Jordan, the difficulties of the couple within the institution of marriage, the schism between Palestinians and Jordanians, his concern with keeping convivial relationships in a world that seems to be rushing headlong toward cold-hearted individualism, the comparison of the Palestinian revolution with other revolutions around the world, different types and different steps.[5] The page I am about to cite belongs to the last subject, but it goes much further than that. Genet comes up with this reflection on the physical conditions of sexuality as a result of his point of view on revolution. The crowded living conditions of the camps prevents the Palestinians from enjoying a complete life, while the moneyed class has both time and space at its disposal:

Only the bourgeoisie can break down moral, sexual and social taboos. For we know full well that nothing pleases us more than breaking down taboos. I even wonder if it's too far-fetched to think that in part what pleases the bourgeoisie has to do with the fact that there's another world who doesn't know this pleasure. The true luxury of the eye is the ability to gaze fondly upon a poor man or his wretched living conditions as though they were a decorative object.

Because we're unable to live in a fully functional universe, we need to rest our eyes on something that seems inert or outside of time. Here too, we're conservative. Don't anyone touch the spectacle I'm busy contemplating! I know it's comprised of suffering and rags, and yet it not only meets my esthetic requirements, but also my need to prove myself superior by showing that I can appreciate the poor man's condition as being there for my own pleasure. Is it a mere coincidence that the Mechouar Palace in Rabat stands over a slum inhabited by 60,000 people? Is it happenstance that some Palestinian refugee camps are so close to the posh high-rises of Beyrouth that Europeans spend more and more time vacationing in under-developed countries, where they can lose themselves in the *souks* while staying in hotels that were built "for Europeans"? It's gotten so that the police are called whenever a poorly-dressed Arab or a shabby-looking black American strays into a residential neighborhood. Here's what a working-class Moroccan told me when I asked him what he feared the most in Paris: "Walking in the street because everyone is watching me."

In the same way, a businessman offers an unforgettable view from his luxury building. What you see is as follows: an old farm and a vineyard where men and women are working. From his apartments, the bourgeois "sees" the landscape, just as Hassan II "is familiar with" the slums. But as for the "unforgettable view," are the farmers and winemakers content to be a part of the landscape?

[And:] I want to return to the idea of a westerner or westernized man who looks out his window, and to that of the Third World at once exploited and watched. If the landscape is simply watched, the one watching it feels a certain serenity. This feeling reassures him, albeit in a slightly sadistic way, that he himself isn't landscape, since he's not part of the landscape. He's conservative in that he refuses to let the landscape change its shape or color. The suffering of the downtrodden provides pretty colors for the tableau—or landscape—that the westerner sees. Also, nothing must change; because, according to the bourgeois, "it would ruin the landscape." After all, it's his landscape we're talking about. If the landscape is exploited by the person watching it, then another type of relationship is created. The observer is no longer the passive guardian of the landscape, but rather, the active master controlling its change, and this change can only have one goal: producing for the master. The goal of all this is to demonstrate that a sensual and passive object is the same as a real, changing object; from the moment the eye sees, or takes pleasure in seeing, he wants to "preserve" the image he sees, just as the master wishes to own it with an eye on using it to turn a profit. Nobody wants to be a powerful man's landscape.

We can hope that henceforth Europeans will never again be in a position to gaze upon the "local color" and the oppressed will never again provide "an unforgettable view." As was the case for the member of the Black September in Munich, wearing a black hood. But does every event need to manifest itself as a threat to the West?[6]

At first reading, this passage seems heavy, overly dense, full of the naïveté of the times. Reading it in all its length, we sense the working out of a method. We can observe Genet in search of a way of seeing; with him we observe the reflection of a reality that he is striving to speak of, and not yet succeeding, a reality he will abide with as long as necessary. Attraction, fascination, and need will not allow him to find an adequate representation. Of misery, no doubt, that could well be sexual. Far from translating the thoughts and experiences of these young students, very quickly he monopolizes the conversation. This is not so much a dialogue as an internal conversation: I arrived in the Middle East, but if I am a believer, why did I leave? Etc. The cited passage proves it; its title could well be "luxury and misery in the writer's eyes."

This fragment arises from the mechanics of the 1970s that prepare Genet's action. The development of the slums is political; it returns in a paragraph in the last book. This is his method. *Prisoner of Love* is the explicit legacy of his conversation with the students. The issue of legacy announces that of revolution. Genet asks, "Whether the king's Palace was an abyss into which the shanty town might be drawn, or the shanty town an abyss drawing down the Palace, in any case one wonders which was real and which only a reflection." A note added to the manuscript leaves no doubt as to the link between these two places. At the point where he returns later in the book to the slums—the echo effect is one of the organizational poles of the work—he writes, "I believe I've found the complete opposite of the aforementioned slums, in the midst of the armed Palestinians."[7] He first noted, "the complete opposite of the Rabat slums I mentioned earlier [...]." Then comes a three-page sequence that doesn't describe either of these political spaces, but the relation between them: a teeming population lives there; a young man will emerge from it and discover himself. The revolution attracts—envy or fear—the Palace toward the slums, and vice versa. It is measured by its gaze: which is the reality, and which the reflection?

The "luxury of the eye," the "superb view," the "man looking out the window," the "tableau," ending with "the landscape as an object of exploitation": in 1972, Genet used this poetically poor vocabulary to "display" rather than show. On this page, Genet wants to show that he is between the "Moroccan" who speaks to him and the hastily identified "bourgeois." The last image is transparent: a black ... member wearing a hood. The event is only an erection. The point, the allusion behind the attack in Munich dramatizes in striking fashion the question of the gaze. Everything is still too obvious; the passage hasn't been crossed, and the misery of the writer's gaze is still visible. For the European, the "luxury of the eye" and the embarrassment of the conversation show the malaise attached to that gaze. For the Moroccan: "the fear of being seen." Fear and terror: the shame of he who sees and the shame of he who is seen. With shame in your eyes, you cannot create political or artistic revolution.

Luxury and possession: in the last book, the same words return but they are no longer separated by shame: "Possessions and luxury would go up in smoke if ever they decided they had nothing to lose."[8] The depth of this eye is blue, it seems suspended from the "wool of the sky." Perhaps it is the lapis lazuli blue of *The Last Judgment* (1536–41); like in the work of Michelangelo, *Prisoner of Love* features a naked heap of men and women. But, as with the fresco in the Sistine Chapel, the idea of judgment seems to dim when faced with the simple presentation of misery. If judgment allows us to rid ourselves of ourselves—our first and last names, our family tree, our fatherland, ideologies, parties, tombstones—then the stripping bare is political: Genet's revolution, or the absolute stripping bare of the gaze that falls upon the other. "O Sun, judge, people!" Osip Mandelstam exclaims in his poem, "Brothers, Let Us Glorify Freedom's Twilight." The writer, or any man for that matter, can at last see himself outside of shame, at least for a moment, facing the sun, "upright, if not kingly."

The temporary form of this transformation can be found in a statement Genet made in 1975 about the French painter Gustave Courbet: "But the only artist who put himself in the service of a revolution as an artist was Courbet, who was a great painter, but not one who repudiated the painting of his age."[9] In 1935, André Breton wrote of the inimitable example of Courbet in this parenthesis: "(the deep faith in the improvement of the world that inhabited him must find a way of being reflected in everything that he chose to evoke, appearing as well in the light he drew down upon the horizon as on the belly of a deer …)."[10] Between the world, the light, and the writer, relations change. The last incarnation of Genet becomes that *reflection of the joy of the rich deep in the eyes of the poor.*

THIRD WORLDISM AND CAPITAL

These days, the tendency is to dismiss the years of the revolution under the heading of Third Worldism; Marxist at the beginning, barbarous at the end. This aspect was quickly mocked, and Genet made fun of it as well, but the problem is that all possibility of revolt is swept away by the same act. We won't let that happen here. "The Black Panther Party was not an isolated phenomena. It was one of many revolutionary outcrops," Genet writes in his last book.[11] To write the word "outcrops" means refusing the title "avant-garde," and keeping the threatening side. Arrested for a theft worth only a few dollars, George Jackson spent his life in prison, where he became a member of the Panthers, then died at the hands of the police. He wrote, "Though I no longer adhere to all of [Sergey] Nechayev's revolutionary catechism (too cold, very much like fascist psychology, revolution should be love-inspired), his first line contains the incontrovertible truth, the black revolutionary is twice doomed."[12] The first sentence of Nechayev's book (written between 1847–1882 and translated by the movement as *Catechism of the Revolutionist*, Oakland, 1968) defines the revolutionary as "a doomed man. He has no personal interests, no business affairs, no emotions, no attachments, no property, and no name." The definition would be disastrous if it signified the disappearance of the personality in favor of the group; it is much more appealing if it means the disappearance of the self in favor of nothing or revolt. Jackson reinvents the legacy by adding the notion of color: black (not red). Genet finds the outcrop. Both blow away the fog of confusion. George Jackson—and his friendship with Genet rests on this last point—wrote, "To the slave, revolution is an imperative, a love-inspired, conscious act of desperation."[13] The author of *Prisoner of Love* can easily recognize revolution as a loving exit from slavery.

Rather than asserting its independence, the principle of the Palestinian revolution makes its own specificity. This is why: the historical leaders of the revolution are part of the generation of the "disaster"—

the *nakbah*. The Palestinians had to translate the crucial event of 1948 and make the connection with the flow of the past as they reconsidered it. A Palestinian refugee in Beirut put it this way in 1970: "Until 1967, the idea of liberation remained immersed in obscurity, naïveté and saintliness. It simply meant a pseudo-verbal return to Arab Palestine as we had left it nearly a quarter century earlier, and so a return to the pursuit of our historical development, as if history had stopped for a period of time."[14] The Palestinian revolution sought to politicize that aspiration to return to Palestine; instead of mythologizing the past, it promised hope for the future. Genet can understand the intervention of posterity over a return to the past.

The revolution viewed as a freeing from slavery (blacks) or a promise (Palestinian): in both cases, there is a new way of relating to one's history.

Between Palestinians and blacks, the relation is one of non-alignment. Malcolm X defined the term: "We're for ourselves. Whatever is good for us, that's what we're interested in. That doesn't mean we're against you. But it does mean we're for ourselves. [...] Egypt is a good example. They take from East and West and don't take sides with either one. Nasser took everything Russia could give him, and then put all the communists in jail. Not that I mean the communists should necessarily have been put in jail."[15] The precision in the example, the nuance; it's perfect. Non-alignment separated the Panthers and the Palestinians from any kind of worldwide revolution along the communist model. But in the same way, what they share keeps them apart, by necessity, if they are non-aligned. Between the movements, between them and Genet, the relation is one of non-alignment: the political translation of the destruction of the alliance, at once imposed by the circumstances and as the only way to preserve the revolt. As George Jackson said, the world is changing around.

"If there were a real revolution, I might not be able to be against it. There would be adherence, and I am not that kind of man; I am not a man of adherence, but a man of revolt."[16] That was Genet in 1975. His is the tradition of challenging, which is not revolt. Often the reader gets caught on these kinds of jokes, and misses the inventiveness that follows, the critique of posing, of mirrors, and the theater of revolution.

During the same interview with the German journalist Hubert Fichte, he calls May '68 a "mimodrama." It's not his word, but he subscribes to it: "Some have spoken of a 'mimodrama,' which seems accurate to me."[17] Which proves that he has something else in mind. May '68 remains the first revolutionary movement he witnessed, and its opposite. He bases his opinion on an event from the same period, when the students occupied the Théâtre de l'Odéon instead of the law courts.

In the last book, the Black Panthers don't escape criticism: "Revolutionaries are in danger of getting lost in a hall of mirrors."[18] When it comes to the Panthers, the word "mirror" pops up because their revolution seems to depend on their elegant style. A beret, combat pants, and a black leather jacket stand for "Panthers" in the public mind, and for their own members too at times. Take the poster that shows the party head, Huey Newton, a poster that was plastered to the walls of the Oakland ghetto, and that believers could purchase by sending a check to *Ramparts* magazine. The image leaves no room for subtlety: Huey is sitting in an enormous wicker chair like a king on his throne. He is wearing the Panther uniform, and there is a panther hide at his feet. In his left hand he is holding a spear; a rifle is in his right. Behind him, on either side, are African shields. The portrait conjures up the Jackson Pollock painting, *Guardians of the Secret* (1943), itself an imitation of Indian art Pollock found in *The Annual Report of the Bureau of American Technology* (1894). The Panthers may remember that painting, or even the Indians, but the portrait is keeping that a secret. The maxim of mirrors stands at the heart of the issue of emblems and archetypes. The issue criticizes images. Its principle is set down this way: "The essence of theater is the need to create not merely signs but complete and compact images masking a reality that may consist in absence of being."[19] Power is quick to use it, for the critique is political.

According to its way of mingling with the tableau it creates, the maxim of mirrors, in Genet's work, reaches its first conclusion in self-criticism. Here is an early moment of lucidity about "these revolutions we watch from plush and gilt stage boxes."[20] Genet himself has nothing against those boxes. When he describes the fedayeen, the word "pose" naturally crops up to help establish his critique. In the last book, Abu Omar talks with Genet. The year is 1970: "As I was saying, the revolution's in danger of becoming unreal through rhetoric, images on screens, and metaphor and hyperbole in everyday speech. Our battles are in danger of turning into poses—they look heroic, but in fact they're performed. But what if our play were interrupted, forgotten, and [...] thrown into the dustbin of History?"[21] The participial phrase "becoming unreal" calls forth a game of clever rhetoric: art, dream, and reality. Their role in fiction, the issue of representation, the opposition between sensitivity and intelligence. The word "pose" underlines the question—light but serious, amusing though grave—of the revolution's vanity. The fighters, Genet among them, recognize the game they are playing.

Mimodrama, mirrors, and poses: the revolutionary may well lose himself in the conformity of revolt, the herd mentality, and the gregarious fold.

"Revolution" is a word with a heavy past. "The Palestinians will never escape the paradox that as the years and the centuries go by, words become charged with emotion, self-interest, scandal, contradictory events, events with different facets. Just as capital acquires interest, so words, too, grow richer. How hard it is to bring about a revolution if you can't move those for whom you're fighting! But when you have to move them with words charged with the past—a past on the brink of tears, of tears that fascinate—then you've got your work cut out!"[22] Genet did not write that the word "revolution" is rich, though he believes it to be true, and his book attests to that fact. The word capitalizes on all revolutions past, the history of movements and countries that have freed themselves, but also on all the meanings of resistance and revolt, and the theater as well, poses, the fashions that spring from those meanings, the twisting around of their meaning. To emerge from the strictly political circle of revolution is the good fortune and task of the writer. In 1983, Genet said, "Listen, the day the Palestinians become an institution, I will no longer be on their side. The day the Palestinians become a nation like other nations, I won't be there anymore."[23] And then this: "And it's in solitude that I accept being with the Palestinians."[24] Does that mean he won't be there because he's dead, or no longer a fighter? Today, the Palestinians are moving toward statehood. In this disinterest, which is primordial, his story begins again. As a man of revolt, Genet cannot join revolutionary groups—the Panthers, the PLO, or any other. And even if he is with them, he is still alone. "It was quite easy to help the revolutionaries, but impossible to become a Palestinian. Isolation was splendid because it was the very nature of the revolution."[25] It is isolated because it is made of bodies. These bodies are not those of the Palestinians, but the result of events. The event of a body is solitude. Once again, as in the displacement of the portrait of the head of the PLO toward the inhabitants of the camps, the writer's gaze moves from the collective to the individual. Genet turns away from the Revolution—an empty word over which the great powers fight—to consider the revolutions of each person, experienced through the body, as an event.

The critique of the global nature of emblems, of revolutionary capital, doesn't mean that a few truths can't be spoken. Mirror or no mirror, for the Black Panthers, "they are necessary, those intervals of sacking and looting." They may strike poses, but the Palestinians' desire to take back the territories leads to a revolution that "though it involves getting the land back, doesn't stop at that." Genet, the spectator, can't help asking a few questions. "What other place are we to watch from if the revolutions are first and foremost wars of liberation? From whom are they trying to free themselves?"[26] Genet discusses the period of Third Worldism, the first wave adopted by a number of militants from the rich nations during the 1960s. He is influenced by its critique, the second wave, carried out by several Europeans some fifteen years later who were groaning under their burden: this was the new international economic order, the World Bank and the debt that constituted the burden for those countries in the so-called "developing world." Once there was blind support for all revolutions, but it was replaced by the isolated gaze of the decolonized individual. Writers struggled against a view of history that labeled a person as "decolonized" even if historically he liberated himself. The relation between Genet and the outcrops of the movements is on the line here; in other words, not all but more than one. In the 1970s, he wasn't trying to be black or Palestinian. A sense of revolt pushed him toward the unknown. Which doesn't mean he didn't know what he was doing.

And then there is that fabric of poverty, the misery that brings Genet together with the members of the movement. Crossing borders, the fabric wraps itself around the world, and Genet wants to be part of that. Here is what remains: necessary politics, the violence of legacy, and the debt to which Genet must now answer.

ENDNOTES

1. "Les Palestiniens" (II), *Shoun Falestine*, 1973; *GC*, 131–132.
2. The Moraly Collection.
3. Republished in the newspaper *Libération*, April 7, 1988.
4. H. Carpenter, *A Serious Character* (Boston: Houghton Mifflin, 1988), 583, 588–589.
5. "Les Palestiniens" (II); *GC*, 99–100.
6. Ibid., *GC*, 140–145.
7. *PL*, 69.
8. Ibid.
9. "Interview with Hubert Fichte, *Die Zeit*, February 13, 1976; *DE*, 129.
10. A. Breton, *Œuvres complètes* (Paris: Gallimard, Pléiade, 1992), 423.
11. *PL*, 246.
12. G. Jackson, *Blood in my Eye* (New York: Random House, 1972), 3.
13. Ibid., 9.
14. N. Picaudou, "Genèse des élites politiques palestiniennes: 1948–1982," *Revue française de sciences politiques* 34, no. 2 (April 1984): 343.
15. *Malcolm X Speaks: Selected Speeches and Statements*, ed. G. Breitman (New York: Grove Press, 1994), 132.
16. *DE*, 132.
17. Ibid., 131.
18. *PL*, 298.
19. Ibid., 302.
20. Ibid., 304.
21. *PL*, 317.
22. Ibid., 178–179.
23. *DE*, 244.
24. Ibid., 245.
25. *PL*, 230.
26. *PL*, 298, 304, 317.

Part Two

The Will to Trial

4 | The Will to Trial

The George Jackson story is political. Working toward his liberation, Genet continued to seek ties linking the poetic and the real world. This trial is really the beginning of a long investigation into the relationship between violence and writing, a concern for the writer. The investigation has three parts: "The Black and the Red" (1971), a response to the circumstances surrounding the opening of Jackson's trial on August 23, 1971; "Violence et brutalité," the preface to *Textes de prisonniers de la Fraction Armee Rouge et Dernières Lettres D'Ulrike Meinhof* (1977); and "Four Hours in Shatila" (1982). These works provide a vibrant depiction of Genet's thought process: was he writing to denounce the effects of violence, or was he aiming to bring violence into language?

THE VISOR

"Another thing worries me: fascism," Genet announced in New Haven, Connecticut, on May 1, 1970.[1] "We often hear the Black Panther Party speak of fascism, and whites have difficulty accepting the word. That's because whites have to make a great effort of imagination to understand that blacks live under an oppressive fascist regime. [...] Black people are right to accuse whites as a whole of this oppression, and they are right to speak of fascism." The sky was overcast when Genet arrived in America. The legacy of violence was threefold: abroad, there was the Vietnam War; within, the struggle with the Panthers; and linking the two was racism, or even fascism. To speak of fascism is to wonder, as did a historian in 1994, if "an authentically popular fascism in the United States would be pious and anti-Black; in Western Europe, secular and anti-Semitic, or more probably, these days anti-Islamic."[2] For three days, from July 18 to 20, 1969, the Black Panthers joined forces with white radicals to form the United Front Against Fascism. Bobby Seale spoke of the "fight against fascism" (September 20, 1969), while David Hilliard named the "political prisoners of fascism" (September 15, 1969). But how did Genet justify the use of the word? Stating, as he did, that the Black Panthers "were right" was a justification inextricably linked to its time and place, and cannot be cast in the same light as fascism. By not creating the political changes required, his words remain fruitless. Nothing has happened yet.

In an interview with *Le Nouvel Observateur* the following year, Genet explained that, "in *fascio*, there is fascination, the fascination of men, especially young men, for a leader. Whatever else, these are human relations. In the United States the cops are there to protect dollars and private property where no one lives. [...] They seem to be referring to nothing."[3] At the same time, the writer knew full well what the reference was: the leader, the police, and fascism. He knew he wasn't alone in seeing it, yet he couldn't truly see it. For Genet, the word still evoked the past. He thought of the old even as he saw the new. He wished to veer away from fascism, or rather, he seemed unable to free himself of it, to the point where he left the word as is, and instead changed the thing it defined. Thus, he found himself in the same relationship with the word as the Italian writer/film director Pasolini, who wrote, in *Pétrole*, "In Fascism there is a fascination that no one has ever had the courage to explain." Like Genet, he felt that the problem had to do with the continuation of the past, its legacy: "What has been lived by the body of the fathers can no longer be lived by ours."[4] Genet spoke of an unnamed correlation.

At this point, the writer experienced the fascist visor: it was impossible for him to see what the stakes were between war, death, and the sky. Being aware of this inability and speaking of it was the dual legacy of his first two American interventions. The first, "A Salute to a Hundred Thousand Stars" (1968), followed by "The Members of the Assembly," also comprised his first attacks on violence. The connection between the two texts, one on the Democratic National Convention in Chicago and the other on the Vietnam War, was not circumstantial. About Vietnam, he wrote, "the dead soldier's family will hang a little star in the window of their house. The death of your child is a pretext for decorating your home. And since nothing in heaven and on earth sparkles more than stars, I imagine that you look forward to the death of many of your sons, in Vietnam."[5] The writer scoffed, repudiating the tradition of American women who hung a star over their doorways when in mourning. The constellation of home, stars, and death is recreated by the simple gesture of the Palestinian women of Jebel Hussein, in Jordan. Time and again, Genet mentioned these widows, gathered around a fire in a small courtyard, having themselves buried their dead. In 1982, he wrote that, "Theirs was a cheerfulness that has ceased to hope." And again, in 1986: "The sun was hot, and the fire burned even though it was out."[6] On their fingertips, the ashes were alive, the dead present. The women were fulfilling the task of mourning as well as tending to tradition. Here, Genet accepted the gesture, while in America, he mocked it. He saw the American constellation as failure, nothing more than "grief in the lap of luxury," what we previously identified as the luxury of the eye. The constellation was denied its simplicity when seen through the eyes of a prisoner of shame.

His complete inability to see things as such—to perceive what was and submit to the real world—was humbly revealed in his other intervention. It had to do with a visor, which he himself saw on August 27, 1968—the day of transformation. About this week of barricades during the Democratic Convention in Chicago, he wrote, "The second day afflicts us with the azure helmets of the Chicago police. A policeman's black leather visor intrudes between me and the world: a shiny visor in whose neat reflections I might be able to read the world, a visor no doubt polished several times a day to keep it in such fine condition."[7] The day following the day of the visor, Bobby Seale spoke in Grant Park; Genet saw a Black Panther but didn't know it. The Black Panthers remained an unseen reality, for Genet was still blinded by the visor. The country was fascist. The visor was fascinating because it was shiny. Genet was fascinated by the effects of fascism reflected in the visor. All three were under the same low and heavy sky, like a lid that was closing. The effects of the visor didn't allow fascination, violence, and death to be linked; they prevented him from understanding the world and consequently submitting to it. The sky was darkened by the lid of fascism, driving, yet holding back, compelling the last Genet. For the moment, he was caught up in something he couldn't see, something that watched him, held by a gaze that he couldn't meet.

In a way, he too was a prisoner of fascism, in the Panopticon of the times. In 1975, in New York, Michel Foucault publicly declared, "I think that what has happened since 1960 is the simultaneous appearance of new forms of fascism, new forms of consciousness of fascism, new forms of description of fascism and new forms of struggle against fascism."[8] Infamy, then fascism; later, terrorism. Neither the philosopher nor the writer made these up. To acknowledge them was to make a political statement. If Genet saw them, he did not yet recognize them. He was more concerned with the visor. He had to learn to see the sky clouded over by fascism. Both philosopher and writer faced the same task: using experience, skill sets, personal choices, and desires, they had to position themselves so that the forms of fascism that were previously unnoticed or too easily tolerated were brought to the fore in order to describe them, to convey them as intolerable, and to outline exactly how the battle against fascism could be undertaken.

Genet's response, which matters to us here, was to turn his gaze upon a single man. The writer's third American venture is titled "Here and Now for Bobby Seale." He gave this man a name—or another,

George Jackson—and established himself in relation to a specific point in the real world. Moved by this living man whose singular death was imminent, possible or impossible, inevitable, he could speak of him. This is how he exposed fascism. With this *one* death, Genet escaped his fascination with the *general idea* of death.

THE GAG

Genet then wrote, "We should never forget [...] that the Black Panther Party seeks to be armed, and armed with real weapons."[9] A sign above the entrance to their Oakland, California headquarters, on 56th Street and Grove Avenue, displayed their full name: BLACK PANTHER PARTY FOR SELF-DEFENSE. The Panthers' newspaper was filled with pictures of weapons, lifted from the National Rifle Association's publication. The January 26, 1968 issue offered an explanation of their methods: "The Black Panther Party is an armed body for carrying out the political tasks of revolution." This statement was meant to dispel false notions that militants either "have the mentality of mercenaries" or "a low political level," or both. It was aimed at those with "over confidence in military strength." The conclusion was clear; it sought the "...weakening or even eradicating the purely military viewpoint."[10] The Panthers looked back to Malcolm X's twofold decision—his refusal to take part in the war abroad and his commitment to act by "any means necessary" at home—as well as Jackson's "perfect chaos." Since war was already here, they had to create either the struggle for liberation, or an exit as a means to escape it. Instead, what awaited them was attrition and elimination.

There is no longer any doubt as to the repression of the Black Panther Party, if ever there was. A recent look at the FBI memorandum concerning the Counter Intelligence Activities (COINTELPRO) reveals that a section known as Radical Intelligence was created to endanger, discredit, and neutralize the black movement's activities. Authorities of the federal government, including the Vice President, labeled the movement as a totally irresponsible group of criminal

anarchists. J. Edgar Hoover saw the Black Panthers as the number one
threat to US security, while John Mitchell, Nixon's Attorney General,
concluded that they had to get rid of them. The methods used by this
FBI section included supplying misinformation to the press, false accusations against individuals, suppressing evidence that could be used
to help the accused and, eventually, assassinations.[11]

Genet was named in these reports by the FBI. Though unaware
of COINTELPRO, his words and actions betrayed knowledge of
the risk involved, along with his desperate effort to stop the repression and his humble attempts to achieve this end. The interweaving
of the writer's trial with that of the Black Panthers began with Huey
Newton, who was accused of murdering a police officer in 1967. He
was immediately incarcerated (and eventually released in August 1971,
when it was revealed there was police provocation). Meanwhile, Bobby Hutton died at the age of seventeen, on April 19, 1968, the first
member of the Black Panthers to be assassinated by the police. Bobby
Seale, whom Genet had heard but not met, was arrested in the wake
of the Democratic National Convention, along with seven other well-
known activists (among them, Jerry Rubin, Abbie Hoffman, and Tom
Hayden). Seale alone was held in jail, awaiting his second trial for being an accessory to murder. (He was cleared of these charges in 1971
and freed.) Erica Huggins and twenty other Panthers were arrested
in New York on April 2, 1969 for conspiracy against their country.
Afeni Shakur was among them (the mother of rapper Tupac Shakur,
who was born in prison.) Their trial began in 1970; bail for the group
was set at $2.1 million (the case would be dismissed in 1971). George
Jackson, whose name would long echo in Genet's consciousness, had
been in prison since 1960 for robbing a gas station. He was handed
a fine and a light prison sentence, but at parole hearing after parole
hearing, he was denied: he would never walk free. He was still incarcerated when, at Soledad Prison on January 13, 1970, a guard named
Miller killed three blacks in the yard and injured one white. Miller was
acquitted. Shortly after, a guard named Mills was shot. Three blacks

stood accused: George Jackson, John Clutchette, and Fletta Drumgo, who became known as the Soledad Brothers (all were ultimately found innocent of murdering Mills, but on August 21, 1971, Jackson was assassinated by prison guards at San Quentin). Jackson's younger brother Jonathan, meanwhile, entered the San Rafael courthouse for James McClain's trial. Armed, he freed McClain and pair of prisoners, took Judge Harold Haley and four others hostage, and demanded the release of the three Soledad Brothers. During the getaway, Jackson, Haley, and two of the prisoners he freed were killed. Angela Davis was accused of having sold the weapons and was wanted by the FBI. On October 13, 1970, she was arrested and jailed, but freed soon after for lack of evidence.

Angela Davis, George Jackson, and Bobby Seale were all imprisoned in Soledad Prison in Monterey County, California. They spent a lot of that time in the "hole," described here by Seale: "The hole itself is a box five feet wide and seven feet long. You have no bed, no bunk, no toilet. There is only a hole in the floor where one could defecate, urinate and this often overflows. This hole was ruled unconstitutional by state supreme court in 1966."[12] To say that "when they join the Black Panther Party, black people know they will be killed or will die in prison,"[13] was simply seeing things for what they were. The author's note can be further interpreted as meaning that all Panthers, or at least most, are parolees or survivors. Eldridge Cleaver, a survivor who went into exile after the death of Bobby Hutton, asked himself, "Why am I alive? Eldridge Cleaver died in that house on 28th Street with Little Bobby Hutton, and what's left is force: fuel for the fire that will rage across the face of this racist country and either purge it of its evil or turn it into ashes."[14]

Genet encountered the justice system countless times. His last book ends on the witness stand, in a trial without charges. "The witness is on his own," he writes. "He has sworn to tell the truth, not to tell it to the judges."[15] The writer attended one of the hearings for Bobby Seale's trial. Seale, along with seven others, was accused of conspiracy and inciting to riot during the 1968 Democratic Convention. Seale was "([...] gagged, an unprecedented event)."[16] The parentheses represent the gag. In a 1970 article, Genet wrote, "In the Bobby Seale affair at the Chicago conspiracy trial, there were eight accused. Among the eight, seven were released on bail in the end. But not for exorbitant and absolutely unpayable bail of a hundred and fifty thousand dollars that are set for blacks. Only one of the accused remains in prison, and for a while the American left lost interest in him; and this man, it just so happens, is black, and the chairman of the Black Panther Party."[17] The article, written in Bobby Seale's defense, was published in the June 1970 issue of *Ramparts* magazine. At the end was a photo and an announcement that read, "As Jean Genet has so eloquently stated, the trial of Bobby Seale and the eight Connecticut Panthers is a test, a moment of truth for white radicals. New Haven should become a center this summer for radicals organizing around the trial. Anyone who can come to New Haven or can help in any way should contact the Panthers Defense Office, 520 Chapel Street, New Haven, Connecticut 06511." It noted the urgency of the struggle. Featured on the cover of the issue was a three-color Paul Kagan photo of an electric chair, similar to Andy Warhol's *Electric Chair* series (1963-1967). Following the article, which was heralded on the cover, the same picture appeared, with the declaration: "*They are planning to kill Bobby Seale...*"

What follows is a moment in the trial of the man described by witnesses as the most important political prisoner in American history. His treatment, in contrast to that of the seven whites also accused, did much to expose the hypocrisy inherent in the system, particularly when Seale found himself shackled to his chair, gagged with plastic wrap, and a cloth placed over his face, forced to answer by nodding or shaking his head. That day, Seale was punished for contempt. Due to this punishment, the law allowed him to speak. The exchange between Seale and the Court went as follows:

The Court: Mr. Seale, you have a right to speak now. I will hear you.

Mr. Seale: For myself?

The Court: In your own behalf, yes.

Mr. Seale: How come I couldn't speak before?

The Court: This is a special occasion.

Mr. Seale: Wait a minute. Now are you going to try to—you going to attempt to punish me for attempting to speak for myself before? Now after you punish me, you sit up and say something about you can speak? What kind of jive is that? I don't understand it. What kind of court is this? Is this a court? It must be a fascist operation like I see it in my mind, you know—I don't understand you.

[...]

The Court: You may speak to matters I have discussed here today, matters dealing with your contemptuous conduct. The law obligates me to call on you to speak at this time.

Mr. Seale: About what? About the fact that I want the right to defend myself? That's all that I am speaking about.

The Court: No, about possible punishment for contempt of court.[18]

What were the effects of this trial? Of the gag, the mispronounced names, the system of repression? The gag inhibited all speech: that's fascism. That day, Kunstler, one of Bobby Seale's lawyers—and lawyer also for Martin Luther King, Stokely Carmichael, and Rap Brown before him—tried to intervene. A noise at the back of the room was cited, and he was denied. The names of the lawyers were constantly butchered; Leonard Weinsglass, for instance, became Weinstein and Feinglass. No doubt, this is where the cruelty began. For the government, the crowning achievement in its repression lay in its use of the court of law to legitimize cruelty against its opponents by shifting the matter of the Chicago siege and its significance to the trial itself. The law is usurped during the process of repression. Genet felt the need to draw a line between law and justice. According to a witness, "The defendants had to face not the abstract majesty of the law but this 'procedure' day after day, week after week. [...] To criticize defendants for not remaining silent reveals the most obsessive clinging to the idea of the intrinsic legitimacy of political institutions. [...] As we listened to the testimony it was almost impossible (morally and emotionally) to remain silent. To listen in silence only seemed to legitimize the authority of a police state. [...] The Dreyfus affair began when the Dreyfus trial ended."[19] In fact, Genet likened this trial to the Dreyfus Affair, claiming that it was "perhaps even more harmful than the Dreyfus Affair in France and Europe." He acknowledged that for Seale, there was "no Clemenceau, no Jaures, and especially, among the intellectuals, no Zola to write *J'Accuse*."[20] By naming Zola, he no doubt wished to repair the mistakes of a work like *J'Accuse*. His need to honor Zola's work while defending Bobby Seale reveals a need to re-establish a link with tradition. Though in the thick of the trial, he was already seeking to understand the will of the trial. Without names, without history, without words, even: a noise at the back of the courtroom.

Genet and the movements were on trial. I say this because, on three occasions, he talked publicly or wrote about the hearing he attended during Bobby Seale's second trial April 14, 1970 with David Hilliard and Emory Douglas, in New Haven. He was present, neither spectator nor witness, but there. All there? Who can say? He first recounted the moment to Americans in his New Haven speech on May 1, 1970. He mentioned it a second time, in passing, nine days later in Paris. The third time, not reprinted in the collection of political texts, appeared in writing in an article for *La Nouvelle Critique* (June 1971).

First, there was *the sign*. "From the moment I entered the courtroom, American racism, which is to say anti-black racism, became apparent to me in all its violence. When I arrived in the courtroom with my black comrades of the Black Panther Party, a cop, without asking me, led me to the first row of the audience, in the section where there were only whites. It's only thanks to the insistence of my black comrades that I was allowed to go sit with them. To you this may seem like an insignificant sign, but to me, having been there as its pseudo-beneficiary, I translated this sign immediately. And when Hilliard and Emory were arrested for disrupting the court while reading out a statement, I myself who had also read a statement before the court— was simply expelled from the courtroom, but left free."[21]

There, Genet also mentions "Judge Hoffman, the judge who had Bobby Seale gagged." Naming this judge complicates the reference to the one in the Dreyfus trial. Second, there's *the remark*. "In the New Haven courtroom, they tried to make me sit with the whites, without asking for my opinion."[22] Third, there's *the meaning*. "Douglas and Hilliard asked if I wanted to see the room. It was big enough for twenty people. The first three rows were occupied by whites, except for one spot. A policeman wanted to put me there: a white among the whites. The rest of the court was segregated too. During the hearing we read a letter. All three of us. Only they were arrested. Not me, the white man. Arrested because, by reading a letter, 'they were disrupting the order of the court.' Six months in jail. I watched the clock as the incident took place. In exactly one and a half minutes, they were bound, arrested and sentenced. A minute and a half, six months in jail, the reading of a letter."[23] The general tone of the first account, the naming of the comrades, and the relating of the circumstances were used in an effort to allow only one possible interpretation of the scene: the racism of whites toward blacks. The remark in the second seems to suggest, within the context of the trial and of racism itself, Genet's racism toward the whites. While blacks were not permitted to sit with whites, he refused to be led to his rightful place as a white among whites. A slight shift, a small transformation: the place he assigned himself throws light on a moment in this story. When faced with blatant racism, he displayed a certain hatred; for segregation between whites and blacks, but also for the writer's being singled out.

Genet stared at the clock, capturing the moment. His presence served to measure time. During the seconds that followed, flowed, and slipped away, he took stock of eternity. Whites were not to be touched. Blacks were to be led to the back. Blacks were arrested; Genet stops time. By watching the clock, by keeping an eye on the temporal aspect of the trial, he was watching history turn its back on the future. Better yet, by watching the time instead of the violence, he stayed true to the temporality of the witness, present to himself alone. In a certain, new way, Genet's gazing at the trial's clock can only mean that *justice had to be created*.

THE ROPE

Beneath the American sky of the seventies, the Black Panthers were the link between the hundred thousand stars of the soldiers killed in Vietnam and the chain of fecal matter, connecting blacks in prison: the high and low. For trying to change perceptions, they ended up in prison and soon after, heaven. From his cell in Soledad, George Jackson wrote a book; to this, Genet added, "Except for Jackson's book, everything I have been speaking of was orchestrated [...] by the guards."[24] From where he stood, neither outside nor inside the movement or Jackson's book, he'd try to break the circle of fascism. In Jackson's name, he sought a way to speak of those locked up; and using the issue of violence, his goal was to make clear what binds art and reality: first, on behalf of the Panthers, and soon thereafter, the Panthers and George Jackson. Genet used every means—oral, visual, written—on a global scale (France, Jordan, Brazil), moving in a way that can only be characterized as panic. His was like a mad chase in the looming shadows of the Panthers on trial, in prison, or assassinated. It's as though Genet wanted to save every black in America, one at time, day after day, word after word. Interventions, attempts and contrite efforts: we must see this as an ongoing misfortune.

In this somber month of March 1971, speaking out on George Jackson's behalf, Genet wrote: "I have come to that part of my speech where, to help save the blacks, I am calling for crime, for the assassination of whites."[25] Silence. Although the manifesto was a response to the likely assassination of Jackson in prison on August 21, 1971, the origins of Genet's incitement to murder go much further back. As noted earlier, Genet did not sign the Manifesto of the 121 (September 1960). Ten years later, he preferred to write this "discourse," a loaded word rarely used by the author himself. He resorted to politics without poetry, leaving the writer off the hook. He had this discourse, or call for murder, signed by the leading Parisians of the day: Maurice Blanchot, Jacques Derrida, Marguerite Duras, Pierre Guyotat, Philippe Sollers, etc. Here, misfortune found expression in humor, albeit macabre, characterized by his prior refusal to sign the Manifesto of the 121, the writing of his own manifesto as a call for murder, the countersigned approval of French intellectuals for this clearly outrageous discourse. Between the call for murder and its approval, is the latter not worse, in terms of responsibility? He who writes the manifesto must know what he's doing, but what of those who sign it? Bitterness and disappointment followed Genet's incitement. Not disappointment from the fact that he couldn't get the signers to write texts on the black cause to be gathered into a book, nor bitterness from the fact that no one, no more than he, committed any murders; the bitterness and disappointment stemmed instead from the very heart of the undertaking, that is, how difficult it is to speak of those who have asked nothing of you. It was pointless to try and enlist others. His incitement was a clear example that *as ever in the history of intellectuals, books are chosen over murder.*

The outcrop called for comment, or rather, two statements about intellectuals in regards to his relationship with violence. The first was addressed to Daniel Defert, to whom he was close at the time. Defert founded the GIP (the *Groupe d'information sur les prisons*, or the Prison Information Group) with Michel Foucault. After the philosopher's death, Defert started AIDES, a foundation that helps those afflicted with AIDS. In lieu of a book on Jackson, a pamphlet for *Intolérable* was published by the GIP, written by Genet and dedicated to the late

Foucault. Genet declared to Defert, "I don't want to publish anything about France. I don't want to be an intellectual. If I publish something about France, I'll strike a pose as an intellectual. I am a poet. For me to defend the Panthers and the Palestinians fits in with my function as a poet. If I write about the French question I enter the political field in France—I don't want that."[26] The assertion about intellectuals must be seen in relation to a theory about murder, which comes later but belongs to the same constellation. In 1975 in Paris, Genet was asked why he'd never committed murder. "Probably because I wrote my books,"[27] he replied. To put it more clearly, "the idea of murder can be beautiful. Real murder, that's something else."[28] He wanted to show the difference between humor and provocation or revolt on the one hand, and humor and political argument on the other. His pressing desire to break away from intellectuals was very real, but it's not his refusal to write on French matters that defines it; it's Genet's relationship with himself and with violence. The question of whether or not one is an intellectual is essentially French. The question of violence is a concern of the last Genet. The writer's role in these two issues is not the same. The terms remain the same (violence, books, oneself), but how he related to each has changed. A distinction must be made between French issues and the foreign cause. The first pertains to a history of intellectuals as well as, in the sense Genet used the term, French political matters. For instance, there was the election of President Valéry Giscard d'Estaing, which prompted Genet to speak out publicly three times. The second pertains as much to issues dealing with foreign politics (i.e., the repression of the Black Panthers) as it does—specifically because of the foreignness—to the relationship with the self, and thus, to violence. In other words, Genet is an intellectual because, against his will, he prefers books to murder. This fact is monumental, indisputable, and inescapable. He wasn't an intellectual (a "poet," if you will) because his relationship with violence as a foreign cause is a means of relating to himself.

As always, such distinctions remain in constant flux. Genet temporarily defined himself as a poet, at once to dissociate himself from intellectuals, especially the French, who are mindful of taking action in France as a means to save or serve their image, and in the name of his status as a writer, in order to effect the necessary changes along with the international movements. He entered the foul-smelling circus of men through a critique of violence, only to immediately capture and imprison himself. He inherited violence as a concern for the self. He had to answer to the violent end.

At the same time, he tried to speak fairly of the Palestinians. The Jackson trial was a link between "The Palestinians" I and II (1971, 1973) and "The Women of Jebel Hussein" (1974). This is not meant to downplay the hardship and suffering of the Panthers and Palestinians as mere grounds for poetic work. Genet's work does not allow such a reading, as it seeks to learn how to break the circle of prison, racism, and fascism. From one to the next, from the Panthers to the Palestinians, from his endeavors on behalf of one or the other to those whom they address, from the written word to the world, a method is honed, violence gains in strength, and the fire spreads.

The method involves an ongoing search; it's part of the process. At that point in time, Genet wrote a text entitled "Problèmes" in 1971 in which he recounts the difficulties encountered when discussing the Panthers. It was published in *L'Ennemi déclaré*, a compendium of his political texts, and was judiciously placed before his incitement to murder, in the form of a facsimile:

> My involvement is becoming more and more mechanical.
> It is time for me to think about these problems and find a
> solution. That I could set against the Panthers' solution.
> The Panthers' political thinking has to pass through my
> life; I want to pronounce living words. I promised myself
> to use only political arguments, but I see that these sorts of
> arguments bore people. I'll have to turn to the emotional
> argument. And that creates confusion, a viscous mess. My

ideas about the Panthers have to be clearer. I need to retain, maintain and increase sensitivity.[29]

To speak of the other, to be true to oneself and remain political; that is the question. Against all odds, the topics broached in "Problèmes" resurface at the other end of Genet's story. In the second section of *Prisoner of Love*, the following passage is said to have occurred in May 1972: "The men inside thought they were taking part in a general orgy, but I couldn't help them transmute it into politics, as they'd have liked. I couldn't give up wandering."[30] Why against all odds? To my knowledge, the name "George Jackson" is never mentioned in *Prisoner of Love*. Yet his name helped Genet establish a position from which to launch his political combat. Better still, Genet sought to describe the pink file of the Moroccan born the same year as he was, wanted to read Nabil Farès' book, see the *Young Thrushes (Jeunes Grives)*: all this I have said. Now he moved from the Panthers to the *single* name of George Jackson. Was he signing this shift, dubbing his political self, or simply signing *J.G.*?

"Problèmes" does not call for solutions. It's a testament to its tenacity that a question that first emerged in a draft text (or a haze) fifteen years earlier reappears as a paragraph in the last book. In the onset of this political memory, Genet stated, very simply, "I sought in other people's eyes the thin silk thread that ought to link us all."[31] The issue is how to transmute police repression and prison bloodshed into reflection leading to an eventual political intervention. In those years, the transition was being made toward the identification of the self through the eyes of another. In other words, the transformation of the prison chains—iron, fecal matter, air currents—into the thin silk thread of exchanged glances.

Now, under the authority of those who had red on their hands and blackness in their hearts, the trial could begin. Genet read George Jackson's letters one last time. "The Red and the Black" was the second installment of his book, previously begun in the introduction to *Soledad Brother*, the book of collected letters. Here, by way of vocabulary, Genet would attempt to exonerate the prisoner, at the risk of death.

As he'd once pointed out, in transcribing the brochure of the Soledad Defense Committee, the equation is simple: "A white man kills three black men: he remains innocent. A white man falls from a wall: three black men will be sentenced."[32] Jackson was one of them. Without preamble, Genet launched his attack: "George Jackson's book is a murderous act, beyond all measure, but never demented, even if Jackson's sufferings and fevers drove him to the door of madness, a door he never entered; it is a radical murder, undertaken in the solitude of a cell and the certainty of belonging to a people still living under slavery, and this murder, which is ongoing, is perpetrated not only against white America, against the American will to power, against what is called the entrepreneurial spirit; it is the systematic and concerted murder of the whole white world greedy to drape itself in the hides of nonwhite peoples; it is the—hopefully definitive—murder of stupidity in action."[33] He insisted on murder to make a clear distinction from another act, the assassination of Mills, the guard. Murder and assassination are therefore opposed as "this sort of digression (assassination) [to] Jackson's long undertaking (murder by means of the book)."[34] In both cases, it is an act. Assassination is an individual act. Murder is undertaken by an individual. The same psychic energy is behind both operations. But because the energy is the same, he said, "The two acts might complement each other, but they were not carried out by the same man."[35] One must accept this premise, make a distinction between assassination and murder, and consider the space between "individual" (as opposed to many) and "same" (as opposed to other) as minute. These distinctions all dwell specifically on the reclusion, reduction, and isolation of the imprisoned man. *Withdrawing into the isolation of the self, just as one speaks of the possible death of another, is truly a political move.*

The task at hand was to save a man from a possible death sentence.

Faced with the impending threat, Genet first isolated himself and then delivered this judgment: "It is obvious that if he wrote his book—and he did write it—he was incapable of carrying out the assassination."[36] *Es ist evident*, as the men of Germany's Red Army Faction were sometimes known to write. Thought, reflection, and analysis have departed; doubt—without a doubt—has been given a leave of absence. Is this the expression of despair, of a desolate attempt, or ongoing misfortune? I don't know. Genet went further. In the same breath, he tried to acquit Angela Davis, also in prison, of having sold weapons. "We can see Angela Davis' work and her alleged gun purchase in the same light. Angela's goals—the liberation of the black ghettos [...]—would be annihilated by the purchase of weapons for any individual, capable of inspiring a fleeting terror that would contradict the full scope of the project."[37] He concluded with an unequivocal statement: "Angela did not buy any guns." Judgment (*es ist evident*) belongs to the circumstances of the trial or the argument between judge and hoodlums. It must not eclipse the project. That is for us to judge.

The visor was both near and far, the object nameless; fascism had to go—such was the scope of the project. At some point during the Jackson affair, Genet's August 1970 assertion that "the entire black community is afraid" gave way to "America is afraid"[38] (August 1971). It was at once small and vast. Blacks were freeing themselves of submission. *Genet and Jackson were no longer talking about the struggle of being born black (race, country, identity), instead denouncing the curse of being held captive (movement, liberation, coming out).* That was definitely new. Would Genet hold to it? That was another issue. The threat Malcolm X perceived—"in America there are twenty million black people, all of whom are born in prison. [...] If you're born in America with a black skin, you're born in prison"[39]—was changing. Prison was now outside the skin.

The actions of Genet and Jackson, seen together, go like this. First, the writer came to the defense of the Panthers, an armed group. Then he defended the prisoners, who were disarmed, by launching a manifesto calling for murder. And finally, he defended a man confronted with death, in the name of writing. Genet made the book the proof of his innocence. Facing the death penalty, Jackson wrote a book. Once assassinated, he would be found innocent of the crime he didn't commit. But would he be innocent because he wrote a book and then assassinated for having written it? That's not really the issue. As Jackson saw it, Genet was trying to go from petty crime to major, even political, offense. In a way, he was now motivated by *truth*, the point of transmutation. Jackson was the one who, still in prison and no doubt working to better himself, transformed the thief's aims into political projects. By rejecting society as it was and needing to make the government capitulate, Jackson wanted to change the government as well as the power structure itself. It was all about liberation from the ghetto. Liberation meant an escape from captivity and surveillance, a move beyond racism and skin, an exit from identity, nation, and state. Who would argue that Jackson wasn't Weidmann, the criminal in the first sentence of *Our Lady of the Flowers*? Though Genet coming to Jackson's defense may have appeared as the smallest of gestures, it should be seen as a monumental undertaking—that of freeing himself from the hole, from prison, from the circle of fecal matter, eschewing the myth of being born in prison to look elsewhere. Jackson wrote his book to show the scale of his political project. Genet came to his defense to free him from prison so he could achieve his political goals. The result of their actions: they were no longer bound by prison's shit-encrusted chains, by the relations between judge and hoodlums, nor by the chain of command.

By making the distinction between murder and assassination, Genet wanted to clear Jackson. In a judicial sense, the impact of the testimony was both immediate and considerable. By establishing the difference between the two acts, he placed himself clearly on Jackson's side, but also with Angela Davis and anyone else willing to be part of the movement, siding with those endeavoring to transform society. In a political sense, the impact was equally immediate and considerable.

Except that he was resisting. A certain *positivity* in the politics of the last Genet would soon fade. His project was neither reform nor change, but a slight shifting of society as it was. His proposals were moveable and could not establish a program. It seems that by differentiating murder from assassination, Genet was, by the same token, separating language and death, the trial forcing him into that separation. In order to save Jackson, he argued that since Jackson had written a book, he couldn't be guilty of murder. Genet presented the book as murder, refusing to leave the topic of violence altogether and maintaining the possibility of violence in language. That is, by insisting on the necessity to check for poetry in the world, he refused any separation. He was only willing to deal with the problem of proving Jackson's innocence by insisting on murder, and by doing so, risking the creation of many more problems. We could even consider whether Genet's words weren't providing enough rope to hang Jackson. Elsewhere, Genet wrote that Jackson's book was "both a weapon in the struggle for liberation and a love poem."[40] It's probably best not to dwell on this too much. Using murder by book as a defense for a man facing a death sentence meant both resisting the temptation of a verbose defense, which would probably have been more humanist, and asserting the possibility of death. The practical effect of the political and poetic act was nothing less than the destruction of a certain notion of the man.

Making any positive assertion regarding Genet's politics is a delicate matter, due to his approach. I described the scope of his political project: abandon the prison system and transform society. The difficult matter of exploding out of jail, away from racism and from fascism—and therefore from shame—was never radical, continuous, or final. Therefore, Genet's political actions were absolutely opposed to murder.

After Jackson's murder on August 21, 1971, Genet reflected, "Recently, I mean when it still seemed possible that Jackson would live, I spoke of his book as murder, and I did not suspect that the murderer would be killed by the American police."[41] Genet never saw George Jackson's body, and could not sit by his side in vigil. In 1983, he said, "Then, when George Jackson died, Bobby Seale asked me to come to the funeral. I went to the United States Embassy and they refused to give me a visa."[42] Jackson's violent end is the difference between the death of the other (always unknown) and one's own death (always impossible). In Genet's text written immediately after Jackson's death, the wavering between the possible (life) and the uncertain (death) is the writer's infinitesimal sign of mourning.

The last word on the Jackson affair marked the end of heroism. It was a temporary, difficult ending, never complete, as we've now learned. The glorification of heroism and death is still part and parcel of the penal system, from which there's no escape. The avenged is no longer the just. Hence, the importance of the phrase "I did not suspect." Doubt does not express pity; it has political significance. In the end, George Jackson could have lived. That possibility didn't come to pass, and the writer took careful note of it. While Genet's subtle gesture concealed sorrow and nameless anger, it dismissed the customary idealization of heroism, vengeance, and death. He simply spoke of *justice as a relationship with others*. He expressed surprise over the death of another man. A possibility no more.

ENDNOTES

1. *DE*, 38.
2. R.O. Paxton, "The Five Stages of Fascism," The Journal of Modern History 70, no. 1 (March 1998).
3. "Jean Genet chez les Panthères noires," interview by Michèle Manceaux, *Le Nouvel Observateur*, May 25, 1970.
4. P.P. Pasolini, *Petrolio*, trans. A. Goldstein (New York: Pantheon, 1997), 226, 224.
5. "A Salute to a Hundred Thousand Stars," *Evergreen Review*, December 1968; *DE*, 276.
6. "Four Hours in Shatila," *Revue d'études palestiniennes* 6 (January 1, 1983); *DE*, 217; *PL*, 327.
7. "The Members of the Assembly," *Esquire*, November 1968; *DE*, 270.
8. D. Eribon, *Michel Foucault*, trans. B. Wing (Cambridge: Harvard University Press, 1991), 312.
9. *DE*, 37.
10. *Black Panther Newspaper*, January 26, 1968.
11. C.E. Jones, "The Political Repression of the Black Panther Party 1966–1971," *Journal of Black Studies* 18, no. 4 (1988); H. Kleffner, "The Black Panthers: Interviews with Geronimo ji-jaga Pratt and Mumia Abu-Jamal," *Race and Class* 35, no. 1 (July–September 1993): 11; and D. Hilliard and L. Cole, *This Side of Glory* (Boston: Back Bay Books, 1993), vii.
12. H.P. Newton, B. Seale, E. Cleaver, *Black Panther Leaders Speak*, ed. G.L. Heath (Metuchen: Scarecrow Press, 1976), 119.
13. "L'Assassinat de George Jackson," in *L'Intolerable* (Paris: GIP/Gallimard, November 10, 1971); *DE*, 91.
14. E. Cleaver, "Three Notes from Exile," *Ramparts*, September 1969.
15. *PL*, 429.
16. *DE*, 63.
17. *DE*, 44.
18. Newton, Seale, Cleaver, *Black Panthers Speak*, 194.
19. L.D. Nachman, "Violence in the Court: The Political Meaning of Chicago," *The Nation*, March 23, 1970.
20. *DE*, 37–38.
21. Ibid., 34–35.
22. Ibid., 45.

23. "Jean Genet témoigne pour les Soledad Brothers," *La Nouvelle Critique* 45 (June 1971): 58.

24. "The Black and the Red," *Black Panther Newspaper*, September 11, 1971; *DE*, 83–84.

25. "Pour George Jackson" (a manifesto mailed in July 1971); *DE*, 69.

26. E. White, *Genet: A Biography* (New York: Vintage Books, 1994), 568.

27. "Interview with Hubert Fichte," *Die Zeit*, February 13, 1976; *DE*, 136.

28. Ibid., *DE*, 135.

29. *L'Ennemi déclaré*, 82 (in original French version only).

30. *PL*, 363.

31. Ibid., 361.

32. "Pour George Jackson"; *DE*, 67.

33. "The Black and the Red"; *DE*, 81.

34. Ibid., *DE*, 82.

35. Ibid., *DE*, 81.

36. Ibid., *DE*, 82.

37. Ibid.

38. *DE*, 90.

39. K.B. Clark, *The Negro protest: James Baldwin, Malcolm X, Martin Luther King talk with Kenneth B. Clark* (Boston: Beacon Press, 1963), 24.

40. "Introduction" in G. Jackson, *Soledad Brother: The Prison Letters of George Jackson* (New York: Coward-McCann, 1970); *DE*, 49.

41. "After the Assassination," August 1971, previously unpublished; *DE*, 85.

42. E. De Grazia, "An Interview with Jean Genet," *Cardozo Studies in Law and Literature* 5, no. 2 (Fall 1993): 307–324.

5 | The ABCs of Violence

"The Red Army Faction seems to be the opposite of May '68, but also its continuation. Especially its continuation."[1] In "Violence et brutalité" published on September 2, 1977 in *Le Monde*, Genet still saw the Red Army Faction (RAF) as "one of the islands of this archipelago of the Western Gulag"[2] and being "inside a giant ear."[3] The May dance led to the German Autumn. The RAF was branded as an event, the defining of a body in space and time, and as memory.

August 17, 1956—the date when the Communist Party of Germany (KPD, or *Kommunistische Partei Deutschlands*) was officially banned— was perhaps the seed of what would later be known as the German Autumn (1977). Genet stated, "It is obvious, moreover, that West Germany's opposition to any Communist Party openly recognized as such is in large part responsible for the existence of the RAF, which proves in a striking fashion that social-democracy is democratic in its discourse but inquisitorial when it sees fit."[4] Allowed to form anew in 1969, party membership rose to 40,000 by 1977. Meanwhile, the Christian Democratic Union of Germany (CDU) and its sister party, the Christian Social Union of Bavaria (CSU), formed the "Union," a parliamentary faction; and Germany was described by Genet as "the Germany of [Willy] Brandt and [Helmut] Schmidt"[5]—i.e., as leftist. At the same time, the Socialist German Student Movement (SDS), offspring of the Social Democratic Party (SPD), began its efforts to better understand the Federal Republic, in particular its police-state character and its neo-fascist process. Ten years later, German students were doubly bent on revolt against their Nazi past and authoritarian present. Unhappy with the government's justifications, aware of the West's hypocrisy toward the East, the call went out for extra-parliamentary action. When the opposition party was banned, a new form of protest was born: the RAF.

Another origin of the German Autumn would be the June 2, 1967 demonstration against the Shah of Iran's visit to Berlin. Writing about Andreas Baader of the RAF, who hid behind the name "Baader-Meinhof Gang," and about the Shah (or rather, his death), Genet noted in his last book, "Saint-Just was dazzling, and knew his own brightness. The Panthers knew their own brilliance, and that they would disappear. Baader and his friends heralded the death of the Shah of Iran."[6] The destinies of the star terrorists unfurled at breakneck speed, making their dazzle deadly. However, the death foretold was that of the *zeitgeist*. A student named Benno Ohnesorg was killed by Berlin police during the anti-Shah protest of June 1967. A year later, on April 11, 1968, an attempt was made on the life of Rudi Dutschke, a prominent spokesperson for the student movement who'd been described as dangerous by the Springer Press. It was under these circumstances and to mark this event that German poet Paul Celan wrote *Mapesbury Road* on April 14:

> The stillness waved
> at you from behind
> a black woman's gait.
>
> At her side
> the
> magnolia-houred halfclock
> in front of a red

that elsewhere took looks for its meaning—
or nowhere perhaps.

The full
time-yard around
a lodged-bullet, next to it, cerebrous.

The sharply-heavened courtyard
gulps of co-air.

Don't adjourn yourself, you.[7]

The red, the black, a bullet—after the attempt on Dutschke's life, Ulrike Meinhof declared to the magazine *Konkret* that, "The bullets fired at Rudi put an end to the dream of non-violence."[8] Meinhof was the second name behind the banner of "the Baader-Meinhof Gang." In Meinhof's words, "If you don't arm yourself, you die. If you don't die, you're buried alive in prisons, halfway houses or the sinister concrete of residential towers."[9] Violent words from a violent world. Gray was the color of the Red Army Faction's gaze. Was it already born, or fading? The Red Army Faction rose from death foretold: of the Shah, of students, of men.

The colonial legacy of the Vietnam War—whose cold winds were felt the world over—and of the war's relationship with blacks in America and the RAF in Germany produced a third birth; from war was born the Baader-Meinhof Gang.

The guerrilla groups that cropped up in the wake of the student movements rejected traditional revolutionary tactics by reintroducing practices reminiscent of the nineteenth-century anarchists; they shook up the established political order by reminding all that social peace in the metropolis could be a fragile thing.[10] On April 2, 1968, Horst Söhnlein, Thorward Proll, Andreas Baader, and Gudrun Ensslin conceived of, planned, and carried out attacks on the Kaufhof and Schneider department stores in Frankfurt. They were arrested less than forty-eight hours later and incarcerated for fourteen months. In

May 1970, Baader was rescued by a commando unit from the library of the Institute of Social Sciences of Dahlem in Berlin, where he'd been permitted to work on his book; one librarian was injured. On May 22, 1970, in the underground journal *Agit 883*, the name *Rote Armee Fraktion* appeared for the first time. The group was immediately declared public enemy number one by German authorities. On the streets, government posters offered rewards of 10,000 deutschmarks for any information on the whereabouts of Baader and some twenty others. On May 11, 1971, three bombs exploded in the US Army's Frankfurt headquarters, killing a colonel and injuring five others. The RAF announced, "Our demands will grow as we stand in solidarity with the victors, with every American plane shot down, with every conscription paper [draft card] burned."[11] From May 11 to 24, 1972, the RAF hit the US Army's European headquarters in Heidelberg (in the process destroying a computer used for bombing Vietnam), followed by a Springer Press building in Hamburg, and the car of the Karlsruhe federal judge. About the Heidelberg strike, philosopher Jean-François Lyotard wrote, "There is a type of violence that, in the end, belongs to the game of war. [...] I do not see what is objectionable about that. When the group Red Army Faction makes an incursion and destroys the American computer in Heidelberg, that is war. The group considers itself at war; it is waging war and it is actually destroying a part of the forces of the adversary."[12] Meanwhile, police shot Petra Schelm (July 15, 1971) and Georg von Rauch (December 4, 1971) in the street. Then, from October 1971 to June 1972, Horst Mahler, Margritt Schiller, Andreas Baader, Holger Meins, Gudrun Ensslin, and Ulrike Meinhof were arrested. On June 6, the courts ordered the RAF group to be kept in isolation; the trial was set for May 21, 1975 in Stammheim. Some twenty years later, the story continued: on June 27, 1993, Wolfgang Grams, alleged member of the seventh generation of the RAF, was caught. Immobilized, wounded, and unarmed, on the tracks of the station where he'd been spotted, he was finished off at point-blank range by a member of the *Grenzschutzgruppe* 9 (GSG-9), the elite counter-terrorism and special operations unit of the German Federal Police. Although the Minister of the Interior Rudolf Seiters was forced to resign as a result, police hailed the murder as a decisive victory against the RAF.

In 1977, Genet grew interested in the RAF, which he described as "the opposite of May '68, but also its continuation"[13]. In other words, he was contemplating the legacy of May '68. Thus he opened the years of *no future*.

It must be said that Genet had been drawn into closer proximity with the members of the RAF, if not actually meeting them in person. In June 1970, Horst Mahler, Andreas Baader, Ulrike Meinhof, and others—as well as Genet—were among the Palestinians at the Al Fath camp in Jordan. The only allusion to this sojourn, unmentioned in any other RAF text, was found in a letter from Gudrun Ensslin to her former companion Bernward Vesper; the reference appears in the latter's book, *Die Reise*.[14] Genet might have failed to mention the RAF's stay at Al Fath or speak of a meeting that did not occur, but if such a meeting remains possible, it affirms yet again an aspect of the times as Genet saw them. The global aspect of the revolution was real. In this regard, for Genet as for the RAF, the Palestinians served as conduit. But without the uprising of the body, or the voyage, liberation means nothing. According to the movement's historian, "It is only after the flight from German reality that the group truly existed in the sense that this was where its story began."[15] After this trip, the RAF launched its acts of violence. The departure from the country shows itself in the clandestine return. Outside the law, its members would neglect the social context and fight illegally. Here, we must point out the complex relationship between the flight from reality, or the journey, the beginning of a story, and the return to society through other channels in order to create a new reality—for the writer, as well as for those of whom he spoke. This was exactly the kind of story the last Genet wanted to tell.

THE EAR

What were the sounds of the times, as recorded in the German courts? A skeletal Holger Meins died after a hunger strike. A philosopher, Michel Foucault, sought to rethink the entire penal system. Genet denounced torture, but not only torture. The debate about prison conditions wasn't his last word; rather, it was a stage in his ongoing reflection on violence. Here, a disagreement with the RAF would be mirrored by a break from Foucault.

The Committee Against Torture and Isolation was formed in Stuttgart in 1972. Starting with the fight against the unusual conditions of the RAF's detention, the committee sometimes worked with lawyers to create political solidarity. After visiting Baader in prison, Jean-Paul Sartre proclaimed, on December 4, 1974, the creation of the *Comité international de défense des prisonniers politiques en Europe de l'Ouest* (IVK), a defence committee for political prisoners in Western Europe. On May 21, 1975, in preparation for their trial, the members of the RAF produced texts that were both a legitimization and a political analysis of their use of force. *Regarding the Armed Struggle in West Europe* and *The Urban Guerrilla Concept* were published in 1971; both titles reflected the gray of their gaze. These were the last texts published by the prisoners. Genet read the first book published on the RAF, *A propos du procès du Baader-Meinhof: de la torture dans les prisons en RFA* (1975). Then, in order of threats or death came *L'Affaire Croissant* (1977) and *Textes* (also in 1977), prefaced by Genet, and after Ulrike Meinhof's assassination, *La Mort D'Ulrike* (1979)—all published by Maspero in France. The project of translating the RAF's prison letters and collecting them into a volume to be published in different countries—the task of informing, transmitting, and explaining—would fall upon various committees until 1977. More than any actual meeting, these committees and this project were at the root of Genet's interventions in the RAF cause. Genet stepped in at the exact moment when *guerrilla actions were replaced with actions undertaken collectively in prison*.[16]

Denouncing torture, tackling the problem of hunger strikes, and defending the prisoners: all were inspired by the committees. Genet would forge his own path. In *Rouge*, Alain Krivine wrote, "The RAF militants are completely wrong. However, that will not stop us from being involved in the battle they are waging in prison."[17] The simplicity of this criticism could certainly not be the last word for Foucault, if his project was to be founded on an archeology of prison, or for Genet, if his attack did not separate itself from a reflection on language in his relationship with violence. Attentive to the birth of prison and the birth of language, the story of the RAF's ear has to differ.

"From reading them, one has the impression that the prisoners are inside a giant ear."[18] Prison vocabulary returns, ever the same. Through the ear, Genet discarded the historical account of the birth of the RAF in favor of his criticism of "depreciation." "Germany has abolished the death penalty. But it brings death through hunger and thirst strikes and enforces isolation through the 'depreciation' of the slightest sound except that of the prisoner's heart. Locked in a vacuum, he eventually discovers in his body the sound of pulsing blood, the sound of his lungs, that is, the sound of his organism, and thus he comes to know that thought is produced by the body."[19] The depreciation the Germans were using was invented by the CIA around 1950 as part of a behavioral modification program called "Project Bluebird." The project was first tried on student volunteers, then soldiers. It was financed by the German Research Foundation (*Deutsche Forschungsgemeinschaft* or DFG) of the University of Hamburg. The United Nations' General Assembly Resolution 3542 in 1975 addressed this type of torture; a man would soon speak of cubic asphyxiation. The penal system gained ground, and the new conditions for detention in Europe worsened.

At the same time, Foucault spoke out on the laws governing the *Quartier Haute Sécurité* (QHS). The establishment of maximum-security wings in prisons was another reform of that period and new to France. Its origins can be traced to a reform dating back to 1975. In

October 1978, Minister of Justice Alain Peyrefitte proposed the QHS law, which was voted through with the appropriate haste for a bill of such importance, and was consistent with the paranoid desire for order that was setting in. *QHS*, by Roger Knobelspiess, then incarcerated for an armed robbery he denied committing, was published in 1980. The manuscript was published at the behest of a defense committee for Knobelspiess that Genet was part of. In the preface, written on March 31, 1980, Foucault said this:

> Knobelspeiss arises from a special new section of the penal
> system: the QHS. This reform was presented in 1975 as
> a necessary part of the humanization of the penitentiary
> apparatus. If it was to be made more flexible, with greater
> day-pass privileges and parole, these half-freedoms, then
> the risks had to be managed. To reassure the penitentiary
> staff as well as the public, it was necessary, or so it appeared,
> to provide prisons with special reinforced programs for
> those to whom the facilities offered only chances for re-
> offending. Logical and reasonable, isn't it? In any case, the
> QHS concerned only a handful of wild animals … The
> QHS created the famous alternative to the death penalty
> […] which allowed a fairer replacement: indefinite and
> full isolation. Life is spared, but in a time without limits
> and a place from which no one emerges. We must read
> the excellent pages Knobelspeiss wrote about this "cubical
> asphyxiation." Day-by-day destruction takes the place of
> execution. It is not easy to eliminate death, but this will
> be death that the prisoner will inflict on himself. […] The
> elimination of death as a means of justice must be radical. It
> means rethinking the entire system of punishment and its
> real function.[20]

What Genet called "aggravation," the "isolation, the monitoring systems […], the surveillance systems, the silence, the lights,"[21] was in line with what Foucault described as "day-to-day destruction." Though not voiced at the same time, together their attacks on the conditions under which the members of the Red Army Faction were being held in Germany and those of Roger Knobelspiess in France were similar. In the ear and in the courtroom, on tape recorders, the criticisms of the fascism of the time resounded: humanization was in peril, or its opposite. Although Genet and Foucault were starting out from a common space and time (the place from which no one escapes), they soon tried different actions.

At the onset of 1977, Foucault undertook to recount the "Lives of Infamous Men." The philosopher's project and the writer's gesture were united on this subject. The oft-repeated word in the life of men of infamy is *battle*, as in defending the RAF's lawyer and criticizing the QHS. With his project linked to the eighteenth century in France, Foucault sought to chronicle the lives of those "monstrous abominations," working from the ashes that remained of their relationship to power. His aim was to use texts to get as close as possible to their reality, "not only that they refer to it, but that they perform in it; that they should play a part in the dramaturgy of the real, that they should constitute the instrument of a revenge, the weapon of a hatred, an episode in a battle, the gesticulation of a despair or of a jealousy, a supplication or an order."[22] Although his goal was to rediscover lives that were now ashes, he acknowledged that he was standing on the side of fire, that he was "always with the same incapacity to cross the line, to pass over to the other side."[23] All that was left of his desire to relate the lives of men of infamy was a fragment of classic writing, on the side of power, the infamy gone.

A year later, Foucault sought to defend the rights of a lawyer and, "doubtlessly," those of his clients. Foucault interceded three times, not directly in favor of the Red Army Faction, but on behalf of Klaus Croissant,[24] one of their lawyers. The philosopher's articles in *Le Nouvel Observateur* focused on a key point in the RAF's trial; he wanted to address the infringement of the rights of the defendants. During the trial, the members were denied three of their lawyers, namely Klaus Croissant, Kurt Groenwold, and Hans-Christian Ströbele. After three years of preparations, the best prepared and most informed lawyers were barred seven days before the trial. This ban was possibly due to the restoration, once more in great haste, of Article 138A of the German Criminal Code, an article that disallowed a lawyer, "when it is obvious that he is suspected of involvement in the events considered by the case, or if it may be assumed that his participation in the defense could constitute a danger for the security of the Federal Republic." The concept of security and its corollary, lack of security, were invoked here to serve the needs of politicians and their power, the deeds carried out with great zeal by the heads of the penal system and reinforced by the police. Fearing for his safety after the trial of the RAF, Klaus Croissant asked for political asylum in France. Instead, he was arrested and threatened with extradition. This is when Foucault intervened.

Klaus Croissant's trial was a small dose of reality in France. It was real because a man's freedom was on the line, and hence, his life. "What is involved here? A right, which is Croissant's, and the lawyers', which is only a part, essential nevertheless, of the rights of those who defend; a right that, more generally, belongs to the governed."[25] In the case of the governed and in particular of the "perpetual dissident," Klaus Croissant, the right must hinge on "a defense against government." Consequently, "In Croissant's confrontation last week with French judges, as in the exceptional measures taken last week in Germany, or in the current project for an international antiterrorist convention, everything about personal freedom that has been upheld by recent law is at stake."[26] The first intervention conveyed the urgency of the situation by providing a historical analysis of extradition rights in general and the rights of the governed in particular. The second came after the extradition, following the noble principle of the weathervane. It briefly drew attention to Marie-Joseph Sina and Hélène Chatelain, two women facing the same ordeal. Foucault wanted the "private matter of the right to asylum" to be defended against the public matter of extradition. The last was an exchange between Foucault and Minister of Justice Alain Peyrefitte. Such dialogue with authority was, of course, foreign to Genet.

Baader was mentioned only once during the numerous publications, and it was in parentheses. His name wouldn't even appear in the index later assembled for Foucault's *Dits et Écrits.* Yet Foucault wrote, "They want to return to a restriction on the right to asylum that recalls 'the fight against anarchists.' (This word was used to label the Baader group, though all their texts prove the contrary.) They want to reverse the trend that, for years, has allowed a necessary political immigration. Not only the movement of those who travel toward power or return, but *those who turn away from it through whatever paths they can find* [my emphasis]."[27] These paths crossed through the lives of the men of infamy by allowing the possibility of "going over to the other side." Foucault wouldn't return to it. He came to a logical conclusion regarding this battle: "It means rethinking the entire system of punishment and its real function."[28] He then moved on to the topic of incarceration.

Archiving was meant to shed light on the ashes of current lives. The fire, though out, could be made to burn anew. Emerging from the circle of power still seemed possible. But during those contemporary years of infamy, Foucault positioned himself with an eye on reforming the system—no more, no less. He didn't come out of the circle of prison, nor from the archives of incarceration. He couldn't even make the link between the two spaces. With a single gesture, he separated the written word, labeled as a document, from reality, described as infamy. Behind these minor distinctions dwelled the apparatus of power, which has a vested interest in the division of thought, language, and action. These divisions were replicated within each of the orders between thought and body, action and language, thought, language, and the world. They ended up conjuring the terrible image of a man split in half, a man locked up. From this separation, from this division or share, flows the paradoxical situation of the philosopher. Foucault oscillated between the criticism of the intolerable and the purpose of the punishment; he described the circle of fascism.

It seems Genet was left behind, but he was there. He listened. What did he hear? A woman. The issue was a surgical procedure to be performed on the person of Ulrike Meinhof in July 1973. It began with a decision by penitentiary law and Judge Knoblich to authorize an examination of the prisoner's brain against her will. This, even if it took restraints or anesthesia. The public finally made itself heard. Ulrike Meinhof, whom the writer liked to quote in his preface, wrote to her lawyer:

> The feeling your head is exploding (the feeling the top of your skull should really tear apart, burst wide open)—The feeling your spinal column is pressing into your brain—The feeling your brain is gradually shriveling up, like baked fruit—The feeling you're completely and surreptitiously wired, under remote control—[…] Speaking at a normal volume requires efforts as if you were shouting, almost yelling—The feeling you're growing mute—You can no longer identify what words mean, you can only guess—The sound sibilants make—s, tz, z, sch, ch—are absolutely unbearable—[…] Sentence structure, grammar, syntax— are out of control. When you write, just two lines, you can hardly remember the beginning of the first line when you finish the second—[…] Raging aggression, for which there is no outlet.[29]

Genet saw the threat carried out on a body—a woman's body. And when the body was suddenly deprived of feeling and language, of the rules of grammar and self-governing, Genet saw a body deprived of syntax. Day and night melded together, and desire was gone. On August 6, 1977, two guards stumbled upon the lovers; Andreas Baader was in Gudrun Ensslin's bed. A fight ensued. The law decided to separate the reunited prisoners by returning to their former prisons those who'd recently been transferred.[30] Although Genet said nothing about this altercation, he spoke of the space of Jackson's solitude: "And yet elsewhere two beings have the need and the possibility of joining together."[31] What was he after? He was looking for practices that were not only sexual and not just within prison, practices that would grant freedom from the confines of prison order. Even though Genet was in a metaphorical prison, and the link between the outside world and the inside had yet to be defined as a promise, his sights were already set on breaking the cage of words which ultimately symbolized norms. He wanted to break through the bars that contained the prisoner's language. As a mark of those who govern the lives of the imprisoned, the minor episode of the RAF's embrace raised the issue of *escaping fascism or abolishing desire itself.* This was where Foucault and Genet parted ways.

Genet watched the actions of the first generation of the Red Army Faction, listened to the members of the Baader-Meinhof Gang, and read the words of the RAF prisoners. He turned his ear away—as he was meant to do—from the sound of torture, punishment, and the forces of security. He moved to a different critical space, where he could act and speak and create an exit. He broke free of the fascist view of life and death as a vicious circle. To put it simply, using the philosopher's words, the places of infamy and the intolerable had entered the writer's vocabulary. About Baader, he wrote, "The greater the brutality, and the more outrageous the trial, the more violence becomes imperious and necessary."[32] In the order of his language, he opened himself to the necessity of thinking of the world, violence, and speech as one; to "make its way," he wrote. This was certainly a turning point. The expression concealed the possibility of the political act—"with all that this implies of solitude, incomprehension, internal violence."[33]

For a split second, Genet and Foucault crossed paths, at the intersection where they met infamy. Foucault veered away. They were faced with a new challenge: not to speak for those who'd asked nothing of them, but to *seek justice from the depths of the unjust.* The committees triggered the involvement of those who could quickly make a previously unnoticed reality too big to be ignored, through books or other means. That was their role. Foucault painted his own gray over the immutable gray of the RAF and the times by condemning the European QHS, defending the RAF lawyers, and suggesting an overhaul of the entire penal system, all of which was in the order of (his) discourse. The last Genet wanted to forge a new path. The difference between the two men was doubtless not the difference between one's notion of law and the other's need for justice. In the world of law, both seemed to recognize the law as it was and as it needed to become. Better still, both spoke of justice as a link to one's fellow human. They were trying to speak the truth. The philosopher's battle, the poet's quarrel, and even the RAF's struggle were all forms of protest, each one humble, desolate, creative, and gray, though not only gray, each one of value for what it said about the political concerns of men of infamy. So many different ways to blast free from shame. More often than not, however, the result is failure.

THE CRYSTALLIZATION

The archeology of the "concept of violence"[34] was at the forefront of Genet's vocabulary. He was interested in the difference between violence and brutality, with an eye on their effects in the vast and terrible world. Political action, when possible, çan only be accomplished if a connection is made between the outcrops of language, humanity, and world. This basic definition came to Genet from observing the Black Panthers' lives in America. "The trend is to call the Black Panthers violent [...] but whites in America have been violent with blacks for over two hundred years."[35] In 1971, the work on vocabulary wasn't finished, but the reality kept coming back, always the same. He felt the need to clarify his attack. "Violence is everywhere in the world. Violence has a finality, brutality does not, or else it destroys itself. The brutality of the whites has been met with a fair and proper measure of violence by the blacks."[36] Beyond the violence, however, appeared the plight of those fighting for survival. Except that his words, though their aim was to escape the ordeal of brutality, were again mere opposition. The dualism between black and white may have returned in a new form as the title of the 1971 article, reducing its scope in the process. This wasn't the last word. The opposition reappeared in 1973, this time in defense of the Palestinians. "By violence, I mean breaking free of the process of closing in on the self which keeps us from truly living: buds breaking open, that's violence; when grains of wheat grow, bursting through the surface of the earth, that's violence, too." Already, this one was set against its own shadow. "In fact, brutality is incompatible with violence." This new definition was framed by a couple of statements that supported it, prolonged it, as well as *limited* it. Genet began by writing, "bearing arms isn't everything in life," and he concluded with a call to discard a falsified story that, in the end, violence and brutality were the real translation. The means? "Carrying out a revolution—rather than a pseudo-revolution—with words."[37]

In 1977, he continued his work. He reiterated his differentiation: "The kernel of wheat that germinates and breaks through the frozen earth, the chick's beak that cracks open the eggshell, the impregnation of a woman, the birth of a child can all be considered violent. And no one casts doubt on the child, the woman, the chick, the bud, the kernel of wheat." He then opposed it to brutality, "the gesture or theatrical gesticulation that puts an end to freedom."[38] The struggle begins once we're free of the dread, the distress, and the intolerable, continues when we perceive the reality of daily brutality, and is extended through the use of vocabulary that enables us to leave the confusion between violence and brutality behind; when we find what we desire. It's a question of learning once and for all what kind of person we are. A woman, Ulrike Meinhof, wrote about this:

> Before us, the big city dweller is revealed: the product
> of a decaying system, alienated, fraudulent and doomed
> relationships, whether in school, university, or revisionist
> groups, during the learning process or the odd job. This is
> what we are, a breed born from a process of annihilation
> and destruction by metropolitan society, of a war pitting all
> against one, of the competition between individuals, of a

system governed by fear, the need to produce, profit at the
other's expense and classify people as either man or woman,
old or young, ailing or healthy, stranger or German.[39]

Genet's long labor opposed the circumstances that link terrorism
and the state: bipolarization, totalization, and crystallization. We start
with *bipolarization*, the first step in clarifying political divisions. The
dialogue, if we can call it that, between those in prison and the ruling
powers consist more often than not of bipolar exhortations. Nobody is
talking to each other, since both are addressing a body of citizens and
calling upon them to either rise against the state or against infamy.
The separation between human and inhuman authorizes us, depending on where we stand, to use violence against the state or brutality
against the infamous. It is necessary to split the world in two if we are
to legitimize brutality. Genet generously demonstrated the impasses
reached by separate judgments, which he called the settling of scores
between judges and hoodlums. The apparent dualism of violence and
brutality does not repeat the binary scheme, but rather seeks to re-
establish the flow between two of the world's states through language.
His precise use of words, his call to judgment and criticism of language
are the very conditions of the dialogue.

The distinction is still opposed to *totalization*. Totalizing is the state
calling for the eradication of terrorism, with no concern for motives,
or the archeology of the intolerable and the origins of infamy. But it's
also how, for the imprisoned, everything is a sign of something else,
a symbol; the Kauhof store and its passersby, a man and even a judge,
for the system. This is what Genet's reflection did not allow. The Black
Panthers, the Palestinians, and the Red Army Faction were interested
in using violence against brutality. It was essential for the writer to dif-
ferentiate the two terms. The Red Army Faction, in or out of prison,
could be faithful to its name; it was a faction, not a whole.

In the end, Genet's actions opposed *crystallization*. "What we owe
to Andreas Baader, Ulrike Meinhof, Holger Meins, Gudrun Ensslin,
and Jan-Karl Raspe—to the RAF in general—is that they have made

us understand, not only by words but by actions, both in and out of prison, that violence alone can bring an end to the brutality of men."[40] Prisons substitute names with identification numbers, the police call strangers by nicknames, the press drops names in passing, and those in power use words for their personal domination. As he wrote what would later be a preface, two of the people mentioned who could legitimately be considered as having been suicided by society—Ulrike Meinhof and Holger Meins—were already dead, one by hanging and the other from a hunger strike, and the other three would also meet violent ends in October of the same year. This fact inspired Gerhard Richter's fifteen paintings, *October 18, 1977*, in 1988. Genet, however, did not speak of Ulrike Meinhof as being Ulrike Marie Meinhof.[41] To speak the names is another way of retelling the deaths, of conversing with them, of always seeking a way of grasping the ashes of legacy. The manner in which Genet addressed the members of the Red Army Faction, by their names, prevented crystallization; it was a self-reflection on brutality or violence as activism. When the RAF identified the target by attacking it and claiming responsibility for its actions, it was also identifying itself as a target. More importantly, the state was even more brutal than the mythologized RAF—all dead or incarcerated— that no longer existed. The principle is terrible: a group is most reviled when it no longer exists. Here, the infamous is confused with the intellectual, or the Jew. Georges-Arthur Goldschmidt, a very accurate witness of the time, wrote in 1977, "We're seeing all the old anti-Semitic patterns returning; the intellectual is as indiscernible as the Jew. Like the Jew, he comprises an element of disintegration. He's always either denigrating or demolishing. The enemy is omnipresent, elusive, and everywhere easily symbolized. Like the members of the Baader-Meinhof Gang, the intellectual is simultaneously evasive and dangerous."[42] As irony would have it, Foucault himself experienced crystallization first-hand, shortly after writing the aforementioned criticism. In December 1977, he and Daniel Defert were arrested in Berlin. He wondered if this was due to the presence of the young blonde girl at their side. Foucault made the mistake of discussing a book about Ulrike Meinhof at breakfast and someone reported it to the authorities. He told *Der Spiegel* magazine, "We did nothing wrong. [...] We were simply a group of French and Germans, obviously intellectuals, who were talking politics out loud, exactly the kind of people who resemble other people who resembled people who, by their words and writings, claim that the others are dangerous. No, not a corrupt race, as they used to say, but a 'dirty bunch.' We felt like pariahs."[43] Even for the last Genet, undoing the dead-end relationship between terrorism and the state and discarding the three characteristics associated with it now meant relating to himself and to inner violence. Seeing what it was, ridding himself of ghosts and concerns of legacy, were all part of the same action that Genet had undertaken, alone.

He returned to his judgment and maintained it. Genet decompartmentalized his critique of violence by raising the issue of learning the mother tongue. During the 1983 interview in Vienna, he remembered, "I'm afraid you're confusing the two words—a confusion I pointed out in an article I published six years ago in *Le Monde* on violence and brutality." Having just said that, he joined action and words. "I'm going to push you—don't be offended. I'm being brutal... [...] If I'm brutal, just like that, on a whim or for fun, I can be brutal, but then it leads to nothing. But if I'm violent, for example when a man or a woman is raising a child, when they teach him '*A, B, C, D*,' the child whines, the child gets bored and the mother insists, '*A, B*,' she's inflicting violence, she's teaching him something when he'd rather be playing. But it's good violence."[44] Here is the last example and the first experience, the *ABCs of the writer's violence*.

An unexpected short-circuit bridged the gap between violence and the learning of language. Stepping through a subjective threshold allowed a creative detachment in the midst of chaos. A child binds humans and the world with violence, permanently. In the end, speech reveals itself to be good violence. It is violence, and it can be seen in the relationship between those who speak, those who stop talking, those who are denied the right to express themselves, those who speak poorly, those who are mute, and those who are locked up. Violence in language binds the wretchedness of the infamous to the power structure. Genet draws our attention to a precise point in the relationship between those in power and those incarcerated: language. This point is political. "I've killed and I've inherited." The cellmate of the Italian philosopher Antonio Gramsci—also a political prisoner of fascism—repeated those words over and over. But language contains legacy, which is violence itself. Poverty and wealth are henceforth bound together as is the possibility of a new relationship between the self and the world. This was Genet's experience, the experience of a man who physically felt the violence of the relation between the world, language, and the self. He felt that violence, he remembered it, and it flowed with his words.

That doesn't mean that he "did nothing," as Foucault declared. Nor does it mean he committed dangerous acts as did some members of the RAF. His actions were real, he was present, and that allowed him a momentary escape from shame. The actions of the last Genet no doubt pointed toward the most inward politics there are. A long silence followed his explanation of violence and brutality. Was his silence caused by a fear of being wrong, or was it the surest confirmation that he'd made a statement that was both imminently political and a complete secret?

THE THORN

Surely the fascination of the extreme left, intellectuals in general, and Genet in particular, with the European Red Army Faction had something to do with the group being German. To the French, the RAF and the RFA (*République fédérale d'Allemagne*, or Federal Republic of Germany) appeared synonymous. The movement's acronym seemed more like an anagram for the country, only angrier. Following the final hunger strikes of RAF members in August 1977 and Klaus Croissant's flight to France, a debate erupted in the French press over the social and political conditions of the Federal Republic of Germany. This debate was interpreted as an anti-German sentiment and an attempt was made to interpret Genet's intervention in this light. Anne Steiner declared: "One particular Genet text brings exasperation to a head."[45]

Nazism will forever lurk in Germany's shadow. Genet was on his guard when he wrote of "a Germany that America has imposed and whose bourgeoisie [...] considers itself absolved of Nazism thanks to its anticommunism."[46] It seems that the "thorn called the RAF sticking in the too fat flesh of Germany"[47] had hit a sore spot, as had Genet. This no doubt pertained to the RAF's relation to Nazism, to the significance of their being Hitler's children. A poorly written book titled *Hitler's Children*[48] was then published, in which the author tried to get to the heart of what the Red Army Faction was about. Unfortunately, the author saw only one side of the story. Hitler's children did not necessarily belong to the RAF. One woman, Catherine von Bülow, the daughter of a Nazi officer who went missing during World War II, also tried to escape the German monstrosity. Von Bülow, whom Genet had met, quoted him at length in her autobiography. She set up Genet's intervention as follows:

> Only the East German Communists were talking to us. There was no shortage of documents. The overabundance of corpses. [...] But the other Germany, "free" Germany as they called it, was silent. In the dictionaries, the biographies of politicians generally stopped at 1930 and resumed in the 1950s. At school we jumped from Goethe or Bismarck to Theodore Heuss. Hitler? Never heard of him. The war? It's better off forgotten, and quick, why waste time talking when we need to rebuild our country, that's our task... [...] And they forgot Rosa Luxembourg, Karl Liebknecht, Pastor Niemöller, the Scholls, [Hans and Sophia] brother and sister, Carl von Ossiezsky, Ulrike Meinhof and Holger Meins. Dead and buried. [Here she adds a long quotation

from Genet's article, and then concludes.] So what happened
then? Who was Stalin? Who was Hitler?[49]

On September 5, 1977, three days after Genet's intervention in *Le
Monde*, the second generation of the RAF abducted Hanns-Martin
Schleyer. They demanded the release of the first generation, imprisoned and soon to kill themselves. Schleyer, serial number 227014,
had been a Nazi officer (*Untersturmführer*), charged with "Nazify-
ing" universities on behalf of the *Reichsstudenten Werk* (the Office of
the Students of the Reich). In 1951, while working at Daimler-Benz,
he became the president of the BDA (*Bundesvereinigung der Deutschen
Arbeitgeberverbände*, or Confederation of German Employers Associations) and the BDI (*Bundesverbandes der Deutschen Industrie*, Federation of German Industries). Schleyer was seen shortly after being kid-
napped in a blue knit sweater and a red jacket, with a sign around his
neck that read "prisoner of the RAF." Years before, in June 1920, the
first Dada art exhibition was held in Berlin. One of the pieces featured
was a sculpture by Berlin Dadaist Johannes Baader (1875–1955). The
sculpture: a stuffed German policeman with a pig's head, hung from
the ceiling and bearing a sign around his neck that read "hung by
the revolution." However, this wasn't the first role reversal to echo a
terrible past; in 1937, another Dada statement was repeated verbatim
on the walls of a Nazi exhibition featuring degenerate art.[50] Johannes
Baader and Andreas Baader are not to be confused, even if the latter
knew about the former. A certain continuity in German history was
at play. Five young Germans who could have been Schleyer's children
came along and disturbed his more-than-exemplary career, as a paper
later written about the *Deutscher Herbst* or German Autumn put it.[51]
Schleyer was executed on October 31, 1977. The RAF's first act of
violence, the bombing, was spurred by crystallization; the second, the
hostage-taking, was a reaction to totalization: "then we are in an altogether different violence that has no relation to the previous one and
which alone, in my view, deserves the name of 'terrorism.' It is of the

same nature whether it is used by the state or by a minority group,"[52] wrote Jean-François Lyotard. Through a certain use of language, Genet expressed a twofold criticism. The blood-red blades were now sheathed, and the critique of violence was now understood as the concern with legacy.

Daniel Cohn-Bendit was asked if Andreas Baader should be perceived as a son of Hitler. A "brilliant pain in the ass,"[53] Cohn-Bendit was behind the May '68 movement and therefore also the cause of Genet's political disappointment. In 1970, Genet declared, "I can now say that in June '68, my sadness and anger led me to understand that I would always wish for the spirit of '68 in Paris to return, whether in France or elsewhere."[54] Or its opposite. Cohn-Bendit's answer connected violence, despair, and memory, stating, "Son of Hitler? I would say he was more a son of Schleyer. By this I mean that terrorism is the end result of political despair; despair in the face of the legacies that bind Germany and its memory."[55] We're struck by the Red Army Faction's relationship with Germany's past, the persistent ties between the RAF and the Third Reich and the will of its members to undertake, in their own way, a process of mourning. The RAF provoked a blank memory in Germany and in anyone who would listen to them (Günter Grass, Joseph Beuys, Genet, etc.). It stopped the hands of Germany's democratic clock. This is certainly what the final words of Genet's intervention sound like: "But to accuse the German government, the German administration, the German people—what does that mean? [...] Or, if you will, I see here a twofold phenomenon of contempt. Germany is seeking to create—and to a certain extent has succeeded in creating—a terrifying, monstrous image of the RAF. On the other hand, and through the same movement, the rest of Europe and America, by encouraging the intransigence of Germany in its torturous activity against the RAF, is seeking to create—and to a certain extent has succeeded in creating—a terrifying, monstrous image of Germany."[56] Judgment, accusation, contempt? In its slavish depiction, the Germany Genet saw was escalating out of control. This was no longer Manichaeism; this was far-removed from his defense of prisoners, from the double-discourse and its mirroring of monstrous images, farther even from the sweeping condemnation of a people. Genet no longer positioned himself in the bond between governed and governing, West and East, or life and death. A new German reality was finally emerging, unlike the idea of Germany that the RAF had condemned, unlike the bright, beaming version the US had wanted, and unlike the Germany of years past. It was a Germany that hadn't always been inhuman.

A more human Germany? One that had been human for thirty years already? The issue was precisely that of history as a means to escape inhumanity. In the matter of inhumanity, the conclusion of the inhuman outcrop lies in understanding the legacy of the monstrous.

Being a son can be understood in three ways. One, the child is the continuation of the parent (reproduction). The members of the RAF were imitating their ancestors by using terror; they were being faithful to eternal Germany. They behaved like their father, Hitler, and murdered Jews, for instance. This was how the author of *Hitler's Children* saw the RAF, as did many others. It has yet to be proven that Andreas Baader's project had anything to do with such politics or any power grab. Two, the child is the death of the parents (destruction). The members of the RAF were only Hitler's children if that meant they were rebelling against the parents. The parents had served the Führer. The children of Hitler literally sought to kill him, as they did when they executed Hanns-Martin Schleyer, for example. This may be true, but one question comes to mind: if silence followed the war, as one generation confirmed (Catherine von Bülow in particular), then how can they be the offspring of an unknown father? How can they take after a father who transmitted nothing? How does this happen and what becomes of the "children of Hitler" theory? This, then, leads us to the third option. The child invents his parents; he is not their creation, but a means of revolt, liberation, and birth, to ensure legacy. Not a legacy that is given away, but rather, that is given to oneself, a legacy that requires violence against the self to come about. To forge a path, as Genet said. But how is legacy invented? How can there be inheritance without death? And what about the birth of the inhuman? So many questions that Genet still couldn't answer directly, unless through counterfeit. Yet his investigation into violence and brutality was definitely built on these terms.

Genet approached the matter of legacy in two ways. On one hand, he connected the RAF story to that of learning (language)—the first experience and final example of violence. On the other hand, he identified the double phenomenon of contempt: depicting eternal Germany as inhuman. Before the birth of the RAF, which may have been May '68, Genet discovered another possible origin: war and Nazism in 1940. The expression Cohn-Bendit coined when he was banished from France in 1968, "We are all German Jews," which was picked up by the youth of the day, testifies to this historical continuity. It forms a bridge that links World War II (1940)—passing high above May '68—to, we could say, a European revolt that did not take place (1977), a revolt the writer was alone in thinking about.

For a European born in the early part of the century, all political thought was relative to World War II. By relating to the RAF, Genet was relating to European history as well as to his own history. His political being was beginning to show evidence of an important resolve that cannot be summed up here, though it's no accident that it emerged in 1977. He was trying to find how the causes that compelled him—here, the RAF, and elsewhere, the Palestinian resistance, an existing interest—were mirrored in his French childhood and in French history. His experience of the Occupation in France was one he could not forget. The issue will later be tackled head-on.[57] Genet's 1977 intervention was pivotal, for it brought him to German soil in the present day. In a manner of speaking, he would never leave. Or, more aptly put, the last Genet remained haunted by his ties with the enemy.

This leg of Genet's journey was capped by a certain display of subjective and political shame. Looking at the Red Army Faction through red-colored glasses, it was not clear that he would opt for resistance. Although that's how he was leaning: toward knowledge, violence, and soon, a bursting forth.

ENDNOTES

1. "Violence et Brutalité", preface to *Textes de prisonniers de la Fraction Armée rouge et dernières lettres D'Ulrike Meinhof* (Paris: Maspero, 1977), published in *Le Monde*, September 2, 1977; *DE*, 173.
2. Ibid., *DE*, 174.
3. Ibid., *DE*, 175.
4. Ibid., *DE*, 176.
5. Ibid., *DE*, 176.
6. *PL*, 206.
7. P. Celan, *Paul Celan: Poems*, trans. by M. Hamburger (New York: Persea Books, 1980), 284.
8. Quoted in A. Steiner and L. Debray, *La Fraction Armée rouge: guérilla urbaine en Europe occidentale* (Paris: Méridiens-Klincksieck, 1987), 25.
9. Ibid., 25.
10. Ibid., 9.
11. Ibid., 67.
12. J.F. Lyotard and J.L. Thébaud, *Just Gaming*, trans. Wlad Godzich (Minneapolis: University of Minnesota Press, 1985), 67.
13. *DE*, 173.
14. B. Vesper, *Die Reise: Romanessay* (Jossa, 1983).
15. A. Steiner, L. Debray, *La Fraction Armée rouge*, 30.
16. Ibid., 59.
17. A. Krivine, "La Fraction Armée Rouge," *Rouge*, September 7, 1977.
18. *DE*, 175.
19. *DE*, 176–177.
20. M. Foucault, *Dits et Écrits* (Paris: Gallimard, 1994), 4:7–8.
21. *DE*, 175.
22. M. Foucault, *Power, Truth, Strategy* (Sydney: Feral Publications, 1979), 78.
23. Ibid., 80.
24. Foucault, "Va-t-on aider Klaus Croissant?" *Le Nouvel Observateur*, November 14–20, 1977; Foucault, "Lettre à quelques leaders de la gauche," *Le Nouvel Observateur*, November 28–December 4, 1977; Foucault, "Alain Peyrefitte s'explique ... et M. Foucault lui répond," *Le Nouvel Observateur*, January 23, 1978; *Dits et Écrits*, 3:361, 388.
25. Foucault, "Va-t-on aider Klaus Croissant?"; *Dits et Écrits*, 3:362, no. 210.
26. Ibid., *Dits et Écrits*, 3:364.

27. Ibid.

28. M. Foucault, *Dits et Écrits*, 4:8, no. 275.

29. U. Meinhof, *Everybody is Talking About the Weather – We Don't: The Writings of Ulrike Meinhof*, ed. K. Bauer (New York: Seven Stories Press, 2008), 78.

30. F. Colomes, "La Fraction Armée Rouge," *Le Point*, October 24, 1977.

31. *DE*, 88.

32. "After the Assassination," August 1971; *DE*, 171.

33. Ibid., *DE*, 176.

34. *DE*, 121.

35. "Jean Genet témoigne pour les Soledad Brothers," *La Nouvelle Critique* 45 (June 1971): 60.

36. Ibid.

37. "Les Palestiniens" (II), *Shoun Falestine*, 1973; *GC*, 133–134.

38. *DE*, 171.

39. U. Meinhof, *Textes de prisonniers de la Fraction Armée rouge et dernières lettres D'Ulrike Meinhof* (Paris: Maspero, 1977), 37.

40. *DE*, 172.

41. *Ulrike Marie Meinhof*, directed by Timon Koulmasis (Germany, 1994).

42. G.-A. Goldschmidt, "'La bande à Baader' et le phénomène de la totalisation," *Allemagne d'aujourd'hui* 58 (May–June 1977).

43. M. Foucault, "Wir fühlten uns als schmutzige Spezies," *Der Spiegel*, December 19, 1977; *Dits et Écrits*, 3:417.

44. *DE*, 245–246.

45. A. Steiner, *La Fraction Armée rouge*, 68.

46. *DE*, 176.

47. Ibid., 177.

48. J. Becker, *Hitler's Children: Story of the Baader-Meinhof Terrorist Gang* (Philadelphia: Lippincott, 1977).

49. C. von Bülow and F. Ben Ali, *La Goutte d'Or ou le Mal des raciness* (Paris: Grasset, 1979), 73–77.

50. M. Dachy, *Dada & les Dadaïsmes*, "Folio" coll. (Paris: Gallimard, 1994), 177–179.

51. *Libération*, September 7, 1977.

52. J.F. Lyotard and J.L Thébaud, *Just Gaming*, 67.

53. *DE*, 20.

54. D. Cohn-Bendit, "Entretien," *Le Nouvel Observateur*, November 24, 1977, 68.

55. Ibid.
56. *DE*, 177.
57. See chapter 8.

6 | Terrorists and Stars

"Stars, that's what we were,"[1] said a fedayee to Genet in his last book. There are names, like fedayeen, that carry a capacity for violence on earth as they do in heaven. Genet spun the violent acts of the time into a web of filigree. The Panthers at the California State Capitol, the planes in the desert, a grenade in a bodice, and the events in Shatila enabled him to conclude his condemnation of violence with a condemnation of images. The final meaning of the will to trial emerged. Genet would return more readily to the perpetual act of the fedayeen going down to the Jordan River; it called for the impossible return of the dead.

ACTS
"When the armed Black Panthers marched to occupy the Capitol in Sacramento, when their athletes stood on the podium in Mexico and defied the American flags and national anthem, when their hair and beards grew, [...] through every possible act, sign and gesture, [the Panthers] made sure that nothing would ever be the same again."[2] This reference to the events at the Capitol appears in Genet's last book during a long study of the black movement. The fedayeen were stars, as were the Panthers. The "colossal event"[3] reflected the hundred thousand stars of those who died in Vietnam, the US, and the Middle East, of all the dead from those no-future years. It was the Black Panthers'

first important message to address all Americans, as well as their first visible action, if not a violent one. In 1967, Huey Newton conceived of a plan to have a delegation travel to the California State Capitol in Sacramento to protest an amendment to the Constitution aimed at restricting the right to bear arms, and to assert blacks' equal rights to coordinate such a struggle.[4] Their objective was to gain the means to defend themselves in the Oakland ghettos. Bobby Seale described the scene; Genet's friend David Hilliard spoke of its legacy. On May 2, 1967, then-Governor Ronald Reagan was also present. He was addressing a youth group on the lawn, which explains why there were "movie cameramen, still cameramen, regular cameras. Bulbs were flashing all over the place."[5] On that day the chant so often repeated on television was first heard: "If I'm not under arrest, you give me my gun back."[6] Bobby Seale, to whom Newton gave the task of delivering a message, later related, "At that time I knew that what Huey P. Newton was saying about the colossal event that had occurred. Because many, many cameramen were there. Many, many people had covered this event of black people walking into the Capitol, and registering their grievance with a particular statement. A message [...] that Huey P. Newton had ordered me to take to the Capitol, to use the mass media as a means of conveying the message to the American people and to the black people in particular."[7] He later added, "Huey found out that the fact that we went to the Capitol was plastered across the front pages of the London *Times*. Things developed from there. We now had a case where some twenty-four brothers were charged with conspiracy: $2,200 bail apiece."[8]

The November 8, 1969 edition of *The Black Panther* newspaper printed a true lesson in politics in an article where Huey Newton discussed the event: "When the Minister of Defense, Huey P. Newton, sent a delegation of armed Panthers to the California State Capitol, this was a process of educating the people by example that Blacks did not have their rights guaranteed by the constitution to bear arms in defense of their lives against racist mobs of fascists in or out of uniform."[9]

Newton then spoke of Bobby Seale, whose rights had been denied, and made a distinction between the law and how the law was applied. Earlier, he'd issued a call to arms by reciting the Declaration of Independence: "'But when a long train of abuses and usurpations, pursuing invariably the same Object evinces a design to reduce them under absolute Despotism, it is their right, it is their duty, to throw off such Government, and to provide new Guards for their future security.' I've just quoted an excerpt from the Declaration of Independence."[10] The action was not murderous. The gesture was both theoretical and practical and served as example, hence making it unique. The sign was clear, as it spoke mainly to blacks and not to the general public. But the presence of a man with a camera immediately transformed the action, the gesture, and the sign into gesticulation. The irony is that the cameras were there for Ronald Reagan. His style, wrote a Panther, was a way of unreality. Political action morphed into a parade.

Genet was nearby at the onset of the second act. "The plane hijacks brought both fame and rejection. I was in Beirut when George Habash's men forced three planes to land in the desert at Zarka. I can still see the weary faces of the three PFLP [Popular Front for the Liberation of Palestine] (Habash) leaders lighting up when I told them how the capture of the three aircraft, tamely lined up in the desert in the sun, had won the admiration of all the young people in Europe. Or at least, I thought, those whose staple diet was comic strips."[11] The youth that was pleased with the fedayeen's actions was European. Dubbed the hijacking of the century, this other colossal event, known as the Dawson's Field hijackings, made September 6, 1970 a very long day. Four planes were hijacked: two planes landed in the Jordanian desert, one in Cairo, and the last in London. The first plane seized by the fedayeen departed from Frankfurt, bound for New York; it was redirected to the Zarka desert in Jordan, where it landed on an old British Royal Air Force strip named Dawson's Field. The second plane was a New York flight from Zurich; it almost landed atop the first. Contrary to what Genet said, the third flight—from Amsterdam to Zagreb—was not rerouted to the same strip; it landed in Cairo. After it was evacuated, the $24 million craft was destroyed by the PFLP. The final hijacking was a failure: a third New York flight from Tel Aviv, with a stopover in Amsterdam, was hijacked by Leila Khaled and an associate; it was diverted to London after Israeli skymarshals stormed the plane.

Of the over 300 passengers taken hostage, many here held in Amman; others were sent to the Zarka camp, also in Jordan, while the remainder stayed in Cairo or London. These operations were all carried out by members of the Popular Front for the Liberation of Palestine to negotiate the release of various Palestinians held in Europe and Israel, including Leila Khaled after her failed attempt. The only fatality occurred during the final hijacking. Israeli guards boarded the El Al plane and shot Khaled's associate, Patrick Joseph Arguello, a twenty-seven-year-old PFLP member and graduate of the University of California at Los Angeles. September proved to be black. In the Jordanian desert, Habash's soldiers occupied the planes as King Hussein's tanks circled; Hussein carried out what would be called the Black September massacre. Around that time, on September 10, Yasser Arafat put forth a motion to suspend the PFLP from the PLO (Palestine Liberation Organization) Executive Committee; the proposal sailed through. As a result, on September 29, once all the passengers had been liberated, the Royal Air Force removed the seven Palestinian prisoners from their cells in Switzerland, Germany, and England. Among the seven: Leila Khaled. The prisoners were taken to Cairo, just in time for Nasser's funeral—and the opening of this story.[12]

Selim, a Palestinian who participated in a similar action on December 26, 1968, in Athens, outlined the political significance of such operations. "We accomplished our mission. We damaged an airplane so that our problem would be 'front page news.' That was our goal, to come out of isolation, to tell our truth to all those who at that point had only heard one side of the Palestinian issue." Why an airport? "It is a crossroads, a public place and it is where events echo most."[13] He added, "Our leader was very clear: *I want there to be a trial* [italics are mine]. I want you to use it to explain the Palestinian problem. I want you to make an appeal for our cause in front of as large an audience as possible. It will be the second phase of your task and it will not be the easiest one."[14] The September 6, 1970 hijackings wove a veil around the world that was both funereal and liberating, ending with a national funeral—Nasser's, on October 1. Under this veil, the mighty were powerless—a committee of five countries comprising English, Swiss, West Germans, Americans, and Israelis, who'd only wanted to observe. The constellation of countries listed seems to be missing a member. Which one? The stars flouted borders, but in the sky sought to draw the country missing here on Earth.

The last action was certainly the most fatal, though the events at the Capitol and in Zarka could well have gone that way. Genet failed to mention that earlier on September 6, 1970, Leila Khaled tried to use the grenades hidden under her breasts. "But describing the dramatic moments of the resistance, as I've been doing, doesn't give any idea of its everyday atmosphere. That was youthful and lighthearted. [...] A great yet almost silent roar of laughter from a whole nation holding its sides, yet full of reverence when Leila Khaled, grenade at the ready, ordered the Jewish crew of the El Al plane to land in Damascus."[15] In the end, it's about an old woman and a young girl. In *Prisoner of Love*, Nabila related, with a "roar of laughter":

> She was very thin round the stomach, and put on a sort
> of bodice with four rows of splinter grenades inside. She
> was probably helped by other women of her own age or
> younger, used to her sex, her thinness and her white hair.
> Then, weeping real tears, she approached a group of Amal
> fighters who were laughing as they rested from shooting
> Palestinians. The old woman wept and moaned for some
> time, until the group of Amals kindly went up to see her to
> see if they could help her. She kept mumbling phrases in
> Arabic that the Shiites couldn't hear, so they had to gather
> round close.

When I read in the papers about a virgin of sixteen blowing herself up in the middle of a group of Israeli soldiers, it doesn't surprise me very much. It's the lugubrious yet joyful preparations that intrigue me. What string did the old woman or the girl have to pull to detonate the grenades? How was the bodice arranged to make the girl's body look womanly and enticing enough to rouse suspicion in soldiers with a reputation for intelligence?[16]

This third and final act needs no comment, or rather, the mythology it utilizes is too obvious to take seriously: heroism, terror, and death. It was most likely invoked by Genet as a way of insisting on the cheerful continuity between the old woman, the young girl, and death, caused by the act of resistance. And yet heroism and sacrifice were first explained in the George Jackson story. The definitive argument against these notions comes with the episode of the fedayeen going down to the Jordan River. Leila Khaled evokes the peasant woman described in two lines of Ezra Pound's Canto LXXIII, a tribute to a young *fascist* girl's act of bravery:

I passed through Ariminum

And met there

A proud spirit

Who sang as though enchanted

By joy!

It was a peasant girl

Somewhat dumpy but good-looking

who had two Germans by the arms

And sang,

sang love

without needing

to go to heaven.

She had led the Canadians

> on to a mined field

Where was the temple

> of lovely Ixotta.[17]

This sample of violence—a walk, hijacking, explosion—revealed an assortment of acts: a symbolic gesture, a concerted action, and a timely intervention. The acts were independent, if not isolated, in pairs or in numbers, and always solitary. Each originated from a precise point of protest, whether it was the number of an Amendment, the name of a prisoner, or a latitudinal point on a map. The terrible gesture spread over the world, its power both real (the airplane) and mimed (the image), mobilizing the police, political, and journalistic forces. All the planet is its playground: *The world ground to a halt while words and gestures unfurled across the retina of humanity.* International terrorism or world revolution, these gestures were woven by image and violence but not always by death; their goal was the trial.

"Hijacking is a strategy of excess, the fluttering poetry of a generalized battle through which humanity, the world and the cosmos itself are whirling along with any orphaned celestial revolutions."[18] These lines about the Palestinian operations can be found in Abdelkebir Khatibi's essay *Vomito Blanco*, whose manuscript Genet proofread in 1974. The same constellation can be found downstream from this story, in Salman Rushdie's *The Satanic Verses*. The 1988 novel begins with a hijacking, using Genet's words: "Then they were in control, three men and one woman, all tall, none of them masked, all handsome, they were actors, too, they were stars now, shooting stars or falling, and they had their own stage names." The narrator adds that, "The young men were too squeamish, too narcissistic, to want blood on their hands. They would find it difficult to kill; they were here to be on television."[19] This wording doesn't have the same power as another text, attributed to an old Palestinian woman, who summed up the Palestinian revolution early in part two of *Prisoner of Love*: "To have been dangerous for a thousandth of a second, to have been handsome for a thousandth of a thousandth of a second [...]. But we were sensible. And dangerous for only a few seconds."[20] All have the merit of drawing attention to a three-way game between fire, fedayeen, and the Western world as spectators. The events of the Capitol (television), Zarka (hijacking), and the bodice (blood) take shape as the satanic issue of image.

Reflected in their actions, we see the terrorist stars desire yet fear the trial, crave yet reject image, and accept, as well as exclude, violence. Genet wrote, "I think most of the PLO longed to create an image that would inspire respect," and also that "they were basking in an image they hadn't earned."[21] As for the Panthers, "they deliberately set out to create a dramatic image."[22] Together, the three reproaches from his last book cast light on the significance that an extraordinary event had on the daily no-future existence of the time. This world was now truly perceived as a constellation. As early as 1970, Yasser Arafat had deemed the Popular Front for the Liberation of Palestine unfit to be a part of the Palestine Liberation Organization, even though some PLO leaders didn't hesitate to hijack funds. All the same, most of the PLO yearned for a respectable image. The fedayeen, on the other hand, accepted an unacceptable image, without daring "the heroism of Leila Khaled."[23] They didn't condemn Khaled's actions; perhaps they lacked the courage to do so. Unlike the PLO, the soldiers didn't create an image; they accepted one. They too were afraid. "You'd turned us into monsters, too. You called us terrorists! We were terrorist stars."[24] Glory and rejection—a single image. But did they have a choice? The image was handed to them. In 1973, Genet was already wondering, "The appearance on TV screens and on page one of the papers of a silhouette hidden behind a mask with two holes cut in it with a kind of 'bun' on top was both frightening and unpleasant. It proves, it seems to me, that Black September refused to be this landscape, this Third World operetta, this local color where death and poverty, seen from afar by European spectators, are pleasant to watch."[25] For the Palestinians, we have long substituted one false image for another, equally false but self-chosen. A silhouette wearing a keffiyeh—male or female?—would appear in the top left corner of the TV screen every time there was talk of Palestinians or international terrorism (a frozen image). This gave way to children, young boys and girls, armed only with rocks, filling the entire screen (news reporting). These two images, whether accepted or not, underscore a people whose very identity was denied.

The Panthers, on the contrary, worked to project an image. They made "many gestures that became symbols all the stronger for being weak. They were quickly adopted by all the Blacks and by White youth. A great wind swept over the ghetto, carrying away shame, invisibility and four centuries of humiliation. But when the wind dropped, people saw it had been only a little breeze, friendly, almost gentle."[26] There was the wind again, only different now. About the Red Army Faction, at the time of Klaus Croissant's extradition, Foucault maintained, "[...] along with the media, the authorities manipulate another scene where they stage a trial which is often without appeal, or at least with any proportionate answer."[27] This other scene, whether beneath or beyond the stellar scene of the disinherited, must not be overlooked. Image itself is never acceptable, noble, weak, strong, or just; it's only an image. All people play with their image. The government projects the image it wants, the press imposes its image, and young soldiers accept the unacceptable if they're fighting to put an end to the intolerable. The strength of the downtrodden was the violent use of the weakness of images. The movements Genet met expressed the anxiety of those who are seen in relation to those who've come to see. The image will disappear.

While Genet didn't dwell on these all too visible actions, was he in some way depriving the stars of their sky? For all these people from far and wide, *the will to image was no different from the will to trial.* In May 1970, Genet reflected on Angela Davis, writing, "There is a question that is hard to answer with any precision: at what moment (if there is one), in what circumstances (if any), does a man or a woman understand that, instead of speaking in vain, they have just come forth to tell the truth?"[28] This line of inquiry is linked to the need to affix words to actions. For Genet as well, the task of writing, of revolting—of inventing a legacy, if you will—was inseparable from the will to trial. *His scrutiny of violent acts was neither moral nor esthetic, but political.* The will to trial calls forth his distinctions between meaningful and hollow actions, the public and people, spectator and witness. It is alien to a certain humanistic conception of the individual. It understands violence, but its goal is not death.

The image, acceptable or not, should no more hide the intolerable than it should infamy and the misfortune that begets it. Though violence is often the only gesture that leads to trial, it is also the impossibility of choosing its terms. Ideally, the method should at once be a *violent act, theatrical gesture, and political sign.* Through image and violence, acceptable or not, the movements displayed the will for *another trial.* While criticizing violence, moved by the concerns of the forgotten, Genet was compelled to mention the manner in which the overlooked got the world's attention. The violence of the stars was the hijacking of the trial of the times by the disinherited. *The will to trial shows the world that which never leaves us: village, language, childhood.*

It was up to Genet's last book to transform this will into a story: the story of an action that did not quite blend in to this will, even if the action and the will and the decision they incited shared a common goal: to explode forth out of shame. Hence, the will to trial of these people and of Genet himself did not conform to ideas of rights or laws. Beyond the rights of individuals and the laws of power, *it called on individuals to make a decision about themselves,* a political decision.

GESTURES

The writer did not go to the Shatila refugee camp to provide it with an image or to make an inquiry. He went "to perceive a reality, a political and human reality."[29] His narrative was not an image of the massacre. Instead, it was the experience of the smell of corpses, of Genet's dead flesh.

"I can't really give a date to the beginnings of this book. Was it after Shatila?" Genet quickly rectified this comment about *Prisoner of Love*: "I started to write the book around October 1983. And I became a stranger, a foreigner, to France."[30] Begun as a revolution, a viral disease, or as the fortunes of a family, the book has various origins. One of which was the name Shatila. The political events known as Sabra and Shatila took place in Beirut between Thursday the 16th and Saturday the 18th of September, 1982. The first mention of Genet's presence in this time and place was in his story "Four Hours in Shatila," published on January 1, 1983 in the *Revue d'études palestiniennes*. "No one, nothing, no narrative technique can ever say," he began. The impossible beginning, the impossible story of this origin, the event of this origin, of this birth or death were still locked within the name Shatila. The issue was the possibility of a Palestinian narration. Salman Rushdie spoke of a "discontinuity of Palestinian existence." Palestinian historian Edward Saïd explained, "There are many different kinds of Palestinian experience, which cannot all be assembled into one. One would therefore have to write parallel histories of the communities in Lebanon, the occupied territories, and so on. That is the central problem. It is almost impossible to imagine a single narrative."[31]

Genet was able to write the story because all his actions had led up to it: his life stages (becoming a dancer, a revolutionary, a witness, and a survivor), his turning points (dance, revolt, and violence), and the general tone of that period in history, as well as that period in his own story (the trial and the disinherited). The excesses of this event, the writer's hyperbole and the negation in the narrative—no one, nothing, not any—were all elements of this story. They interlocked in a short narrative that was both impossible and improbable and told by no one, with his sights set on investigating death.

The key event of 1982 was the war in Lebanon. This story finds its roots in a new space and time, in a geographical situation that was tortuous, if not intolerable, in the so-called "external sanctuary." For a people deprived of their land, this entailed finding safe quarters in which freedom fighters could organize the politico-military infrastructure necessary to reclaim their rights. These quarters would be subject to the twofold hostility of the host country and of a part of the country wanting to be reclaimed; in this case, Lebanon and Israel. The terms of the accord, as set by US envoy Philip Habib on August 20, 1982, called for the PLO to pull out its combatants. In exchange, the Israeli army would promise to stay out of West Beirut, which would instead be watched over by multinational forces. The evacuation ended on September 1. Even though the peacekeepers' mandate concluded on September 21, the US contingent withdrew eight days early. The lingering trauma of the Vietnam war and Israeli pressure were invoked to justify the hasty departure. In the general exodus, Italy and France withdrew their troops as well.

The bloodbath in Sabra and Shatila lasted thirty-six hours. Lebanese numbers put the death toll at 460, whereas Palestinian sources claimed the body count rose to 5,000. According to Israel's Kahan Commission, named after the judge charged with leading the inquiry, less than 1,000 died.[32] Plus one, no doubt. Now over forty years old, Genet's memory grew hazy. The war, of which this massacre was a part, brought great destruction. In all, there were 19,000 Lebanese and Palestinian casualties, more than half of them civilians, while 30,000 were wounded. Hospitals, social services, administrations, offices, and most of the PLO infrastructure in Lebanon were destroyed.

The Lebanese government chose the period after the war to rid itself once and for all of the Palestinian problem, using terror, exile, and emergency laws. In Beirut, Amin Gemayel, brother of the assassinated president, decreed that passports would be denied to Palestinians abroad. Only Palestinians who'd arrived before 1948 were allowed to stay. That day in September set off the third Palestinian exodus, ever farther from Palestine, toward Tunisia. Afterward, the conflict was extended in the form of invasions into occupied territories, in what proved to be the most sustained attack against Israel since 1967. On

September 19, 1987, the anniversary of the Sabra and Shatila massacres, the intifada began in the West Bank and Gaza.

Were the PLO, Israel, and France responsible? From the Palestinian perspective, it was not until the Eighteenth Palestinian National Council Congress on May 20, 1987 that George Habash declared, "[The Palestinian movement] must answer the following question: what do we want from Lebanon? Why do we insist on maintaining a Palestinian armed presence in Lebanon? How do we perceive our relations with the LNM [Lebanese National Movement]? [...] During its presence in Lebanon throughout the seventies and until 1982, the Palestinian revolution made mistakes. These mistakes must be identified, acknowledged, and rectified."[33] The mistakes? The Palestinian domination over the Lebanese National Movement, the wrongful use of arms, the decision to use shelling over cross-border infiltration, the pressures on Amal, the numerous cease-fire violations, and the discord among the Fatah members.

On the Israeli side, a columnist in the *Ha'Haretz* newspaper wrote, "Behind the official excuse of 'we shall not tolerate shelling or terrorist actions' lies a strategic view which holds that the physical annihilation of the PLO has to be achieved. That is, not only must its fingers and hands in the West Bank be amputated (as is now being done with an iron fist), but its heart and its head in Beirut. With the loss of its physical strength, in their opinion, the PLO will lose not only its hold over the territories but also its growing international status."[34]

In his last book, Genet cast an accusing eye and saw hogwash. He considered France: "We wait for the first of these events to emerge more plainly: France's betrayal of the civilian population when its soldiers slipped away and eclipsed themselves as soon as they'd cleared the Museum Corridor of mines in East Beirut."[35] He called this conjunction an eclipse. September, sanctuary, war: the event with untraceable origins was in itself a beginning for Genet. This beginning was in turn an origin, *tajawuzat*. The excesses described by this word were already visible in the hostility of the host.

Genet watched from a balcony. He entered the camps, one step at a time. But was his presence there that day coincidence or propaganda? To ask the question is to ponder the final consequences of what he would later call "play-acting." The memory of the event would make this Frenchman write in his last book: "The big Israeli demonstration in 1982 against the Lebanese war was planned before the invasion began. Everything was worked out in advance: the invasion, the raids in Beirut, the murder of Bechir Gemayel, the massacres at Shatila, the ostentatious horror of world press and television—even the world's revulsion, the demonstration itself and the final whitewash."[36] The Palestinian Liberation Organization knew that preparations for the invasion were underway.[37] Indeed, it had amassed a good deal of information about then-Israeli Minister of Defense Ariel Sharon's military plans. In Beirut, Arafat and others drew up plans for reporters and Arab and Western diplomats in the desperate hope that media knowledge of the details might delay the invasion. Leila Shahid gave her account of Genet's timely arrival in Beirut: "I wanted to use Jean's being here and his knowledge of Beirut and Lebanon, and I asked him if he wouldn't write an article on what the siege of Beirut represented. He told me he would try but that he hadn't been back since 1970. I would have to help him and provide documentation."[38] They decided to go by plane to Lebanon. Genet made it even clearer, stating, "No, I wasn't there by chance. I had been invited by the *Revue d'études palestiniennes*. We left for Beirut together with Layla [sic] Shahid."[39] They entered Beirut via the Road to Damascus on September 12, 1982. Leila Shahid said, "Jean was very excited, he wanted to see everything." Was the meeting propaganda, coincidence, tactic, manipulation, circumstance, or chance?

Genet later put dates to his stay.

If you like, I'll retrace the chronology of what happened during my stay there. We arrived in Damascus on September 11, 1982, then went by road to Beirut, on

September 12. And on Monday, September 13, we visited
the city. [...] On Tuesday, Bashir Gemayel was assassinated.
[...] The next day, Israeli troops crossed into the Passage
du Musée, passed through other parts of West Beirut, and
occupied the camps at Shatila, Sabra, and Bourj al-Barajneh,
among others. [...] There was a moment of flux between ten
a.m. and a quarter after ten on Sunday, and this allowed me
to go in.[40]

He still expressed doubt: "It is difficult to say that the Israelis wanted this massacre. Indeed I'm not sure of this myself. But they allowed
it to happen. It was carried out, in a way, under their protection. Since
they lit up the camps at Sabra, Shatila, and Bourj al-Barajneh. When
you send up flairs, it's in order to do reconnaissance, it's to help the
people who are on your side. The people on Israel's side were obviously
the ones who committed the massacre."[41] Finally, the historian Amnon
Kapeliouk, who studied the massacre, cut to the heart of it: "To use an
Israeli soldier's expression, from the top of the buildings [those of the
closest command post], it was like watching from 'the front-row seats
in a theater.'"[42] Entering the camps is crucial to the story of Genet's
political emergence.

Genet went down into the streets. Having entered both the camp and
the story, he said, "I was struck by a kind of faint attack of madness that
almost made me smile." He marched, as he put it, into the "fairy tale" of
the massacre.[43] Perhaps the term "fairy tale" was his tribute to Céline,
who was mentioned at the beginning of this story.[44] Genet's arrival in
the camps was in some ways a nod to Céline; not a moral nod to the
"nobility" of the causes he espoused, but rather a farewell, as he set out
to bear witness to the slaughter of innocents—it was a political nod.

In this garden of love and death, Genet came across a dead body:

The first corpse I saw was that of a fifty- or sixty-year-old
man. He would have had a ring of white hair if a wound (an

ax blow, it seemed to me) had not split open his skull. Part
of the blackened brain was on the ground next to his head.
The entire body lay in a sea of black, clotted blood. His belt
was unbuckled, only one button of his pants was fastened.
The feet and legs of the dead man were naked, black, purple,
and blue: perhaps he had been taken by surprise at night or
at dawn?

And then he looked upon a second corpse: "The body of a thirty- or
thirty-five-year-old man was lying on its belly." The third body was a
woman, a "Palestinian woman [...] stretched out on her back, laid or
left there on top of the rubble, the bricks, the twisted iron rods, no
comfort. [...] The black and swollen face was turned toward the sky,
black with flies, with teeth that looked very white to me, a face that
seemed, without the slightest movement, to be grimacing or smiling
or screaming a silent and uninterrupted scream." And then he saw "the
corpses of four men piled on a single bed, one on top of the other, as
if each had made an effort to protect the one underneath him or as if
they were gripped by some erotic lust now in a state of decomposition."
Much farther, several pages later, he continued, "My description of
Shatila was interrupted for a moment, but I must finish it. There were
the dead bodies I saw at the end [...]. I thought I saw a black boxer sitting on the ground, stunned from a knockout [...]. If at first I saw him
as a black boxer it was because his head was enormous, swollen, and
black, like all the heads and all the bodies, whether in the sun or in
the shadows of the houses."[45] The corridor of corpses mimicked a museum corridor. Genet borrowed from the masters for this remarkable
description of descriptions: Fra Angelico for the old man split open by
the ax, Goya for the pile of terrified corpses, and Bacon for the boxer.
The colors black, violet, and purple appear in visual art throughout the
ages. Though the style was Florentine, the tone was modern. These
terrible changes in the head, face, and hands do not apply to all types
of death indiscriminately; they belong to violent death exclusively. The
exact nature of the text highlights the poetic aims of the description.

However, it also acquires political value when presented in a way that offers legal corroboration to the terrible rumor that rose swiftly from an act of terror, if not a terrorist act, bearing an official character and pertaining to the state. Poetic and political, the description of descriptions was meant to say only one thing: "All of them—and I mean all of them—had been tortured."[46] Black, violet, and purple were the colors of Shatila. Genet also had in mind the "yellow and blue and black"[47] that T.E. Lawrence used to describe the massacre at the Turkish barracks. Separating political and human realities and the living from the dead were now the same task.

In the end, he could not count them all. "I had spent four hours in Shatila. About forty corpses remained in my memory." The nameless experience of the massacre was simply that of the impossible debt owed to the dead and to death itself. He wrote, "The stench of death was coming not from a house or a tortured victim: my body, my being, seemed to emit it."[48] The foul winds were now blowing from the Palestinians' lungs into Genet's. All senses were called into play in this story of invasion: sight, hearing, and smell. And their roles were switched. With the eyes now acting as hands, the whole body was touched. The event was important because all five senses were alive in the face of death. Genet was engulfed by his actions, both on a microcosmic and macrocosmic level, in the realms of language and death; the man and the world were swept away.

Death was last to be eclipsed. At the heart of the tale lay the twofold affirmation: "The worst was on its way. I saw it." As an elderly Palestinian woman told Genet, "Please don't tell me what you saw in Shatila. My nerves are too sensitive, I have to stay calm so that I can bear the worst that's still to come."[49] The name Shatila now meant the worst that was still to come, much later, in a distant present. Like the acts invoking, provoking, and awaiting it, the worst was now always possible. Genet wrote, "Love [*l'amour*] and death [*la mort*]: these two words are quickly associated when one of them is written down. I had to go to Shatila to see the obscenity of love and the obscenity of death."[50] The experience of Shatila was not that of a mass grave, of a small community slaughtered by another and witnessed by a third. To Genet, this wasn't simply a massacre carried out in a ghetto (the camps) on foreign land (Israel) upon the Palestinians by the Phalangists (the Lebanese militia), under the floodlights of the Israel Defense Forces. To the writer, the event was the perception of the obscenity of love and death. The two words evoked the awareness of a body. "In both cases, the body has nothing left to hide: positions, contortions, gestures, signs, even silences belong to both worlds."[51] Faced with human deaths, writing is transformed, one word pushing aside the other that becomes the last. He spoke of the acts, gestures, and symbols[52] of the Panthers. Faced with the Palestinians, he spoke of gestures, signs, and silences.[53] Entering the camps meant entering two corresponding worlds.

Human and political realities were taking shape. According to the above logic, from the reflection of the joy of the rich deep in the eyes of the poor, Genet now saw the Phalangists' bayonets in the eyes of the fedayeen. At the end of *Prisoner of Love*'s second part, "The wide eye can still see the shine of the knife or bayonet. The brightness that slowly approaches, pales, blurs, disappears. Then the knife, the hand, the sleeve, the uniform, the eyes, the laughter of the Phalangist have ceased to be."[54] It's the death of the world. "What was missing here, I realized, was the cadence of prayers."[55] The eclipse meant that no one was looking. Unless the writer invented it, there would be no eye. Yet, after the event, if God was not dead, everything was possible. One simply needed to call on the name God or "No One."

Leaving the grammatical world and entering that of the living, trying to see death—a single action, no doubt as simple as these words suggest. Experiencing the debt now meant recognizing the summons of responsibility, testimony, and legacy. A legacy that would forever keep its secret. The writer as a boxer—KO'ed or almost, if not totally mad.

SIGNS

Most combat took the form of shots in the night from both sides of the border.[56] The attention Genet gave to the fedayeen going down to the Jordan River must point to something other than sorrow. The constellation of shots, borders, and the descent into night calls for the impossible return of the dead.

Genet lost many friends in the war. Burials, like prayers, were not enough. He chose to veer away from self-pity and instead told the oft-repeated tale of a timeless action without precedent, of the scores of attacks, operations, and massacres, and ultimately, of the return—or endless returns—from going down to the Jordan. Between myth and reality, is the end heaven or hell or chaos?

"When we went down the steps of the Jordan at night to lay mines, and came up again next morning, were we ascending from Hell or descending from Heaven?"[57] The Jordan is a river but also a border; it is the setting for a struggle over land, traced by a river with its black waters. Except for when the snows are melting, the Jordan is more stream than river; thirty to fifty feet wide, it runs for 118 miles between the Sea of Galilee and the Dead Sea. It's a red line, a security line, and a borderline.[58] The sole reason the fedayeen going down to the Jordan belongs to Genet's story is because he saw in it a descent into the self: "To go back so far in time is the same as descending deep, deep into yourself, unto death, so as to find the strength to fight."[59] The Jordan River was a golden gateway to both dreams and reality. Jordan, *Al-Urdunn* in Arabic, means "descending."

As the fedayeen gradually disappeared, the writer's words on the matter followed suit: two voices, one silence. In 1977, Genet reread notes from 1970 for the first time, and in a postscript, note, or fragment that would also vanish, he wrote, "The zone I spoke of, flanked by the Jordan River, I did not yet know that with each night it was becoming more sparsely populated: fedayeen of fifteen, sixteen, seventeen, eighteen, nineteen, twenty years old would cross the river, would kneel down to kiss the Palestinian earth, and would go, always at night, to explode an Israeli target. Many did not come back. Very few knew the happiness of return, the kisses on the cheeks and the great glad slaps on the back."[60] He was assessing the matter of the Jordan for the first time.

The postscript calls for a parenthesis. In 1982, he recalled the arrival of visitors to the bases near the Jordan, greeted by laughter and kisses: "(the one they embraced was leaving at night, crossing the Jordan River to plant bombs in Palestine, and often would not be coming back)."[61] That the death in language should take the form of a parenthetical note has meaning in this story, too. His return to this image in his final book was his last. The returning was approaching chaos:

> Several images throw themselves at me, and I don't know
> why I choose the one I'm about to describe for the last time.
> The vapor from a boiler steams up a window, then gradually
> disappears, leaving the window clear, the landscape
> suddenly visible and the room extended perhaps to infinity.
> Another image: a hand and a sponge move to and fro over
> a blackboard rubbing out the chalk writing. That's all. The
> farewells the fedayeen who are leaving take of those who
> will leave later seem to have the same effect. First they
> all embrace. Those who are going to stay behind stand
> motionless on the path, and those who've been chosen to go
> down to the Jordan retreat backwards into the distance with
> a smile, both groups waving their hands in front of their
> faces as a sign of farewell, of effacement. Like the writing
> on the board and the steam on the window, all their faces
> disappear, and the landscape, all its tears wiped away, is
> restored to itself. The fedayeen to be sacrificed have been
> the strongest. Tired and waving the childish "Bye-bye,"
> they have resolutely turned their backs on their comrades.[62]

The only thing typical about the second type of disappearance lies in its reference to Abu Kassem's death. Earlier in the book, the craftsman had made a cane for the writer. After the same image—the blackboard, the chalk, the farewell—Genet wrote, "A man doesn't return from Israel. I've often noticed that gesture of farewell wiping out a face and a body. And seen the face and body appear again the next day. I don't know why, but the camp took on a mischievous air then. But Abu Kassem never came back from the Jordan. He was twenty years old."[63] At times, going down to the Jordan meant going to Palestine and at others, to Israel. In those dazzling moments, Genet felt himself becoming a Palestinian. The resistance was also fought in language. The writer goes down deeper, nearly hitting bottom.

The final example of disappearance is also its opposite. It is one of the outcrops of the book, at the end of the night. "When the fight was over," Genet wrote, "how was it that none of the dead, whether friend or foe, got up and went and washed the blood off? I saw and still see the fedayeen as capable of being angry with the Israeli dead for not being able to wake up; for not being able to understand that death should last only a night at most. Otherwise fighters would become murderers. [Abu Omar added that] 'just because you kill someone there's no reason for them to stay dead forever.'"[64] In the face of death, language was suddenly erased and the landscape cleansed. Subjected to the real world, Genet fell silent before death. He tried a last shift from the question of violence, seen here as disappearance and violent death, to the possibility of return. The distinction here could be seen as a concern with resurrection, a desire to come back, in human form, as well as a promise of kisses and hugs from son to father.

Going down to the Jordan comprised the mystery of the Palestinian resistance. It's a kind of revelation that Genet returned to repeatedly; its significance is ours to uncover. But instead of bringing order to chaos, here the song *is* chaos. Like an echo, repeating as it fades out, the last book sings of disappearing into the river. The tragedy of the disappearance is opposed to a joy, born of a projected return, being denied. Whether as father or son, Genet saw the impossibility of return as chaos, as violence. Faced with the impossible, a transformation was in order; the need to return became the need to create a legacy. Coldness and sorrow had to secretly coexist, as with his detachment and his detachment from his detachment, without the possibility of renaming what others call love, friendship, and mourning.

Near the very end of his last book, Genet humbly concluded, "That was what I thought, or rather something like it, yet I knew I'd never be cured. The fedayeen who'd become my friends, but with a friendship that was never labored, were dead, imprisoned, or on the run, or had regrouped to fight other battles in other countries."[65] The end of this critique of violence could be seen as friendship with the dead. Genet's dance was comparable to that of the Bedouins, recalled at the very moment of this farewell; the dance was never morbid, nor even nocturnal. It was light, and sought "direct contact [...] with the death of the victim."[66] Now, every word counted if the dead could not all be counted. What remained was the impossibility of knowing death.

This message must remain on the pediment of this moment in the writer's experience: "The world can be changed by other means than the sort of wars in which people die. 'Power may be at the end of a gun,' but sometimes it's also at the end of the shadow or the image of a gun."[67] Choosing the shadow of the gun over the gun itself meant rejecting fascism while remaining a threat.

Yet the vital hostility toward the enemy remained; what we'll "never know of the enemy." That is the problem. The terror, the burden, and the wonderment when faced with the impossibility of knowing the enemy, or others, comprised a mystery and must now orient our inquiry.

ENDNOTES

1. *CA*, 12.
2. Ibid., 251.
3. B. Seale, *Seize the Time* (New York: Random House, 1970), 154.
4. D. Hilliard and L. Cole, *This Side of Glory* (Boston, New York: Little Brown and Co., Back Bay Books, 1993), 122–123.
5. B. Seale, *Seize the Time*, 157–158.
6. Ibid., 159.
7. Ibid., 162–163.
8. Ibid., 177.
9. D. Hilliard, "The Ideology of the Black Panther Party," *Black Panther Newspaper*, November 8, 1969.
10. D. Hilliard, Editorial, *Black Panther Newspaper*, February 10, 1967.
11. *PL*, 372.
12. E.F. Mickolus, *Transnational Terrorism: A Chronology of Events, 1968–1979* (London: Aldwich Press, 1980), 208–213.
13. Mahmoud Issa (Selim), *Je suis un fedayin* (Paris, 1976), 79–80.
14. Ibid.
15. *PL*, 133.
16. Ibid., 60.
17. E. Pound, "Canto LXIII," in Massimo Bacigalupo, "Ezra Pound's Cantos 72 and 73: An Annotated Translation," *Paideuma* 20, no. 1–2 (1991): 17.
18. A. Khatibi, *Vomito Blanco: le sionisme et la conscience malheureuse*, coll. "10/18" (Paris: Bourgois, 1974), 42.
19. S. Rushdie, *Satanic Verses* (New York: Viking, 1989), 78.
20. *PL*, 269.
21. Ibid., 262.
22. Ibid., 97.
23. Ibid., 262.
24. Ibid., 14.
25. "Les Palestiniens" (II), *Shoun Falestine*, 1973; *GC*, 136.
26. *PL*, 51.
27. M. Foucault, "Va-t-on extrader Klaus Croissant?", *Le Nouvel Observateur*, November 14–20, 1977; *Dits et Écrits* (Paris: Gallimard, 1994), 3:365, no. 210.
28. "Angela et ses frères," *Le Nouvel Observateur*, August 31, 1970; *DE*, 57–58.

29. "Une rencontre avec Jean Genet," *Revue d'études palestiniennes*, Fall 1986; *DE*, 234.

30. *PL*, 388.

31. S. Rushdie, *Imaginary Homelands: Essays and Criticism, 1981–1991* (New York: Penguin, 1992), 179.

32. M. Naïm, "Les massacres de Sabra et Shatila," *Le Monde*, September 13–14, 1992, in a feature entitled "Il y a dix ans."

33. R. Brynen, *Sanctuary and Survival: The PLO in Lebanon* (Boulder: Westview Press, 1990), 193.

34. Y. Marcus, "The War Is Inevitable," *Ha'Haretz*, March 26, 1982; R. Brynen, *Sanctuary and Survival*, 153.

35. *PL*, 377.

36. *PL*, 130–131.

37. R. Brynen, *Sanctuary and Survival*, 153.

38. *GC*, 30.

39. *DE*, 232.

40. Ibid., 232–233.

41. Ibid., 233.

42. M. Naïm, "Les massacres de Sabra et Shatila," 2.

43. *DE*, 214, 228.

44. See Chapter 3.

45. *DE*, 209–210; 210; 213; 214; 223–224.

46. Ibid., 227.

47. T.E. Lawrence, *The Seven Pillars of Wisdom* (New York: Anchor, 1991), 726.

48. *DE*, 223 and 227.

49. Ibid., 222.

50. Ibid., 210.

51. Ibid.

52. *PL*, 51.

53. *DE*, 210.

54. *PL*, 378.

55. *DE*, 214.

56. J. Bowyer Bell, "Arafat's Man in the Mirror: The Myth of the Fedayeen," *New Middle East* 19 (April 1970): 22–23.

57. *PL*, 13.

58. M. Foucher, "Israël-Palestine: quelles frontières? Géographie physique et humaine de la Cisjourdanie," *Hérodote* 29–30 (September 1983): 98.

59. *PL*, 375.
60. "Près d'Ajloun," in *Per un Palestinese. Dediche a più voci a Waël Zouaiter* (Milan: G. Mazzotta, 1979); *DE*, 158.
61. *DE*, 228.
62. *PL*, 375.
63. Ibid., 264.
64. Ibid., 390.
65. Ibid., 427.
66. Ibid., 426.
67. Ibid., 97–98.

7 | Jean Genet's Covert Operation: Supplement to the English Edition[1]

On the subject of Israel's April 10, 1973 attack on Beirut, Jean Genet wrote in his final book, *Prisoner of Love*, "It's because of this act that Murder may be considered as one of the Fine Arts. And like all works carried out under the aegis of the Beaux-Arts, Murder deserves a medal or two."[2] The reference to Thomas De Quincey comes late, in the second version of the manuscript, but Genet knew of De Quincey's 1827 essay, *On Murder Considered as One of the Fine Arts*. He might have read the paperback version of the translation that came out around that time, in 1975. The essay belongs here the way a thread belongs to a tangled skein in the scene we are about to witness. De Quincey attracts our attention to a distinction he makes. Like all things under the sun, he says, murder can be considered in one of two ways: "Its moral handle, and that, I confess, is its weak side; or it may also be treated aesthetically, as the Germans call it—that is, in relation to good taste."[3] The two sides belong to the judges: the gaze of morality and law, or the German or aesthetic aspect. What's curious is that the German side, toward which De Quincey leans, will bring Genet from Beirut to Germany—to Munich, more precisely.

The major difference between De Quincey's essay and Genet's

story is a question of political order. While describing a triple political murder, Genet departs from the absolute principle of good taste when it comes to murder. About events in Ireland, long before the IRA, De Quincey declares that a murder in Ireland can never partake of the qualities of Art: "Tithes, politics, something wrong in principles, vitiate every Irish murder."[4] In his essay, the British author warns us, "Assassination is the branch of the art which demands a separate notice; and it's possible that I may devote an entire lecture to it."[5] He never carried out this wish. Genet took charge of it instead, and we will soon read his thoughts on the subject.

The two writers are not opposed to one another simply because Genet so noisily departed from the aesthetic principle according to which political assassination cannot be considered as one of the Fine Arts, or because he dedicated a political essay to a branch with which De Quincey did not care to concern himself. The distinction between them arises because, unlike the British writer, Genet, instead of separating the two spheres, considers aesthetics and political murder together. This is not some fascist principle. For Genet, particular reality must be minutely observed in its specificity through language. The small scale, the issue of vocabulary, calls forth the great, the wide and terrible world. Here, the three capital letters that await in the foreword (Murder, Fine, Arts) are also the initials of the three murdered Palestinians. This transition is possible only because Genet's politics are tied to the practice of language.

The dimension that sets apart the British essayist and the French writer does not depend on the latter's separation between the aesthetic and the moral, but rather on Genet's will to consider the two spheres together under the heading of a third. This is Genet's choice; neither moral nor aesthetic, his gaze is political.

The universe is changing, and now Genet has returned to the Middle East; the winds of trial are blowing around the world. Let's give this scene, in its first version, the dimension it was lacking. Beginning anew in his last book, Genet writes, "Here I shall speak of the deaths of Kamal Udwan, Kamal Nasir and Muhammad Yusif al-Najjar, three leading members of Fatah."[6] On both sides of this scene, the writer walks with his friend Hamza, H., the revolutionary, a son. The road, the verb "to walk," are the signposts of this passage: "It was October 1971." At this point, the scene appears like a stop along a stroll made for two men; untimely wanderings, a step off the road that gives meaning to the walk taken by Genet and the son. But the stop hangs on to the walk by a mere hair. We see the son again in and off-scene, even if, in a certain way, Genet never abandoned this minor motif in the last book. The hirsute line, if I may put it that way, seems to be the very structure of his memoirs. *Prisoner of Love* opens with wild youth gathered around a casket. The intelligence of this scene is possible only if we recognize the disheveled hair. And here's why: previous to this walk, Genet spots the soldiers of the Saïka, a Palestinian organization entirely dominated by Syria, "huge fellows with slight mustaches [...] with rifles in their hands. Their hair came down to their shoulders and ranged in color from light brown to ginger." On the stage of this scene, the soldiers of the Mossad, named as such and we'll soon see why, appear this way: "Two English-speaking hippies with fair curly hair." The soldiers of the Saïka will soon prove to be traitors, those of the Mossad high-ranking spies, and between them the relation is that of a man and his shadow. They resemble each other; they are brothers, yet enemies. Hamza steps out from the crowd as the one whom Genet has elected as his son, to have "a conventional haircut."

Hair is present as fashion and from it, Genet extracts the particular circumstances of the times, which must remain. Such is his work. It is a kind of code. After conjuring up the extravagant styles of the 1970s, Genet brings the paragraph to a close this way: "But here the youthful flowering was no spring: it took place in a Middle East where it was already summer, nearly autumn, and heading for a hard winter." The spring was not youthful, he writes, like the name and the step of that interrupted walk. "Spring of Youth" was the code name given by the Israeli secret services to the Beirut operation that cost the lives of three important members of Fatah.

Both the date (April 10, 1973) and the operation's name ("Spring of Youth") are explicitly or literally written, though both are present. The scene is organized as a covert operation carried out by Genet.

The amused telling of this operation is not Genet's doing, though he seems to be praising it. The wonderment, the work, the theater, and the reward are motives for praise or its contrary. Genet narrates it for a first time in his book:

> This is what Daoud told me: "After dark two English-speaking hippies with fair curly hair appeared with their arms round one another's necks, laughing and exchanging kisses. They staggered up to the two guards on duty at the foot of Kamal Udwan's stairs. The two guards shouted insults at the two shocking queers, who promptly showed the excellence of their training by whipping out revolvers, shooting the guards, rushing up the stairs and killing Kamal. Much the same thing happened at the same time to Kamal Nasir and Muhammad Yusif."

The story told by a third party—and not just anyone—features couples: three times two men who make seven with the teller; guards and hippies either trying to fend off or committing three murders. Genet states his preferences and provides some details about the reflection of these acts in the eyes of the Palestinians in Beirut. "Kamal Nasir, whom I met, was the one I liked best. The one I liked least was Kamal Udwan; his blunt questioning got on my nerves." We see, on a small scale, that brutality can flow from language, and it bothers Genet. He adds that the killing was insufficient to create in the streets of Beirut a sense of dismay that you might have expected. Edward Saïd, the author of *Orientalism* (1978), who met Genet in Beirut in 1972, related that he had seen Kamal Nasir the very evening of his death, for the latter was a member of his extended family.[7] On the other side, the Israeli Chief of Staff Ehud Barak, who served as Prime Minister of Israel from 1999 to 2001 and who was responsible for the operation, was happy to tell the story of how he disguised himself as a woman to execute the three executives of the PLO.[8] Later, he was put in charge of peace negotiations.

The story of the Beirut attack was told by a third man. Certain episodes of Genet's last book are related in other books: Rachid Boudjedra's *Journal palestinien*, Leila Khaled's *Mon peuple vivra*, and Mahmoud Issa's (Selim) *Je suis un feddayin*. Let's turn to this latter book. Dated 1976, it is a transcription of notes written down in student notebooks, and reread only to check a name, date, or place in which the author presents the situation in Lebanon. A complex situation that mirrors this small country's image: fragile because of its inadequate army, torn apart because of a system of governing based on the balance of religious communities, threatened on its southern border by reprisals and intervention, buffeted by foreign interference. In other words, a perfect setting for quarrel, intrigue, and false solutions. This author's story is nearly identical to Genet's:

> It was the month of April. One night, around two o'clock in the morning, there was a knock at my door. Even before I opened it I knew something serious had happened. Yet the news that my friend brought me left me speechless. Three of our leaders had been assassinated. They weren't just political chiefs but personalities who had civil responsibilities. Abu Yusef looked after Palestinian refugees in Lebanon, Kamal Udwan Palestinians in the occupied territories, Kamal Nasir was a speaker and writer. Muhammad el-Najjar was among the victims too. He was neither political nor a combatant. Certain that they were not a target for the Israelis, these Palestinians lived on the same street in Beirut, without any other protection than the local police station. None of them was armed except for Kamal Udwan, who had a pistol. I was all the more surprised since neither

I nor anyone else had caught wind of what was about to happen. The accomplices on the ground had done their jobs well. Several days earlier, the Israelis who carried out the mission arrived with tourist visas and French or Belgian passports. There were quite a few of them and they had a "correspondent" at the American embassy. That evening, just before midnight, they went to the houses of the Palestinians in rented cars. The operation was extremely easy to carry out successfully. The police station was deaf and blind. The district was deserted. Muhammad el-Najjar was shot with his wife who had opened the door. Then it was Abu Yusef's turn, as well as a neighbor woman who was murdered for imprudently trying to help him. Kamal Udwan died trying to defend himself. He must have killed or wounded some of his attackers, since bloodstains were found in the stairway. As for Kamal Nasir, he was sitting at his desk, writing an article when the Israelis burst into his home. He was found lying on the floor, his arms crossed, his face riddled with gunshot wounds. Kamal was a Christian. I knew him well; he was an excellent speaker. Despite the noise as the Israelis retreated—they covered their retreat by shooting at everything that moved—neither the police nor the army was alerted. It was as if the operation took place with the authorities' protection. The rented cars were found abandoned near the beach, which led people to think that the Israelis had withdrawn in boats. But we soon realized we were wrong. One of the aggressors arrested by our men confessed and told us that the commandos had hidden in Beirut once their mission was accomplished—some at the American embassy—and had not returned to Israel until the next day. This man, who is still in prison, recanted his version of the facts at a later date.[9]

Genet's comment about the dismay that no one suspected takes on, in this author's words, a political significance. The killings were made possible by the complicity of established governments, the United States in particular. The enormous difference in the way Genet and

Issa treat the subject is the same as that which separates the wind of what is about to happen (the rumors) and the wind of trial, tied to a critique of violence.

Let's bring together, for the first time, the features of the Beirut scene in regards to the criteria set down by De Quincey. "First, the kind of person who is adapted to the purpose of the murder; secondly, of the place where; thirdly, of the time when, and other circumstances": the place, the time, and the vestments, rather than the man hidden behind. The space and time: three private apartments in Beirut, at night, around two o'clock in the morning. Genet, or rather the actors of the crime, will have respected the rules of the art form if "the good sense of the practitioner has usually directed him to night and privacy."[10] The perfection of the assassination, the operation's success and Mossad's success as well—Genet sees them all in Daoud the taleteller's eyes. Daoud, he points out, "showed a certain admiration for its audacity and style. Such perfect execution implied the hand of a single great artist; [...] as well as admiring it he was amazed that such a swift and violent deed could be accomplished almost playfully by slaughterers with long fair corkscrew curls." Such success, paid for with such effort—"You may suppose that Israel praised the exploit in the newspapers"—demands recompense: "the six chests were duly decorated."

Rarely does Genet hand out medals; very few laurels for anyone. Yet he wrote, "And like all works carried out under the aegis of the Beaux-Arts, Murder deserves a medal or two." The critique of commemoration, which is neither the memory of legacy nor memory's movement, comes just after the passage in Beirut: "The Palestinian leaders were simply imitators. Their monument to the martyrs—to the dead—in the Beirut camp, made of wood and sheet metal, a small light bulb, always lit, seemed enormously moving to me by its poverty." A veiled criticism, indeed, but real if the monument is the "imitation of French monuments to the dead from the First World War." The other side of the decoration, or medal, an imitation, but of what?

"Newspapers all over the world described the assassination, but none of them called it terrorism on another country's sovereign territory." Genet went on to write, "You may suppose that Israel praised the exploit in the newspapers in Jerusalem and other cities. It probably does the same thing now when it stops and sinks Palestinian boats at sea." Praise or something else, the question remains unanswered. Let us now enter into the veiled but real critique of state terrorism. This is the time, not to give a third version of the story, though we have it before our eyes, but to point out at least where it might be found. Reading it, we will see that on that April day, six Israeli agents carrying South American passports, staying in Beirut's Coral Beach Hotel, rented three Buicks and went fishing as they waited for the commando group that would arrive by sea. Genet wrote, "We know what happened to the three PLO leaders and one of their wives." He does not say that the neighbor, an Italian woman, was also killed. Issa notes this. The styleless story of that day, or of that day without style, can be found in a sinister book by E.F. Mickolus, *Transnational Terrorism: A Chronology of Events, 1968–1979* (London, 1980). In this work, every terrorist operation is classified and numbered, from one to four thousand. We find the story of this event, dated April 10, 1973, but not its number. The Beirut operation is classified in this work of history between Affair 1521, an attack on April 9, 1973, against an El Al airplane in Cyprus, and Affair 1522, April 12, 1973, in Greece, when Ahmed Abusan, an unknown Arab soldier, was killed in his hotel room. A fair exchange, you might say. But why is the number missing for the Beirut operation, so important for Genet? The historian of terrorism—and it is a trade these days—points out in his introduction, "Scattered throughout the chronology are descriptions of incidents that were or are suspected of having been the work of governments. These listings are by no means exhaustive of the examples of state terrorism; they are included to provide readers a sense of the environments in which nonstate terrorist organizations operate."[11] It wasn't until November 1993 that Israel recognized this triple assassination. General Aaron Yariv declared, "We methodically organized an operation whereby we would liquidate the leaders of Black September, without concern for geography. We liquidated them wherever they were." Responsible for these operations was, besides Ehud Barak, Mike Hararaï, a member of Mossad who became an advisor to the Panamanian dictator Manuel Noriega. According to the expression in common use, the General went on to say, "Golda Meir gave the green light for each assassination, one at a time, in order to avoid errors and complications on the territory of States that were the theaters of these assassinations."[12] And so Golda Meir, the spider in Arafat's web, signed, signed, and signed again: for the assassinations of Kamal Udwan, Kamal Nasir, and Abu Yusef Nedjar. But also for the assassination in Paris in 1972 of Mahmoud Hamshari, Genet's friend.[13]

Now the question must be asked. What other event might be hiding behind the story of that particular day in Beirut? In other words, as Genet put it, "Why did I have to write about the murder after describing the Saïka soldiers' long hair?"

It seems easy to travel from Beirut to Munich, taking the route indicated by Genet. But the journey carries its share of weight. Surprisingly, De Quincey himself indicated the possibilities in his essay: "Riding one day in the neighborhood of Munich, I overtook a distinguished amateur of our society, whose name, for obvious reasons, I shall conceal."[14] The name of Daoud; the mention of the six Israelis charged with the Beirut operations as athletes; the general unexpected and exemplary tone of the text as a secret—all these encourage us to journey with Genet on German soil.

What is the name De Quincey has chosen to hide for obvious reasons—or rather, who is the man Genet met whom he calls Daoud the tale-teller? Abu Daoud, using the name Saad ad-Din Wali, along with Abu Iyad and Fakhri al Amari, is considered to be the mastermind of the September 5, 1972 attack on Israeli athletes during the Munich Olympic Games.

The code name of this attack, more down to earth but with echoes that live on today, was "Irkit and Birim," the names of two Arab villages occupied since 1948. Daoud bought the weapons in Sofia, put them in the Saudi Olympic installation that was next to the Israeli delegation, and made the hotel reservations for the Palestinian commandos. He left Munich before the attacks began. Who were the three men assassinated in Beirut? Abu Yussef (also known as Muhammad Yusif al-Najjar) and Kamal Nasir were both members of Fatah, and Kamal Udwan was one of the chiefs of Black September, the organization behind the Munich attack. Three times two couples in Beirut? The Palestinian commando was composed of six men in Munich. Did they receive medals, these golden athletes? Nine Israelis were taken hostage. In all, in Munich, eleven Jewish athletes and coaches were murdered: David Berger, Ze'ev Friedman, Yossef Gutfreund, Eliezer Halfin, Yossef Romano, Amitzur Shapira, Kehat Shorr, Mark Slavin, André Spitz, Yacov Springer, and Moshe Weinberg.

Youth without spring, since the attacks of Irkit and Birim took place in September. Did Genet speak of Munich? He explicitly named "Daoud Thalami, one of the leaders of the Popular Front for the Liberation of Palestine." Were Daoud the tale-teller, Abu Daoud, Daoud Thalami, and Saad ad-Din Wali one and the same? Listening keenly, earlier in the last book, we can read this warning: "Kamal Udwan [...] I'll tell later on how they were killed by Israelis pretending to be queers, perhaps in retaliation for the murders in Munich during the 1972 Olympics."[15] It's all been written.

We have to wait until 1992 to read what Genet wrote about Munich. He did it in a text that was not included in *The Declared Enemy*, his political writings; it is called "Les Palestiniens II." Three intersections in this 1973 piece merit particular attention: drowning, the effective critique of Europe, and war. Genet writes in his white-hot way:

> The Munich episode was hardly surprising. I was in Italy.
> If you want to know, I'll say a few words about it. It's often
> been said that the Olympic Games are nothing more

than a for-profit operation, a show of prestige. They are competitions, and therefore a form of international one-upmanship through sports. The games are a sort of United Nations of sports where small nations can compete, but the only real rivalry is between the two super-powers. If the Munich events created a storm of protest, it wasn't because of the games themselves, but because of the Western press, more or less directly linked to Tel Aviv by a complex organization of editorial directors, editors in chief and journalists.[16]

Let's slow down now. This is a false solution, and not Genet's last word. Did you note that the 1973 drowning—"the Western press... linked to Tel Aviv"—remained in the 1986 book? Some noticed that, speaking of the magnified exploit, Genet wrote, "in the newspapers, in Jerusalem and elsewhere, Israel [...]." Stylistically, an inversion is a form of rejection. Would this be the only trace of Munich in the last book? Genet can't stop himself from writing it. The constellation contained in the sentence, the anti-Semitic cliché about the Jewish control of the media, the old saw about the international plot, all these things that keep Genet from thinking about the limits of his own thought and life—let's not forget them. This kind of drowning challenges the collapse of vocabulary linked to the names of territory, homeland, and nation. "It's often been said," Genet writes, and forgets to think. In fact, he's simply copying the editorial written by Jean Lacouture and published in *Le Monde* on September 6, 1972, the day after the Munich attacks. Lacouture wrote, "The Olympic Games have paid the price for their monstrous exaggeration ... Black September used the opportunity provided by the huge concentration of mass media ..." And on it goes. The Olympic theme and the games and medals hide something else. Speaking of the "operation" is an understatement, for the Games take the place of assassination, murder, and death. By hiding the real significance of the event that took place during the Games, in the 1973 text, without the posterity of his last book, Genet misses his target twice: he gives in to the cliché about the plot, and offends death. Though he's speaking of sports, Genet isn't in the pool. Instead, he's drowning in his own words.

In 1973, Genet picks up where he left off, revises himself, pursues and elaborates his critique of the reflection of violence in vocabulary that finds its form—if not definitive, at least original—in the archeology of the legacy of the Red Army Faction. At the time, the form was simple. Genet reads the paper and concludes with an attack. Still regarding Munich, he quotes, then writes, "'All the hostages were killed.' Four 'Palestinians' were shot. Three others fled, a 'policeman' was killed and a pilot seriously wounded (*Le Figaro*, September 7, 1972). Each word has been deliberately weighted with infamy and opprobrium […]. In the newspapers, after Munich, words were chosen to portray the Palestinians as outlaws. To describe any event in those terms is to associate them with an underworld that is simply the Third World."[17] In this context, the critique of the use of vocabulary by the masters takes on a new meaning.

In these 1972 events, Genet discovers the origins of the "Internationale policière" that began in 1977 in Germany, and then elsewhere in Europe as the "Quartier de Haute Sécurité" (QHS). He writes, "It's clear that European union will prevail, but only as a union against a common enemy: the poor, the humiliated, the Black, the Arab, the Yellow, everyone who has 'slant eyes.'" War has been declared. "You know that, as far as I'm concerned, the combatants of Black September died like soldiers and that the Palestinian nation, whose only territory is Arabness and dreams, must be extremely dear to every Palestinian to make men so resolved to die for their beliefs. Now dialogue with Israel is impossible."[18] War is the last word. Fratricidal war, the war of language, to which Genet answers with a quarrel.

Before ending this short elucidation of the scene, a final reflection and another envoy. The reflection: in a certain way, Beirut and Munich do not constitute just a couple—April 9 and 10 are also the anniversary of the massacre carried out in 1948 by the Irgun and the Stern Gang at

Jean Genet and William S. Burroughs at an anti-Vietnam War protest in Chicago, Illinois, 1968. Copyright © Raymond Depardon/Magnum Photos.

Jean Genet at the Black Panther Demonstration at Yale University, 1970.
Copyright © Leonard Freed/Magnum Photos.

Jean Genet at BAKA camp (80,000 Palestinian refugees), near Amman, 1971.
Copyright © Bruno Barbey/Magnum Photos.

Palestinian refugee camp of BAKA, in Jordan, near Amman, 1969. Training of Al Fatah fighters. All these young people come from Palestinian refugee camps—most of them are orphans, their fathers having been killed in fighting. Many come from Karame, a bombed village near the Jordan River, victims of March 1968 fighting. Copyright © Bruno Barbey/Magnum Photos.

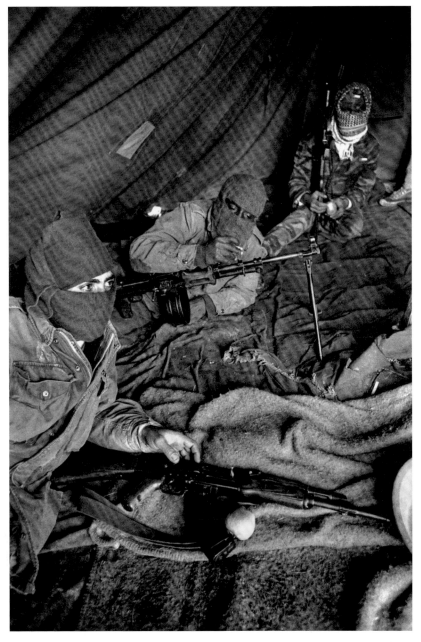

Palestinian military camp of BAKA, in Jordan, near Amman, 1969. Copyright ©
Bruno Barbey/Magnum Photos.

A poster shows an unveiled woman raising the Algerian flag to lead men into the war for independence from France. Algiers, 1990. Copyright © Abbas/Magnum Photos.

Andy Warhol, *Birmingham Race Riot*, 1964. Screenprint on white paper.
Courtesy: The Andy Warhol Foundation, Inc. / Art Resource, NY.

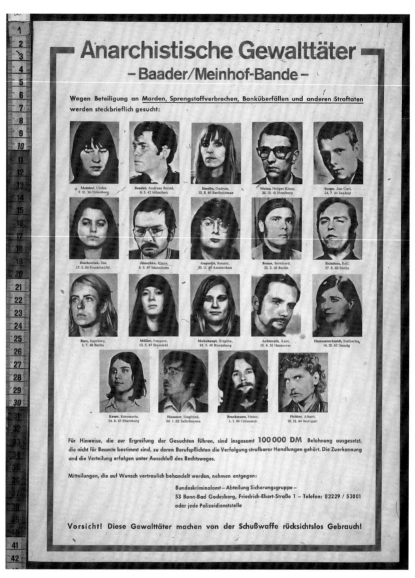

The Baader-Meinhof Gang, 1970, 1972. Courtesy: Bundesarchiv.

Gerhard Richter, *Confrontation 1 (Gegenüberstellung 1)*, 1988. Oil on canvas.
Courtesy: Marian Goodman Gallery, New York.

Gerhard Richter, *Confrontation 2 (Gegenüberstellung 2)*, 1988. Oil on canvas.
Courtesy: Marian Goodman Gallery, New York.

Gerhard Richter, *Youth Portrait (Jugenbildnis)*, 1988. Oil on canvas.
Courtesy: Marian Goodman Gallery, New York

The tomb of Jean Genet overlooks the Atlantic Ocean in Larache, Morocco, 1987. Copyright © Harry Gruyaert/Magnum Photos.

Deir Yasin. This is part of the text the Black September soldiers threw out a window of an Olympic building in the direction of the authorities: "We are neither killers nor bandits. We are persecuted people who have no land and no homeland ... We are not against any people, but why should our place here be taken by the flag of the occupiers? ... Why should the whole world be having fun and entertainment while we suffer with all ears deaf to us?"[19]

The Munich communiqué demanded, besides the freeing of 236 Palestinian prisoners, "the liberation of Andreas Baader and Ulrike Meinhof." Hence, the will to trial. What Genet calls dying like soldiers and being men of resolve. Who ever denied that the history of men of infamy, and infamy in vocabulary to which it is tied, does not present a true political stance? Not only seeking death, these men wish to present to the world that which they must not be separated from: suffering, language, home, childhood.

In his last book, Genet did not return to the circumstantial fragments about Munich. Instead, he chose to comment on Daoud's brief story. The choice is a rich one; it is poetic, tactical, and political. Here, Genet is carrying out a work of counter-praise, the overstated yet true praise (admiration, wonderment, success) of the Israeli operation rather than the laudatory story, which would have been possible, of the Munich attack. By moving from Europe to the Middle East, and keeping his eye fastened on the reflection of the Arab world in the Western world, Genet brings the whole world to trial. Daoud's name links the stars in the constellation of the time: assassination conjures the names of George Jackson, Munich, the Red Army Faction, and Beirut; the names of Black September, the Mossad, and Europe that looks on. Changing De Quincey's title from "murder" to "assassination" takes on its true meaning here. If Genet has a memory—if the distinction drawn in 1971 already did spring from the British writer's essay—he must have thought of the work done for George Jackson and the distinction between the two acts. Just as he must have remembered the importance of Germany in developing the difference between violence and brutality. Genet's aim is not to orient a practice; he wants judgment to be exercised.

Man, Genet insists, will be beautiful. Two long paragraphs added to the manuscript of the last book speak about the Israelis' preparation and disguise. These additions, typed onto the page with little leading, are unique in their kind. Here is how his last book resembles one of Proust's manuscripts: lines added at the last moment, cut out and stuck onto an earlier version of the text, form a single long page, Proust's palimpsest or paper banner. Man will be beautiful—De Quincey insisted on the same point: "Titian, I believe, certainly Rubens and perhaps Vandyke, made it a rule never to practice their art but in full dress: point, ruffles, bag-wig and diamond-hilted sword."[20] Just like the assassin, he will wear silk stockings and slippers. The Israelis? Genet wrote, "They all agreed to undergo the necessary training. To make their caresses plausible, each couple had to get used to kissing and being kissed on the mouth. The muscles of their arms and legs, their agility, the innocence and hairlessness of their faces—all had to be brought to perfection. Above all, their voices had to sound feminine and not falsetto." Or this: "Six curly blond wigs, a bit of red on the lips and black round the eyes." And then, "Divided up into three couples they'd given perfect performances as queers in love."[21] All that's missing are De Quincey's ruffles, rings, and diamond-hilted sword; the clothes make the murderer, but skin is a disguise too, a disguise of muscles, and the hair not their own if you decide to accept the idea of a wig rather than natural growth. "Queer" is an insult only in certain mouths. If Genet uses this well-known word, can we feel contempt for those labeled that way? They were perfect in their role. Now praise is competing with a language that would be insulting or full of contempt for anyone other than Genet, who loves men.

One remark here: Genet's drowning, that we pointed to earlier, is still visible here in the slight slippage between the first and second versions of the manuscript. At the beginning and at the end of the latterly added first paragraph, Genet literally rewrites the same sentence about the difficulties of choosing the members of the Israeli commando: "There was no shortage of blonds." And this because of the way the sentence ends: "Lots of young Sabras were of Ashkenazi origin," that is, German, if Germans are thought to be blond. We return once again to Munich. In the same way, between this paragraph and the former state of the scene, the same words return concerning the commando retreating back to Israel. By sea, in a boat, Genet hammers, they "sailed back to Haifa under the dark sky." Perhaps Genet was fatigued, unless fatigue was tired of Genet. More like a fascination, a slippage and lack of clarity when faced with the destination of these men sailing between light (blond) and shadow (dark sky). No doubt Genet is already wondering about the people who say they are Chosen, from the days when darkness was on the face of the deep.

The disguise—ski mask or wig—is a motif whose radical meaning is drag, or even transsexuality. Bobby Seale had considered freeing Huey Newton by dressing him as a woman; cloaked in a dress, he would have walked free as the police looked on. He himself wore a disguise to go and visit imprisoned Black Panther members. Arrested in Berlin, Horst Mahler, the lawyer for the Red Army Faction, hid behind a fake beard and a wig.[22] Dressing in drag is part of the times. Imitation and trace, incarnation, pastiche, assassins and martyrs—we don't know how to distinguish. Genet dresses, then undresses the Israelis. To contempt for queers comes the taste for pastiche, or vice versa. In fact, describing a man—six Israelis, in this case—implies, for Genet, preparation, work, an operation. Assassination is the end result, though drag is the process. The operation succeeded, but in the end we don't know which of the two, assassination or dress-up, was the most difficult and therefore most admirable.

Faced with the momentary and desired impossibility of choosing, Genet asks at the end of the passage, "I wonder if it isn't comparatively easy and pleasant to slip into tender femininity, and hard to throw it off to commit a crime." Here, the writer is closest to the issue. Like questioning the abyss: the question involves relations with others, by reproducing the separation between life and death, through sexual difference. Is murder tender compared to the difficulty of feeling the difference between the two sexes? Is wearing drag tender if the passage from life to death is difficult? Murder and assassination, violence and brutality, pushed by the winds of trial, the issue will change: Genet will soon come up against the obscenity of love and the obscenity of death. What would beauty be if it did not also recognize itself as ugliness?

Reread the scene in its entirety, the Middle East with Europe, with the names of Beirut and Munich together. Consider the long list of the dead, as long as the hours in a day. Determine, if you can, the difference between praise and contempt. Such a judgment depends on the way you see the assassins. It varies according to whether you see them as "six Israelis," "six athletes," "six blond wigs." Who will win the laurels of Murder considered as one of the Fine Arts? To whom will you give the medal—to Genet, to the Israelis? Why not to De Quincey? Instead of athletes, you have martyrs.

Definitely, it would seem that in this scene, just like De Quincey with his fictional society of friends gathered together with the same aesthetic taste for murder, Genet makes two toasts: the first to the Israelis, the second to the Palestinians. On one side, according to De Quincey, "the Jewish school of murder," and the other, "the fanatical Mohammedan sectaries, called The Assassins." Genet's double praise for the Assassins is obvious: that Iranian branch of the Ismailis, Mohammad's fanatics, who existed in the years 1090 to 1259 in Persia and Syria, and also for the Zealots or Sicarii, a Palestinian Jewish sect under Nero's reign, partisans of Judah of Galilee, who also specialized in the art. What is interesting, as De Quincey points out to his audience, is the archeological fact according to which, in Palestine, "the Assassins, as ancient as they are, had a race of predecessors in the very same country."[23] Through Genet's sleight of hand, faithfulness to oneself, the Assassins, an Arab sect, becomes Israeli, whereas the Zealots, a Jewish sect, stand in for the Palestinians. Opening this telling, the resemblance of the soldier or the man with his shadow attests to the fact that the two circumcised nations share a single fate. The quarrel knotted up in ancient words, those of the predecessors, first and last, their becoming, everything is hanging here, by the hair, if I may say, be it a wig or not, including the collapse of Genet's vocabulary. Not surprising that we discover the "need" at the origin of this scene.

In the notebook that holds the seven final transformations of Genet's manuscript, we find a page that was meant to take its place among the overburdened sheets, at the end of an added-on paragraph, before the retelling of the Beirut scene, as it was told a first time. At the center of the telling, though added on at the end, Genet imagines himself as a son and grandson, both Jewish.

Shortly before his death, he wrote, "Instead of having me baptized, the orphanage, even though it didn't know whether my mother was Jewish, might have had my body marked with the 'shallow slandered stream.' [...] My son would be a major spy in Mossad, working in the Israeli Embassy in Paris, and my grandson would be a Mirage pilot, smiling as he dropped his bombs on West Beirut." The line from Mallarmé taken from his poem "Le Tombeau de Verlaine"—"this shallow slandered stream that is death"—can be found in one of Genet's notebooks that dates back to the beginning of the 1970s. In a brief note on the white page he wrote, "circumcision: this shallow slandered stream." Birth has gone off with death. Genet's oldest questioning returns at the last: the end witnesses the beginning. Why write if not to speak of birth—to write one's own name cleanly?

Now the wind whips through the wheel of the war between the sons of darkness and the sons of light: they are the same. The goal is certainly to become a warrior who exists to kill and leave dead bodies. In the history of Murder—or Assassination—considered as one of the fine arts, the extermination of families is always part of the drama: the genealogical object of the last book. The order of free minds, Israelis or Palestinians, in both Genet's and De Quincey's eyes, is a unique case in the history of an army of murderers and assassins who have come together *a justus exercitus.*

What about justice?

Genet is now divided into three: the father, son, and grandson of himself. Let's just remember to name the three dead men, and capitalize their names.

ENDNOTES

1. Unpublished in the original French-language edition of this book, this chapter was my thesis director Jacques Derrida's favorite one.
2. *PL*, 183.
3. Thomas De Quincey, "On Murder Considered as One of the Fine Arts" (1827), 4.
4. Ibid., 29.
5. Ibid., 8.
6. *PL*, 181–182; all subsequent quotes are from this passage.
7. Edward Saïd, "Orientalism and After," *Radical Philosophy* 63 (spring 1993):22.
8. In *Tsahal*, directed by Claude Lanzman, 1994.
9. Mahmoud Issa (Selim), *Je suis un fedayin* (Paris, 1976), 218–220.
10. De Quincey, "On Murder," 17, 19.
11. Mickolus, *Transnational*, 37, 384–385.
12. *Libération*, November 23, 1993.
13. Elias Sanbar, *Les Palestiniens dans le siècle* (Paris, 1994), 90.
14. De Quincey, "On Murder," 15.
15. *PL*, 110.
16. *GC*, 147.
17. Ibid., 149.
18. Ibid., 152.
19. Mickolus, *Transnational*, 341.
20. De Quincey, "On Murder," 35.
21. *PL*, 183, 185.
22. Reported in *Le Monde*, October 10, 1970.
23. De Quincey, "On Murder," 27.

Part Three

The Man Who Gave Birth to Humanism

8 | The Dawn of Time

"The Jews have been living warmly wrapped in unreality for nearly 2,000 years, spinning around weightless in the sky as in a Chagall canvas,"[1] writes historian Alain Dieckhoff. He goes back to a time before the creation of the state when, "Having been wiped out politically, they had continued to subsist through the mind and had become true living dead, ghosts whose supernatural appearance frightened other peoples." He defines Israel "as a people by default," as "a defunct nation, or rather a ghostly nation."[2] For a long time, blacks in the United States were invisible too. In Genet's first text on the Palestinians in 1972, he noted that, "The helical or spiral movement by which the people of an Ottoman province became a true nation without a homeland mirrored the Jewish movement that led to Zionism. By mirrored, I mean an inverted image—the Palestinian population [...], a ghost."[3] In a 1983 interview in Vienna, he added that, "Each Palestinian is real. Like Cézanne's *Sainte-Victoire Mountain*."[4] Finally, in *Prisoner of Love*, Genet asserted, "And so the very real state of Israel finds itself shadowed by a ghostly survival."[5] He spoke of the Palestinian reality mirrored in Israeli eyes. Political Zionism could not free itself of metaphysical Judaism. Furthering the idea of the mirrored reality, Genet emphasized the fact that the Palestinians had to rid themselves of Arabness and dreams rather than faith. The movements' fables and Genet's fictions proliferated, eager to counter a falsified history.

At the same time, Genet evoked the weight of the Palestinians and the need to tell it "with words that are mine. But in order to speak of a reality that was not mine."[6] Being "more in reality"[7] is a single imperative, both poetic and political; it is one of the origins of this story. For greatest impact, Genet put all his weight into the juxtaposition, judiciously picking both the artist and the painting. No mere mountain, he chose Sainte-Victoire, or *Saint Victory*, a splendid sleight of hand meant to give voice to a new volume, despite the fear.

Chagall and Cézanne, the angels and the mountain; they were invisible men, ghosts and spirits chasing each other almost malevolently. From then on, the Palestinians' Sainte-Victoire was also Genet's mountain. In the end, this phantasmagoria invited fratricide.

FABLES

So Genet came to the US in 1970, seeking words stripped of "biblical rags," voices that were "starker, blacker, more accusing and implacable, tearing out every reference to the cynical conjuring of the religious enterprise and its efforts to take over."[8] These words pertained to the Black Panther movement. The voice's cruelty was proportional to its distance from religion. It was Genet's intention to keep the "myth-making function" away from perception, memory, and logical thought, wary of the fictions and fantastical depictions it fueled. This function was the source of novels, dramas, mythologies, and all that came before. While novelists have not always existed, humanity has always had religion—"very likely, therefore [...] religion is what accounts for the myth-making function."[9] The universe appears to be a god-making machine. Casting it aside is not easy. Though Genet heard and sought this voice, it's not clear if he spoke with it. The raw, black voice remained something like a promise.

Too much love

too much love

nothing kill a nigger like too much love.

Thus spoke Julius Lester. Malcolm X later declared, "The Christian world has failed to give the black man justice."[10] From 1961 to 1964, in the wake of this failure, the black population in America shifted from Christianity to Islam. This tide made it as far as Jacques Berque's book, stored in Genet's library in Larache.[11] In *L'Islam au défi*, the Islamic scholar wrote that for black Americans, "Converting to Islam showed a new form of combativeness." According to Berque, the well-tried combativeness "of Islam in the face of Western doctrines tipped the scales in its favor as an ideology for change."[12] Genet chose to commit both this statement and its consequences to memory. Christianity's failure cropped up constantly in Malcolm X's discourse. As mentioned in his *Autobiography*, the black leader's father was a pastor. The publication of *The Negro Protest* in 1963 allowed Genet to read these words from the pastor's son: "I firmly believe that it was the Christian society, as you call it, the Judaic-Christian society, that created all the factors that send so many so-called Negroes to prison."[13] In 1964, Malcolm X joined the Black Muslims, a political and religious group founded by the "Honorable Elijah Muhammad." Referring to Muhammad's teachings, he said, "Well, number one, the Honorable Elijah Muhammad teaches us that the solution will never be brought about by politicians, it will be brought about by God, and that the only way the black man in this country today can receive respect and recognition of other people is to stand on his own feet; get something for himself and do something for himself." Identity wavered between God and nothingness; only solitude could provide a solution. Along the way, politics were thrown out. Once Christianity was condemned and politics were abandoned, an even more interesting knot formed: "The solution that God has given the Honorable Elijah Muhammad is the same as the solution that God gave to Moses when the Hebrews in the Bible were in a predicament similar to the predicament of the so-called Negroes here in America today, which is nothing other than a modern house of bondage, or a modern Egypt, or a modern Babylon."[14] The goal of this sweeping oratorical motion is to seek "[c]omplete separation; not only physical separation but moral."[15] The looming entanglement calls for definite separation and manifests itself as *typical of Judaism, made in the same motion that distanced Christianity for the sake of Islam.* The war between myths has always existed. In the United States, where Genet witnessed the black movement, it was a *three-way war.*

A first fable illustrates the relationships with religions maintained by Genet and the movements he met. In *The Autobiography of Malcolm X*, the son of a Protestant devoted all of Chapter 17, titled "Mecca," to his conversion to Islam. In April 1964, he flew to Cairo on the German airline Lufthansa. Typically, this involved a stopover in Frankfurt. During the flight, the future *haji* was so overwhelmed by a feeling of welcome that he would later comment, "The effect was as though I had just stepped out of a prison."[16] After Frankfurt, the plane resumed its course. The black leader went on to become Hajj Malik El-Shabazz and had his turn at the Black Stone.

In *Prisoner of Love*, Genet set off for Japan on the same German airline on December 22, 1967. The plane was forced to "go back to Hamburg."[17] It then resumed its course. During the night, he went to the toilet at the back of the plane: "I got up to go and have a crap in the rear of the plane, hoping to get rid of a tapeworm three thousand years long."[18] What was he trying to get rid of? "A thick black layer of Judeo-Christian morality."[19] Malcolm X's journey through the skies was mirrored by Genet's; hope extended the struggle. The quasi-Christmas fable was at the fore because it came early in the last book and proved pivotal. Everything happened against the backdrop of that night, which may have been in the dawn of time: its recollection, its fading entirely, and the story that vanished with it.

For the writer, the war was primarily fought between different narrative forms. The plane, the story of the "pure head"[20] and Genet's other inventions were fables, which together told a different version of the story. Through them, the concern of the disinherited for creating a legacy was extended. In a mythological sense, their purpose was to provide liberation or escape. But in the case of Malcolm X, the experience led to the harsh return of the myth-making function. The conclusion, then, was clear: "The first humans, Original Man, were a black people."[21] The end of the fable returns, ever the same.

In 1970, Genet was in the United States when a member of the Black Panthers heckled an old black minister in the streets of New York, shouting, "Bullshit! What has the Bible ever done for me?"[22] Bobby Seale, the founder of the Black Panthers, best expressed how the Panthers distanced themselves from religion. What follows is psychedelic prose from a chapter titled "Free Huey!" in Seale's history of the Black Panthers, *Seize the Time: The Story of the Black Panther Party and Huey P. Newton*. Genet told the tale of Huey Newton, imprisoned and on trial for being a member of the Panthers.[23] Here is Bobby Seale's fable:

> So, as Huey said, let's go back, back, back. Let's go to Europe. Let's take Europe and let's take Africa. Let's take two different peoples, even before they met each other. Let's take Europe. Europe had the one-headed god concept, the all-pure god, right? The pure blood, and my son of pure blood will become king, and my daughter of pure blood will become queen. This is the thing that went down through history. This is directly related to this purity of god bullshit, the single-headed god, the one-headed god. It's not just the idea of the one-headed god, but what people projected and put into it. People said, "I'm made in the image of god." Boom. They're made in the image of this pure head who's absolute, who's all superior, who's all pure, so goddamn pure that people began to read things into the bullshit, and they began to reject their basic animal drives. But even the masses of people in Europe screwed. They had a tendency to accept the so-called bad things about themselves. It was that

monarchy, that government, that king, queen, and hierarchy that laid the rules out, and they themselves projected themselves in this puritanical image of god. They were created in the image of god and they had the power and the guns and force to see that everybody stayed pure. And if you didn't stay pure, then you were a witch, and you were burned at the stake. This happened even before they met black Africans. Europeans were lynching people then.

I'm not saying all societies in Africa didn't have this puritanical concept, but many societies they call primitive, even some outside of Africa, had what many people define as pagan gods; a two-headed god system or a three-headed god system, but they also said they were made in the image of god. You look at the society, and the way people develop, and you look back in history, and you can find these things out. This head was a three-headed god, with a neutral head, a bad head, and a good head. They said they were made in the image of god, so they were able to accept the bad things and the good things about themselves; but the European monarchies perpetuated this purity bullshit, tabooing things, like sluts or those who were downgraded and under their feet. "You're a vassal!" This projection by the monarchy of "I am the greatest" and all that shit was very bad for human society, because it was a process [of] chopping the head from the body, and the government heads being cut away from the masses of the people.

The Africans mostly had the two-headed god system, bad and good, and said they were made in the image of god. Maybe it developed out of the fact that they had so much fucking food and fucking land down there, they didn't have to worry about a bunch of bullshit. It may be related to industrial development and poor peoples, I don't know. So when the European met the African, when the whole economic development of using slaves came about, these taboos were ingrained in the minds of the people in European society, especially with the monarchy projecting that purity for the people.

"Ah, he's different than I am. He's *black*." In the kind of
system that has a two-headed god, that's impossible. But if
the god is one-headed, pure-headed, he's absolute. They put
taboos on the Africans the same way they put them on their
own people, in their own society, with the witch concept.
They were burning white people at the stake in their own
society even before they met Africans. That even got
transported over to America, this thing about witches. They
even have a tendency to carry it on now. They superficialize
the witch, like the one on TV. Samantha. A good little
puritanical witch. It's a thing with them. You have to
understand society and have a concept of how human beings
function, to be able to see them, and to be able to define
how things will go, especially if you try to relate directly to
it.

When the Panther Party first came on the scene, the man
said, "They're all anti-white. They're a bunch of black
racists!" We *never* considered ourselves a bunch of black
racists.[24]

Ghosts, if not witches, constantly return. The "purity of god
bullshit," European history entwined with the monarchy's historical
dominance, its conquests and the deadly exporting of its purity, in
addition to the three-headed gods and, of course, fear itself, make up
this history lesson. Huey spoke, Bobby wrote; the fable, part oral, part
written, was already under the authority of a two- or three-headed
god. Friendship was speaking. The thrust of the story was a leap out
of monotheism, a place where Genet's thoughts could land. The attack
on monotheism was woven from all fabrics. Although it touched on
racism, it was also an attack on Judaism, even if the fable doesn't name
it. In it, every dance was called for, revelry on the Sabbath, all religions
overturned. A chaste prayer, it said this: there were lynchings and
burnings before whites and blacks ever met, and there was destruction
before and after the contamination from without. The critique of the
myth-making function stated that purity never existed.

Now let's listen to another dialogue, a much older one, between Ezra Pound, a poet imprisoned north of Pisa, and another prisoner, a black one. In 1945, the American writer offered to help the inmates with their correspondence and also with their *ABC of Reading* (1934). The following exchange from Canto LXXIV was originally jotted down on toilet paper: "Hey Snag wots in the bibl'? / wot are the books ov the bible? / Name 'em, don't bullshit ME."[25] Genet and the black movements retained the memory of the fight for civil rights, from Malcolm X's debate all the way to the Panthers' three-headed god, through the interrogation of a black prisoner and the heckling of a black minister. The fedayeen version, repeated by Genet, was, "Why Muhammad and not me?"[26]

Arab is not synonymous with Islam and vice versa. The Palestinians, who aren't entirely in either category, have a more complex relationship with the myth-making function. The political use of religion by African-Americans was relatively simple—their people's resurrection according to Christian, Muslim, and atheist dogma, perceived by Genet upon his arrival—whereas the Palestinian movements had a more delicate relationship with religion. It might seem that, when he was with the blacks, Genet attacked the church in an almost Voltaire-like manner, while with the Palestinians, he found himself entrenched in a truly metaphysical battle. The question was his to confront. From the onset, the issue was less about describing the relationship with the sacred than it was about seizing, at the moment Genet first encountered the movements, the will to trial and the creation of legacy, both concerns of the disinherited in regards to the myth-making function. The outcome was of great importance, with escape on the line.

In terms of religion, the PLO and Fatah were to the Middle East what the Black Panthers were to the United States: the last to arrive, they rejected the myth-making function, perhaps in a bid to find the fable more easily. Genet's last book is often cited outside the context of this struggle: "The Palestinians still haven't woken up yet. They're still completely drunk. Still poets."[27] How to escape the fable if the goal is a return to Palestine? It had to be possible, now that the real question was autonomy. Historian Maxime Rodinson argues that religion has remained a major issue in the Middle East for so long because "[h]istory has so arranged matters that the onset of new crises [Algeria, Egypt] has not allowed a sufficient time for the secularization process to be completed or for the various confessions to be closely integrated."[28] Rodinson also underlines the time it took Europe to achieve this. He writes, "The political and juridical influence of confessional structures has been particularly strong in Lebanon and [even more so] Palestine."[29] Rodinson seems to suggest that if this reality was imposed by colonization, it's because powerful groups of clerics pressured their respective states to recognize, through clauses in their constitutions, Judaism and Islam as official religions. Although the political and religious maps did not mirror each other, geography remained sacred everywhere.

In 1970 especially, Palestinians fought as much with Arab states (Lebanon, Syria, and Jordan) as with Israel. In the wake of the 1979 Iranian revolution, thousands in Iran volunteered to go to the camps and help the Palestinians. Their Islamic credo was a source of tension with other fedayeen. Khomeinists wanted to turn the PLO into an "Islamic Liberation Movement," stop speaking of an Arab nation (*al-oumna al-arabiya*) and a Palestinian homeland (*al-watan*), and instead demand an Islamic nation (*al-oumna al-islamiya*).[30] Arafat refused on diplomatic, political, and, most likely, religious grounds. In Lebanon, the Iranian group known as the *Hezbollah* set itself apart from the Palestinian organizations in Beirut. The Palestinian movements Genet encountered in Jordan and Lebanon, and particularly in Morocco and Tunisia, over the course of fifteen years must not be mistaken for religious organizations. But in this region, the war against Arab states in the name of Palestine's unique character has been defined as a war against *Arabness*, and above all against Islam, deemed to be its basis. Similarly, the war against Israel can be viewed as a war against a fable that has its religious purpose, but whose political use excludes the Palestinians. Tactics have shifted in such a way that the argument used against the latter (the Palestinians) was first rejected by the former (the Israelis); Islam against Judaism. Hence, the war cannot be won.

However, the strong ties of certain Palestinians with Islam escape me. In the Koran, we read, "We know the promptings of his soul and are closer to him than his jugular vein" (50:16). During a 1972 conversation that Genet later transcribed, an Algerian officer told him, "The Palestinians frighten them all, great and small monarchs alike. So they tell people like you. They tell the Muslims something different."[31] Yasser Arafat wanted to change his name to Abu Ammar, to reaffirm his identity by going back to traditional Arab ways. The name of his organization, *Fatah*, was an inversion of the Arabic acronym *Harakat al-Tahrir al-Watani al-Filastini* (meaning the "Palestinian National Liberation Movement"), by the same token referring to a line in the Koran which reads, "When God's help and victory come" (110:1). The movement was born in the Nile Valley;[32] the political palindrome doubled as a religious palimpsest. To present Yasser Arafat's movement, which Genet was close to, as more political than religious and to try and separate—particularly for the Palestinian political effort— religious from secular history, as I believe we should, is an immediate attack. In a way, the religious war between Israel and Genet was entirely Genet's doing. He was associated with a realistic and relatively moderate movement. If there was a radicalization, particularly on the Israeli question, it was his creation, and not the movement's. The consequences of this are not just political, but religious.

The question of what the Palestinians and Genet collided against when they attacked religion and Israel bears scrutiny; the state has rather singular ties with the myth-making function. After much debate on the wording of the Declaration of Independence of the State of Israel, it was decided that God would be called the "Rock of Israel." For the religious, the consecrated term evoked *Achem*, or God; for others, the spirit of the land. The Declaration states, "'The State of Israel will be founded on the principles of freedom, justice and peace envisaged by the prophets of Israel." The Law of Return (1950) grants all Jews the right to immigrate to Israel. The nationality law (1952) guarantees citizenship to all who invoke the Law of Return to immigrate to Israel. The only criterion that the founders of the state used to count the Jewish people was religion. A 1970 law states, "A person is considered to be a Jew who is born to a Jewish mother or who has converted to Judaism, and who does not belong to another religion."[33] Consequently, conversion is the only means to rejoin the Jewish people in Israel. This law, then, has major implications for Palestinians in Israel. Identification cards all reflect the double status of citizen and *le'om*, a personal status that ascribes nationality in an ethnic sense. The typical Israeli is therefore someone with Israeli citizenship and Jewish nationality, the latter acquired through Judaism. What about Palestinians? "To be described in any other way [than this type] is to be significantly different and, it must be admitted, to a disadvantage."[34] Rather than clamor for equal status within Israel, which was never Genet's goal, Palestinians fought to form their own state. Against this Rock, this impossibly entangled nature of Israel's religious (prophets, rabbis) and political (kings, judges) orders, Genet collided.

Another fable was used to recount a moment in this struggle. Two versions of the amphora fable exist: the Jacques Givet version, about Arad, and the Genet version, about the Tunisian potters. Givet was the staunchest of the small number who supported Israel against the anti-Zionist left in the 1970s. The year 1968 saw the release of his book, *La Gauche contre Israël*. The author attacked the leftist ideas of the time, perhaps targeting Genet himself; the latter was named in this piece, and he may well have read it. Givet's parents died in the concentration camps and his son moved to Israel. He wrote, "Ours was a miracle generation: we returned to Zion after 2,000 years." The statement weighed heavy with meaning, and it was one that many Israeli citizens might have expressed. The source of confusion (or the long hesitation) revolved around carrying on as the last Hebrews or starting anew as the first Israelis:

> I witnessed the birth of a city named Arad, in Israel. We were surrounded by desert, as far as the eye could see. The Israelis chose this spot in the sand because according to the Bible, there had been water here. We dug until we found it. Close to the source, we discovered pottery dating back 3,000 years, bearing the name Arad in ancient Hebrew. Hebrew was the language of the builders of the new Arad, the Bible was their book, the potters who had inscribed the name of the city were their ancestors, as much as Charlemagne and Vercingétorix were the ancestors of the French. From then on, the new inhabitants of Arad would drink from the same source as the former inhabitants. I ask all who have a country (and who sometimes feel they could do without because no one contests it), what is a country if not this?[35]

This tale is possible because in Israeli geopolitics, current geographical spaces are perfectly mirrored by those in the Bible. As a result, since 1967, the districts in the West Bank have also had new administrative divisions whose names and territories are usually those of ancient Israeli tribes. For instance, the Arab town of Ramallah is also the district of Benyamin. One historian refers to this toponymic practice as *political archaeology*.[36] The counterpart of the fable of pottery or amphorae appeared in Genet's last book. In Tunisia, 1968: "In every village along the coast and from north to south, potters indefatigably turned out millions of jars—replicas of the age-old amphorae that sponge fishers are always finding at the bottom of the sea, full of oil preserved by the mud since the days of ancient Carthage. Every morning there were more jars, still warm from the just-quenched oven. I could see Tunisia dwindling away: all its clay being sold to girls from

Norway in the form of terracotta amphorae. In the end, I thought, it'll disappear altogether."[37]

He felt the need to give the fable a further twist. "I'm still itching to say a few more words about amphorae," he wrote. "I saw them being made. [...] [H]e had to start all over again, or the amphora wouldn't live up to its supposed three thousand years." He concluded with this attack: "To the other reasons I've given for the more lively part of Tunisian youth going to fight with the Palestinians, we might add that it was fed up with age-old amphorae."[38] A new and ever-fleeting political constellation was shaping up: *J.G.*, Givet and Genet, or the struggle between two perceptions of history, or rather, legacy. Every nation is founded on similar myths, on this kind of political archaeology. Together, these fables cast light on the Palestinians' relationship with the myth-making function; they could only oppose it with political creation of a different nature. Genet's twist saw him turn away from a religious and nationalistic view of history, and beneath his feet was water, not earth. Givet chose to draw attention to the fact that Hebrews and Israelis drank from the same source, if not the very same water. In modern times, oil was found in Arad. According to Givet, land is the basis for country. Like a drowned man, Genet cherished the sea, where all countries would disappear.

Apocryphal? An interpretation of a passage in his last book? Genet warned, "If Palestinians act like moles, they will turn into Zionists."[39] The scriptural writings—Jews from Medina, Christians from Byzantium, Muslims from Mecca—are opposed by all those excluded by the promise: what has the Bible (Koran) ever done for me?

THE RAMADAN WAR

"One question I will not avoid is that of religion,"[40] Genet declared in 1973 when he met the Palestinians in Paris. His presence with the Black Panthers on one hand and the Palestinians, facing Israel, on the other, linked the three monotheisms: Christian, Islamic, and Judaic. It sparked Genet's war on Ramadan.

In a letter about Paul Claudel sent in the 1970s, he wrote what already sounded like a refrain. "Claudel as a poet betrays his religion. He makes it go sour. Religion can't accommodate poets. Poetry cannot serve any ideology. It sticks in the gullet of all [...]. The poetic passages in Claudel are irrelevant to religion."[41] If nothing else, writing that Claudel betrayed his religion was stating that he had one. The sacred doesn't end where literature begins, evidenced by the conflicting religions in Genet's heart. Better than a historical analysis on the question, his investigation was expressed as exchanges and dialogues. Religions loathed each other: "Men have divided themselves into factions, each rejoicing in its own doctrines" (Koran, 23:49). Solitude in the face of religion was the writer's last word. Genet dealt with the topic in an uncharacteristic manner, almost unrecognizable, when he spoke to the Palestinians in 1973:

> Were we to try and downplay the question of faith, we'd
> see that it's actually a simple matter that could almost be
> reduced to the precepts we learned as children. Children
> inherit their father's faith, in the same way they inherit
> his morality and behavior. Where does that leave my own
> experiences in matters of faith? Though I was raised in the
> Catholic religion, I had exactly as much—or as little—faith
> as any young peasant my age. Around fifteen or sixteen,
> however, I understood that faith had disappeared, and that
> this disappearance coincided with my newfound ability to
> laugh at myself and make light of sacred topics. My waning
> faith caused no tragedy, either within me or around me. So
> what really happened?[42]

Faith is a matter of legacy. But why did the young Genet inherit his father's beliefs and not his mother's? He was not Jewish. He was not raised in faith, but rather thrown into the Catholic religion. Having spent time in the Mettray Penal Colony from 1927 to 1929, Genet wrote *Le Langage de la muraille* (1981), in which he cited the precept of the colony: "Isolation is the best way to undermine the spirits of children; this is where the voice of religion, having never spoken to their hearts, finds all its emotional resonance."[43] The dogma instilled in Genet by the establishment served the Catholic church, the dominant one in France at the time, the church of the State: "Having once been subjects of the throne and the altar, the former Mettray boys are now subjects of the colonial army."[44] Genet needed to rid himself of it.

On October 14, 1969, Genet gave his friend Mohammed Choukri a French translation of the Koran, saying, "You've read the book in Arabic, of course? It must be marvelous."[45] He read it, along with notes and commentary. Later, in August 1974 in Morocco, Choukri related this conversation between Genet and a mutual friend, El Katrani:

> Genet drew the map of the Kaaba on a piece of paper. Then he sketched out the four points of the compass and looked at El Katrani.
>
> "Where is the Black Stone?"
>
> "I don't know."
>
> Genet pointed the pen to the east.
>
> "It's there."
>
> Then he drew two arrows, one toward the south and the others toward Syria, the north.
>
> The name Yemen comes from yamine, the right, because the country was situated to the right of the Kaaba. Before Islam, the Kaaba was used to help find the four points of the compass. And how did the Arabs turn around the Kaaba?
>
> "From right to left," El Katrani answered.
>
> "Not at all. They turned from left to right until Mohamed changed the direction."
>
> "Why did he do that?"
>
> "He wanted to change their cultural habits."

"You know all that about Islam and you don't convert?" El Katrani asked him.

"Put God in your heart."

"I put myself in God's heart." [...]

[The conversation continues the same evening.]

"Do you know Jesus?" El Katrani asked.

"No, I don't know him," Genet said.

"How can that be?"

"Not personally. I've only heard about him."

"And Moses?"

"The same thing."

"Which one do you prefer?"

"Neither. I told you I'm an atheist. You make your Islamic religion sacred, and I make my atheism sacred. That doesn't mean believers and atheists can't live together."[46]

At the time, Choukri detected a "slight animosity" toward the Jews, but not toward Arabs. Yet the duo of Jesus and Moses was cast out from the moment Genet declared himself an atheist.

In *Prisoner of Love*, the exchange continued under the guise of meetings with different men. Abu Omar was Arab, but a "Palestinian Christian" as well. Mubarak was Sudanese, Palestinian, and Muslim. Genet, uncircumcised, was Christian, but did not believe in God. He remembered his "conversations with Omar and Mubarak."[47] The latter was black and feared racism. During one conversation, Genet recalled a definition for the term that had appeared fifteen years prior in the US: "racism means the contempt one bears one's fellow men the better to exploit them."[48] Attached to the issue of religion, involved with the Panthers and the Palestinians, the question of racism haunted Genet.

Abu Omar, Genet's friend, was also a friend of Edward Saïd.[49] In Genet's testament, which he claimed no Arab would read, or anyone else for that matter, Abu Omar said on one occasion, "Quick, come and look—the lights of Jericho!" He saw "across the gorge through which the Jordan flowed. Some of the lights were moving. 'That's where I was born.' He was so moved I owed it to him to be silent. I found out later that the only lights you could see at night from Ajloun were those of Nablus."[50] Now Genet felt the impossibility, both geographical and political, of looking at Judaism in the same way as the other two monotheistic religions, the impossibility as well of throwing down the walls of the sacred and, finally, of seeing the place of one's birth again. Religion has disappeared, the sacred and atheism gone; all that's left is doubt. He touches religious devotion thanks only to the issue of origins that lives on in him. Dispassionate but poignant, simple though desolate, Genet's faith does not flow down from above; it is not eternal, it evolves from meetings and exchanges with men from many places, and alone as well. The quarrel over religion is spontaneous. Origin, legacy, the promise—nothing more than a questioning of and from childhood.

A predisposition for making ironic, economic, and political critiques of the church, an attachment both to a certain idea of faith and the need to name God, a nascent inquiry into the Beginning: all coexisted within Genet, despite earlier signs of rejecting all churches, whose shadow is the unavoidable rejection of all faiths. The 1970s saw the Church, the religious institution, become as intolerable as the police and the university. That same year, Genet declared to Americans, "The Church, born from an Eastern fable perverted from its original meaning by Westerners, has become a tool of repression, especially here against blacks, to whom it preaches evangelical gentleness out of respect for the master—the white man—and to whom, with the Old Testament, it promises the fires of hell to those who revolt."[51] His critique of what he called "evangelical blackmail"[52] was akin to Voltaire's attack on sectarianism. He sounded like the author of *Micromégas* (1752) when he evoked, through the ironic circumlocution, "that ungraspable being who, in the Arab world, is recalled several times a day by means of loudspeakers attached to the tops of minarets."[53] He was no longer Voltaire-like when he recalled that some "very poor people may need to indulge in the luxury of having fat princes above them, waddling through their cool invisible gardens, just as other poor folk save up and ruin themselves for Christmas."[54] The disdain of the disinherited is the ideal manure for making light of matters like Christmas and the manger in Bethlehem.

In the US, Genet condemned the Church for meddling in politics in the name of "repression." His goal was the separation of two orders: revolt and religion.

This allowed him to condemn the Old Testament. The book preached morality to slaves while promising fire to those who revolted. Genet later renewed his attack and narrowed its focus: "The Catholic Church is the incarnation of authority and Biblical morality, and any representative of those superpowers [is] my enemy."[55] Herein, the clash with biblical morality, and with those who represented the Torah, is clear; surely the enemy lived across the Jordan River. The struggle against fables wore on, and Genet seemed to discard them all. The innovation in his discourse came from having read those who'd spoken before him, most notably Malcolm X. In the same critical vein as the black movements, Genet's raw discourse said something else in the end: the ideal solution is complete separation from any religion. But he didn't maintain this separation when he was with the Palestinians. He had to find the fable at worst dull, at best explosive.

Genet related in his last book an event that happened during his first trip to Jordan, in 1970. It was at the evening meal, the breaking of the Ramadan fast, "not far away from the place between the Damia and Allenby bridges where John had once baptized Jesus, that the fedayeen decided to change my first name to Ali."[56] The significance of his religious questioning is as clear as day. The scene was sacred: the location (between Jordan and Israel, on Palestinian soil), the comparison (Jesus and John), and the verb (to baptize). But the moment was not: it was the breaking of the Ramadan fast (*Eid ul-Fitr*). Whether fable or myth-making function, is the end of Ramadan still within the realm of religion or at the threshold of the secular? *Between Ramadan and the end of Ramadan, Genet most often stood at the unhealed scar that divided two eras.* As Ramadan ended, he changed, becoming Ali. In the Middle East, no doubt all boys are called Ali. That was decided by the fedayeen. Really, all they did was give him a name, out of friendship. The verb "to baptize" was foreign to their vocabulary, which is why the writer did not attribute it to them. He wrote it instead. The issue of origins forced a word on him and the event applied it to the fedayeen as well: baptism. A moment of rupture, a hesitation between giving a name and being baptized, uncertainty over choosing the name of *the* son, Jesus, or the name of *a* son, Ali. Islam and Christianity; the scene played out on Israel's doorstep.

Students in Ibadan, Nigeria welcomed Malcolm X in 1964. They nicknamed, if not rechristened him, Omowale, meaning "the son who has returned." The black leader apologized for mispronouncing the name, stating, "I haven't had a chance to pronounce it for four hundred years."[57] He added that it was an honor to be hailed as a son who'd been smart enough to return to the land of his ancestors. Like Genet, Malcolm X could not lay claim to any ancestry; the African legacy of an African-American needed reinventing. Genet was compelled by the need of the disinherited to create a legacy. He was denied the possibility of returning as a son.

In the last book, and for fifteen years, every instant for Genet was the beginning and end of Ramadan, the *Eid ul-Fitr.* He wrote, "I'd forgotten—this morning is the beginning of Ramadan."[58] Genet's passing attachment to Islam was simple; he was in Jordan among the fedayeen during the month of prayer. According to the lunar calendar, Ramadan in 1970 lasted from October 31 to November 29.[59] Genet arrived on October 20 of that year. He witnessed Islamic practices. Day after day, phrase after phrase, the writer's precious moments were held by this strange temporality. Of the opening and closing of Ramadan, to-gether, the author spoke of "the strangeness of the Muslim world, [...] when I was in the midst of it during the desert of Ramadan."[60] He stood in the eye of sacred time, a time of fasting and prayer. This coincided perfectly with the discovery that those representing biblical morality were the "enemy." Simple, but as he also pointed out, strange. Perilous too. Outside, the battle between Jordanians and Palestinians raged on. Across stood Israel. Inside, the inquiry of an unreconciled man.

As the legacy of the religious question asked by the black move-ments on one hand and the Fatah on the other, the author's Ramadan war could only lead to *the twofold inquiry into the fiction of race and the myth of origins.* The latter would soon be linked to Judaism. For Genet, the fiction of race and the myth of Judaism no doubt merged into a *question of origins.*

PIETÀ

A man with a black beard tells Genet, "When you came [...] you told us that you didn't believe in God. But if you ask me, if you didn't be-lieve in Him you wouldn't have come."[61] The setting: Ajloun, Jordan, 1970. In a way, the passage we are about to read responds to this al-legation in the last book. But if the answer took some time coming, the interval was justified by the journey, a descent into the self, toward nothingness, which is the rhythm of *Prisoner of Love*: "The last few lines were an attempt to put off asking the following question: would the Palestinian revolution have exercised such a strong fascination on me if it hadn't been fought against what seemed to me the darkest of peoples?—a people whose beginning claimed to be *the* Beginning, who claimed that they were, and meant to be, the Beginning, who said they belonged to the Dawn of Time? To ask the question is, I think, to answer it."[62]

The tremor that shook Genet reverberated throughout the book. First, Part One evoked the time before God, "back amid the so-called 'dawn of time,' when God didn't yet exist."[63] On the other side, Part

Two described a battle: "the metaphysical struggle goes on, impossible to ignore it, between Jewish moralities and the values [...] of Judaism and those of living revolutions."[64] Faced with these two notions, panic won out. The Palestinian revolution became a metaphysical struggle when it ceased to be a fight for stolen land; hence, the critique of religion also served to create the foray of a fable. I believe this fable addressed Genet's most remote questions. His brief move into metaphysical comedy was born from a tale of coming out.

Genet's *pietà* pertained to the hijacking of the myth-making function in favor of the fable; the embodiment—during the course of a long inner quarrel—of the mythological notion of the dawn of time and the appearance of a figure, not new but created by a son and pronounced a new man, and a mother become sorrowful, the couple joined on wood. It called for a new archaeology and sought to fix a flawed origin.

A long, long time ago, in 1970 and in America, Genet drew attention to something "new," identified as a new form of discourse, raw and religion-free. A political promise was announced at the beginning of these pages. In August 1971, he wrote about George Jackson and his book *Soledad Brother* in which he lauded "the 'new man' [Jackson] was able to become,"[65] putting the term in quotation marks. Perhaps Nietzsche had created this new man. (Leila Shahid got Genet the German philosopher's works from the French publisher Gallimard in the last months of his life.[66]) But African-American history, like others, is full of messiahs come to announce deliverance. For instance, in 1925 Marcus Garvey announced from his cell in the Atlanta Federal Penitentiary, "If I die in Atlanta my work shall then only begin [...]. For in the new life I shall rise with God's grace and blessing to lead the millions up the heights of triumph with the colors that you well know."[67] Whatever the case may be, the myth-making function was launched, the pale outline of a giant.

In May 1971, with George Jackson still on his mind, Genet wrote about the Palestinians and the fedayeen in particular: "In the Middle

East a new man will perhaps emerge, and the fedayee, in certain of his aspects, would be for me the prefiguration and outline of this new man."[68] The second step of the metamorphosis was violent, the good news muffled by all the temporal and lexical indicators. This was a possible world, not a truth. However, the new had emerged from its quotation marks. The transformation was underway and could not be stopped; the figure was becoming clearer.

Genet returned to this birth and gave it a name. In 1977, still speaking of the Palestinians, he expanded on notes dating back to April 1971: "This new beauty comes from revolt. [...] Feraj and Hamza are very beautiful, lively, precise, and their beauty is one that no longer owes anything to the dawn of time. They do not come to the surface to be enveloped by this darkness, they have already escaped from it."[69] The new man was made flesh, and a new expression came to be, not in capital letters: the dawn of time. The future giant had explicitly encountered Genet's remote question for the first time. For now, the dawn of time had to dissipate for the new man to be born. During these years, the words followed from text to text. The struggle of the myth-making functions was still present, in small letters within the vocabulary, between a term (new man) now free from quotation marks and another (dawn of time) awaiting its capitals. *A giant had arrived, a new man who emerged from the dawn of time. His name: Hamza.*

As a result, Hamza could return transformed. In "Four Hours in Shatila," Genet took what he believed to be one of his white hairs and put it on Hamza's knee: "'A hair from the beard of the Prophet is worth less than this.' He takes a slightly deeper breath and starts again. 'A hair from the beard of the Prophet is not worth more than this.' Although he was only twenty-two years old, his thoughts leapt with ease far above the forty-year-old Palestinians, but there were already visible signs—visible on himself, on his body, in his gestures—that linked him to his elders."[70] Was he a messiah announcing the new man? In that instant—with a transformation that hung by a hair—Genet momentarily took the prophet's place. The only characteristic linking the poet and prophet is that of being equally slow to reflect their times. Expressing the political demands of their times meant asking themselves the same question: am I late?

Although Genet wanted the dawn of time to dissipate, he was drawn to the conflict with the Dawn of Time (i.e., Israel and the Jewish people). A god was born from this combat. In Hamza's actions, Genet saw signs of the elder. Soon, Genet would come to see him as a son and stigmata would appear on his hands.

Missing here, with Hamza and the writer—if not the prophet—was a woman. But not for long. The figure had a new ramification; the event concealed in a 1974 text would never leave him: "H., twenty-two years old, had introduced me to his mother in Irbid. It was during Ramadan, one day around noon. 'He's French. Not simply French, and not a Christian either; he doesn't believe in God.' She looked at me with a smile. Her eyes grew more and more mischievous. 'Well, since he doesn't believe in God, we'd better give him something to eat.' For her son and for myself she prepared a lunch. She didn't eat until evening."[71] Around this couple of Hamza and his mother—for this was now a two-part figure—the mystery was deepening. The scene replayed itself at various times in *Prisoner of Love*.[72] In one version of the Ramadan story, he changed the introduction: "A friend. A Christian. But he doesn't believe in God."[73]

The year 1974: "not a Christian either." And 1986: "A Christian." Somewhere between the two versions of the fable, *the author became a Christian again; this was a problem.*

The war in Irbid continued. Part One of *The Prisoner of Love* tells of the mother's return. Genet was lying in the absent Hamza's bed when, over the sounds of battle, he heard a knock at the door: "Then in the midst of this aural chaos two little reports from nearby seemed to hurl the din of destruction back. [...] The mother had just come in. Had she come out of the now ear-splitting darkness, or out of the icy night I carry about with me everywhere? She was carrying a tray, which she put down on the little blue table with yellow and black flowers, already mentioned." He drank and closed his eyes. Then: "Another two little taps at the door, just like the first two. In the light of the stars and the waning moon the same long shadow appeared, as familiar now as if it had come into my room at the same time every night of my life before I went to sleep. Or rather so familiar that it was inside rather than out-side me, coming into me with a cup of Turkish coffee every night since I was born." And finally: "Because he was fighting that night, I'd taken the son's place and perhaps played his part in his room and his bed."[74] Maybe all of history had scripted and announced this presence, like a shadow heralding the body that casts it. The shadow was giant, with enough might to drive the war back, to thrust Genet all the way back to his birth, back to that frozen night, to the very dawn of his time. The character of the fable slowly settled into the writer's temporary room. Genet played the role of the son. The room with the shadow, the little blue table with yellow and black flowers he mentioned and the cup of Turkish coffee: the goal of sixty years' worth of confused anxiety had been to compose this *tableau*. The arrival of the mother who had stepped out of the fable sparked a camaraderie between the war—without, within—and Genet that had everyone happy to play their parts. He could lay down his arms and die. It was the fable's func-tion: the colossal retreat of destructive chaos.

Genet's final return to Irbid and to this room in 1984 is told in Part Two of *Prisoner of Love*. No exact date was given; the fable had to be timeless. If, as he indicated, he returned the day after the anniversary of King Hussein of Jordan's grandfather's death—killed coming out of a mosque in Jerusalem on July 20, 1951—then the later meeting with the mother took place on July 21, 1984. He had to identify himself. His interpreter and guide during his last journey told the woman, "'Your son introduced you to the Frenchman, and told you he was a Christian but didn't believe in God.' [...] 'Hamza didn't believe in Him much either.'" And, once recognized, Genet recalled: "The fact that she'd said I must be given something to eat showed she knew that unbeliev-ers were in the habit of carrying on as usual during Ramadan. That answer of hers had seemed extremely broadminded on the face of it, whereas in fact it was the logical consequence of her twenty-year-old son's independent ways. He'd discovered atheism at the same time as revolution, and Islamic customs had gone by the board."[75] The son's "discovery" was itself a memory of the experience mentioned in the earlier discussion with seven Palestinians in 1973: "Around fifteen or sixteen, however, I understood that faith had disappeared, and that this disappearance coincided with my newfound ability to laugh at myself."[76] Genet concluded the scene of his return to the house with a logical interpretation of the mother's reply: "Her first words to me long ago turned out to be less striking than I'd thought at the time, when I put it down to typical Palestinian sensitivity and tolerance, a quality always discovered sooner or later in the struggle that leads to practical wisdom. But I didn't think any less of her now I knew what had really led to her brilliantly simple answer. She was still Palestinian, but *she might have been a loving Christian mother whose adolescent son had lost his faith, and perhaps his reason,* [italics are mine] and insisted upon eating meat on Good Friday."[77] Through Genet briefly likening himself to the son of a Muslim Palestinian mother turned Christian, we see the return of the heavy-handed Judeo-Christian morality. The symbol of tolerance, momentarily transformed with dazzling simplicity, morphed just as quickly into a Christian icon. Pure gold. Love, Christian love: the two terms are easily associated when written. For Genet as well. *The Hamza-and-his-mother couple filled the void in the dawn of Genet's time.*

The penultimate ramification of this unusual icon was the son's torture, wounds, and suffering. Genet curbed all invention when it came to torture. Yet a letter is mentioned in the last book that might have depicted the abuses, without the reader knowing it: "Who were Hamza's jailers? What suffering was being inflicted on him?" Torture was a recurring theme and integral to the picture: "Hamza-and-his-mother. As I read Daoud's letter, each of the elements of the couple was being tortured separately and in different ways."[78] He revisited the subject, evoking only a blackened body, wondering "what kind of torture had left his legs black?"[79] In the end, during his last stay in Ajloun in 1984, he concluded the final version of the fable: "The worst had been death, alone, under torture. So the worst wasn't always inevitable. Or had the worst really happened anyway, *in that Hamza wasn't dead?* [...] So part of Daoud's letter was true."[80] Torture was an integral part of the figure because it portrayed Hamza, the new man, as the son, the cruci-fied one. Why the hesitation about his death? He reflected, "I couldn't resign myself to changing him into a silent doll, but nor could I forget him, alive or dead. Should I bury him deep inside me? If so, in what form?"[81] If Hamza was alive, he had risen from the dead.

On the last page of his book, Genet wondered, "But why is it that this couple is the only really profound memory I have of the Pales-tinian revolution?"[82] However, he made a last-minute addition to his manuscript: "What bothered me most was the strength of the Hamza/mother image, linked to that of the Pietà and Christ."[83] The figure is revealed, Genet did not invent it; it is written in the Koran: "We made the son of Mary and his mother a sign to mankind." (Koran, 23:50) It is in the *sura* of the Believers. Morroccan writer Abdelkebir Khatibi ad-dressed the heart of the matter in *Vomito Blanco* (proofread by Genet, whom he'd met around September 1974): "[...] there is a temptation in Christian circles sympathetic to the Palestinians to Christianize Islam and liken the fate of a Palestinian people to that of the Cross."[84] "Em-blem of the revolution," the religious figure is political. Repairing an identity, it is national, even nationalistic. Claudel returns, and brings the worst with him. The fable has played itself out.

Yet Genet's last book has at least two endings, once with the pietà, another time differently. A similarity in vocabulary binds these two endings of *Prisoner of Love*. The last paragraph of Part Two declares that the "only really profound memory"[85] is the couple, the Virgin and Son. The outcrop of the last page of Part One, also the first ending of the book, describes "what remains in men's minds."[86] The memory of men and the memories of Genet: here is a vestige, one and the same, the fable's final ramification.

At the junction between parts One and Two ("Souvenirs I" and "Souvenirs II" in French) of *Prisoner of Love*, after the words "he overcame oblivion," *Hitler* provides the break. A blank page marks the separation between the two parts. In the manuscript, however, the narration continues. The partition, the choice of having Hitler's name divide the book in two, is a late gesture imposed on the self, a political *decision* made by the last Genet:

> What remains in men's minds, what they deliberately erase, and what disappears of its own accord, may be either subject, cause, occasion or circumstance. It's hard to say who or what creates a glory or an echo, what somehow sets memory in motion when you read, aloud or to yourself, the story of the Kiss bestowed on the Leper.
>
> The leper in his cowl yields himself the Cid. Similarly, out of courtesy, a dead man is replaced by Antigone, a wounded man by the stretcher-bearer, a drowning man by the lifeguard, the wolfhound by Hitler. What am I saying?—by Hitler's hand, by just his little finger stroking it. But the dog has vanished, and all that's left suspended in mid-air is the caress, the eternal caress that is at once a proof of the magnanimity and the means by which it will go on existing for ever.
>
> You'll never know anything about the beggar into whose hand I dropped a couple of dirhams—neither his name, nor his past, nor his future. All we know about the Cid is that he kissed the leper—apart from a tragedy famous for several centuries. What do we know about Hitler, except that he burned Jews or caused them to be burned, and that he stroked a wolfhound? I've forgotten all about the beggar this morning except for the two dirhams. And what's a wolfhound doing here, biting the legs of a Greek shepherd?
>
> There must be another story struggling to get out from

> beneath the one I've been telling. There are still two or
> three hospitals where they look after lepers. But do they
> really look after them? Perhaps the experts inject people
> with the virus so that future Cids can show what heroism
> and Christian charity an Arab's capable of. Through leprosy,
> which conferred another sort of obliteration, he overcame
> oblivion.[87]

Was this the legacy, memory and oblivion? This page is revolting; Genet endows Hitler with magnanimity. One last time, if this was the last book, he couldn't help kissing the mouth of the leper, be it the beggar or Hitler. This old kiss tastes like ashes. Genet compared the dead in a far too predictable way, even though he wrote it between the lines. Under Hitler's spell, his memories conspired to equate the piles of Palestinian corpses and the Jews who were burned, mountains and ashes.

The accord and kinship that existed between Hitler, Hamza, and the Palestinian *pietà* are unspeakable in Genet's eye. But the accord was undeniable. On a smaller scale, they were part of the same "remains." On a larger scale—of his arrival at the house where Hamza's mother lived, the most critical juncture of his last book—he wrote, "'That's Hamza's house.' [...] I still don't know how, but that Palestinian house in the camp at Irbid had something German about it." He then dispelled any doubts: "The house wasn't built with materials from the Black Forest, but I sensed a parallel between it, or rather between the sight of it and the sound of the word Germany. Perhaps I even had a presentiment of the present-day link between Germany and the Grand Mufti of Jerusalem."[88] Zionists cultivated public relations with Nazi Germany as well. The basis for this coalition was simple: "Our obligation was to fight the enemy. We were justified in taking aid from the Nazi oppressor, who was in this case the enemy of our enemy—the British."[89] The same ties with the enemy, but this time Zionist, incited the Grand Mufti of Jerusalem, Haj Amin al-Husseini, to meet with the national socialist leaders. In fact, the German Secretary of State wrote to him in March 1941, "Should the Arabs need to fight the British in order to achieve their nationalist goals, Germany would be willing [...] to provide both military and financial assistance." In November 1943, in Bosnia, the Grand Mufti declared to the German Army's first Muslim volunteer troops: "You must serve as example and guiding light in the struggle against the common enemies of national-socialism and Islam."[90] The collusion between Germany and the Grand Mufti of Jerusalem served to illustrate how close Hitler and the *pietà* were. In a manner of speaking, the Germany of the 1940s is the one Genet would never leave, especially since his 1977 intervention on behalf of the Red Army Faction. This is the Germany Genet deemed "monstrous"[91] in "Violence and Brutality."

In the end, who wouldn't wish, for Genet's sake, that if he was going to take leave of himself and his art, he would have done so differently, not with a *pietà*, but in a surer, more triumphant way? With something less deceptive, less equivocal in relation to these dominant trends, less nihilistic?

In going east, to Irbid, to Jordan, Genet found a basic conjunction. It was his, but not only his, having to do with his subjective disposition: "Something very powerful happened there, converging in a life with great emotional intensity,"[92] as his friend Leila Shahid asserted. "Palestine was no longer a country—it was an age. Youth and Palestine were synonymous,"[93] Genet wrote. He was no doubt echoing Gérard de Nerval's sentiment and modesty: "[...] when I set foot upon this eternal land and immersed myself in the venerable source of our history and beliefs, I felt as though my years would stop, I would return to infancy in the cradle of civilization and be young again amid this eternal youth." Genet, like Nerval, could proclaim, "I feel younger, and indeed I am; I am only twenty years old!"[94] The myth-making function was set in motion, resulting in the fable of the *pietà* in Genet's last book. As the reader will recall, Genet entered the Virgin's house the first time he met Yasser Arafat: "Do this in remembrance of me."[95] The *pietà* now gives flesh to the words spoken to the son, and in a certain way they were Genet's last answer to the political leader.

Hitler and the *pietà* were the political and religious sides of a fable designed to fill a single void. The *pietà* enabled Genet to become the son, and at the same time, claim the mother and a house. The "emblem of the revolution" was collateral for the family, property, and society. The Palestinian way of life became the implicit response to European politico-religious hierarchy. But that's not all. By likening the fate of the Palestinian people to that of the Cross, an enemy of Israel, Genet's *pietà* cast the Jewish people as *deicidal*. At the same time, just as the fable of the *pietà* was linked to the Christian future of the Palestinian people, the Hitler fable condemned the disinherited to an anti-Semitic fate. After all, the Hitler fable represented the possibility for believers of a worst-case scenario: the extermination of non-Christians. Thus, the *pietà* restored the European trinity—country, identity, family— while the name Hitler served to fill the void left by these values, re- placing them with hatred, destruction, and death.

The *pietà* was a sort of Islamo-Christian Sign, while Hitler was the very real Name behind the extermination of six million Jews. The houses of the *pietà* and of love (mother, son), of Hitler and death (the final solution), were temporary homes for the writer. *Would Genet's fable lead to the writer's dark farce: blood, country, and God?*

ENDNOTES

1. A. Dieckhoff, *The Invention of a Nation: Zionist Thought and the Making of Modern Israel*, trans. Jonathan Derrick (New York: Columbia University Press, 2003), 93.
2. Ibid., 24.
3. "Les Palestiniens" (II), *Shoun Falestine*; *GC*, 108–109.
4. *DE*, 241.
5. *PL*, 349.
6. *DE*, 240.
7. Ibid., 241.
8. Ibid., 52.
9. H. Bergson, *Two Sources of Morality and Religion*, trans. R.A. Audra, C. Brereton, W.H. Carter (New York: Henry Holt and Company, 1935), 98.
10. Malcolm X, *The Speeches at Harvard* (New York: W. Morrow, 1968), 122.
11. C. Dagher, *Al Hayat*, August 1992.
12. J. Berque, *L'Islam au défi* (Paris: Gallimard, 1980), 67, 102.
13. K.B. Clark, *The Negro Protest: James Baldwin, Malcolm X, Martin Luther King talk with Kenneth B. Clark* (Boston: Beacon Press, 1963), 22.
14. Ibid., 28.
15. Ibid., 29.
16. Malcolm X, A. Haley, *The Autobiography of Malcolm X: As Told to Alex Haley* (New York: Ballantine, 1992), 328.
17. *PL*, 51.
18. Ibid., 53.
19. Ibid., 52.
20. B. Seale, *Seize the Time*, 249.
21. Malcolm X, A. Haley, *The Autobiography of Malcolm X*, 168.
22. W. J. Weatherby, "After the Panthers – What Next?" 322.
23. See Chapter 4.
24. B. Seale, *Seize the Time*, 248–250.
25. E. Pound, *The Cantos of Ezra Pound* (New York: New Directions, 1996), 450.
26. *PL*, 334.
27. Ibid., 341.
28. M. Rodinson, *The Arabs*, trans. Arthur Goldhammer (Chicago: University of Chicago Press, 1981), 29.
29. Ibid., 156.

30. F. Grimblat, "La communauté chiite libanaise et le mouvement national palestinien 1967–1986," *Guerres mondiales et Conflits contemporains* 151 (July 1988): 81.

31. *PL*, 423.

32. A. Perlmutter, "The Crisis of the PLO," *Encounter*, February 1988, 26.

33. A. Dieckhoff, *The Invention of a Nation*, 131.

34. G. Weiler, *Jewish Theocracy* (Leiden: Brill, 1988), 239.

35. J. Givet, *La Gauche contre Israël? Essai sur le néo-antisémitisme* (Paris: Pauvert, 1968), 29, 48.

36. M. Foucher, "Israël-Palestine: quelles frontières? Géographie physique et humaine de la Cisjordanie," *Hérodote* 29–30 (1983): 105–108.

37. *PL*, 20.

38. Ibid., 21.

39. Jehad, *Al yom assabeh*, April 20, 1987, 38–39, trans. B. El Omari and Hadrien Laroche.

40. "Les Palestiniens" (II); *GC*, 117.

41. E. White, *Genet: A Biography* (New York: Knopf, 1993), 521.

42. "Les Palestiniens" (II); *GC*, 120.

43. É. Ducpétiaux, *Exercice* (1841), quoted in J. Genet, *Le Langage de la muraille* (IMEC manuscript, 1981), 264.

44. *Le Langage de la muraille*, 345.

45. M. Choukri, *Jean Genet in Tangier*, trans. P. Bowles (New York: Ecco Press, 1974) 48.

46. M. Choukri, *Jean Genet et Tennessee Williams à Tanger* (Paris: Quai Voltaire, 1992), 76–80, 87.

47. *PL*, 225.

48. "Jean Genet chez les Panthères noires," *Le Nouvel Observateur*, May 25, 1970; *DE*, 45.

49. E. Saïd, "*Orientalism* and After," *Radical Philosophy* 63 (Spring 1993): 22.

50. *PL*, 219.

51. "May Day Speech" (speech given in New Haven, May 1, 1970); *DE*, 40.

52. "Les Palestiniens" (I), *Zoom* 4 (August 1971); *DE*, 71.

53. "Près d'Ajloun," in *Per un Palestine. Dediche a più voci a Waël Zouaiter* (Milan: G. Mazzotta, 1979); *DE*, 154.

54. *PL*, 115.

55. Ibid., 197.

56. Ibid., 126–127.

57. *Malcolm X Talks to Young People: Speeches in the US, Britain, and Africa* (New York: Pathfinder Press, 1991), 12.

58. *PL*, 229.

59. Service religieux de la Mosquée de Paris (personal communication, November 13, 1994).

60. *PL*, 197.

61. Ibid., 115.

62. Ibid., 166.

63. Ibid., 41.

64. Ibid., 381.

65. "The Black and the Red," *Black Panther Newspaper*, September 11, 1971; *DE*, 83.

66. E. White, *Genet: A Biography*, 727.

67. V. Harding, "The Religion of Black Power," *The World Year Book of Religions* (London: Evans Brothers, 1969) 1:13.

68. "Les Palestiniens" (I); *DE*, 74.

69. "Près d'Aljoun"; *DE*, 157.

70. "Four Hours in Shatila," *Revue d'études palestiniennes*; *DE*, 226.

71. "Les Femmes de Djebel Hussein," *Le Monde diplomatique*, July 1, 1974; *DE*; 117.

72. *PL*, 81–82, 181, 186–188, 192–193, 201–204, etc.

73. *PL*, 187.

74. *PL*, 192–193.

75. *PL*, 403–405.

76. "Les Palestiniens" (II); *GC*, 120.

77. *PL*, 405.

78. Ibid., 294.

79. Ibid., 354.

80. Ibid., 409–410.

81. Ibid., 354.

82. Ibid., 430.

83. Ibid., 296.

84. A. Khatibi, *Vomito Blanco: le sionisme et la conscience malheureuse*, 142; Khatibi, *Figures de l'étranger dans la littérature française*, 196.

85. *PL*, 430.

86. Ibid., 271.

87. Ibid., 271.

88. Ibid., 401.

89. Quoted in T. Segev, *The Seventh Million: the Israelis and the Holocaust*, trans. H. Watzman (New York: Holt Paperbacks, 2000), 33.

90. M. Ferro, *Colonization: a Global History*, trans. K.D. Prithipaul (London: Routledge, 1997); Y.-M. Ajchenbaum, "Une division SS islamiste en Bosnie," *Le Monde du dimanche*, November 14, 1993.

91. "Violence et Brutalité," preface to *Textes de prisonniers de la Fraction Armée rouge et dernières lettres D'Ulrike Meinhof*; DE, 177.

92. *GC*, 66.

93. *PL*, 305.

94. G. de Nerval, *Voyage en Orient*, in *Oeuvres complètes* (Paris: Gallimard, Pléiade, 1984, t. II), 504, 515.

95. *PL*, 141; see Chapter 2.

9 | Anarchy

Jean Genet did not join the resistance in 1940. He said as much, forty years later to the day. In the intervening years, he tried coming out into the world, an action that took him to other ghettos (the Black Panthers) and other camps (Palestinian refugees) to bear witness to other histories. Who would deny this? We need to unravel this particular aspect of his politics and learn how, in Genet's eye, the causes of the blacks and the Palestinians were reflected in the former plight of the French, reduced to shambles by the Nazis. Genet carried both the thrashing and the victory, the defeat of a hated France and the triumph of a people he loved.

The realities of Hitler, genocide, and Israel, reflected in the life of the Palestinians, caused Genet's vocabulary to crumble. This was the political aspect of an essentially religious conflict. Faced with Hebrew that was linked to the question of origin, Genet was more interested in the enemy's tongue than in questioning the "languages of paradise."[1]

Now, we must review the story of his coming out in light of what emerged from politics founded on a struggle against the *verb*.

GHOSTS
Genet first spoke to Americans on Thursday, March 12, 1970 at New York City College. On this occasion, he urged the students "to do

everything possible [...] to prevent the brutal genocide of the Black Panthers and of black people."[2] This speech, or exhortation, does not appear in the collection of his political texts published in French. Yet the matter is essential. Its history differed from the relationship of Jews and blacks, from the well-documented relationship of Jews and Arabs, and of Jews in Europe.

In 1960s America, in the wake of accusations of racism leveled against Black Muslims, Malcolm X was asked if he felt *"any* white men had ever done anything for the black man in America."[3] He answered unequivocally, "Yes, I can think of two. Hitler, and Stalin." During the third speech he gave at Harvard, on December 16, 1964, Malcolm X elaborated on the Hitler paradox: "In those days, a black man could have a job shining shoes or waiting tables [...]. Only when Hitler went on the rampage in 1939, and this country suffered a manpower short-age, did the black man get a shot at better jobs." He also told the stu-dents, "But this advancement never was out of Uncle Sam's goodwill. We never made one step forward until world pressure put Uncle Sam on the spot [...]. You have been as cold as an icicle whenever it came to the rights of the black man in this country. (Excuse me for raising my voice, but I think it's time. As long as my voice is the only thing I raise, I don't think you should become upset!)."[4] Along with the paradox and the witticism applied to Hitler, a wind both hot and cold blew over the assembly. These increasingly dark words were laced with a growing panic.

In the US, Hitler's name invoked racism rather than anti-Semi-tism, and was linked to the black leader's conversion to Islam. In 1964, Malcolm X discussed his pilgrimage to Mecca in his autobiography, writing, "America needs to understand Islam, because this is the one religion that erases from its society the race problem." Then he add-ed, "With racism plaguing America like an incurable cancer, the so-called 'Christian' white American heart should be more receptive to a proven solution to such a destructive problem. Perhaps it could be in time to save America from imminent disaster—the same destruction brought upon Germany by racism that eventually destroyed the Germans themselves."[5] This second movement identified Americans with Nazis, as the enemy. The historical reality evoked by these two attacks—Hitler, Nazi America—was genocide. Shortly after, Malcolm X's house burned down, leading him to wonder how to tell the story of his life in a world that was changing so fast.

A December 1969 petition, signed by Huey Newton and Bobby Seale on behalf of the Black Panthers, declared:

> The savage police, based upon official policies of Federal, State and City governments, has resulted in innumerable beatings, frameups, arrests and murders of black Americans, the classical example of which is the Black Panther Party. [...] The Genocide Convention adopted by the General Assembly of the United Nations on December 9, 1948, defines as genocide "killing members of the group and any intent to destroy in whole or in part a national racial or ethnic or religious group." And further, according to the Convention, "Causing serious bodily or mental harm to members of the group" is Genocide. We assert that the Genocide Convention has been flagrantly violated by the Government of the United States. [...] The racist planned and unplanned terror suffered by more than 40 millions of black, brown, red and yellow citizens of the United States cannot be regarded solely as a domestic issue. The continuance of these practices threatens the struggle of mankind throughout the world to achieve peace, security and dignity. On the basis of simple justice, it is time for the Human Rights Commission of the United Nations to call for universal action, including political and economic sanctions against the United States. We further demand that the United States government make reparations to those who have suffered the damages of racist and genocidal practices.
>
> Huey P. Newton, Bobby Seale, UNDER THE AUSPICES OF: The Committee to Petition The United Nations, of the

Conference Committee, 33 Union Square W., New York, NY.[6]

Genet met with the Panthers a year later. That's when he pronounced his appeal at New York City College. Perhaps his later use of the word "genocide" was inspired by point seven of the Panthers' Ten Point Platform and Program: "We want an immediate end to police brutality and murder of black people."[7] The word came into common use after World War II; its use by the Panthers demonstrated that it could be applied to all oppressed peoples. The birth of the United Nations and the motion concerning genocide invited other peoples in other places to use the term. In the Party's petition, the word "reparation" (*shiloumim* in Hebrew) draws a connection to those paid to Israel by Germany. Such debts indicate a legacy.

Spoken by the Panthers in 1970, the word genocide was not a Hebrew word, but it did call to mind the Nazi plan to annihilate the Jewish people. However, the reference to genocide also evoked the actions of Hitler, the good man. The analogy's limitations are apparent: the notions of the Jewish people (genocide) and Hitler (good man) are incompatible. Between the United Nations motion and the anti-Semitic notion, one may well question the use of the term with regards to black people in America. Does the "classic example" of the Black Panther Party, whose members were decimated, indeed warrant the use of the word genocide? Charles R. Garry, the Black Panthers' lawyer, deplored the fact that, "Unfortunately, the Party did not begin to keep records at its inception of the men and women who were harassed and killed."[8] It was best not to count the dead; Genet already knew all too well how impossible it was to tally the debt owed the dead. In an interview in *The Guardian* after the assassination of young Fred Hampton, Bobby Seale declared, "An estimated 80,000 people went through the house where Hampton was shot dead and actually saw the bullet holes in the wall. These people received a first-hand experience of genocidal tactics."[9] It seems he did little to clear up the confusion. Better to speak of an unwanted war, of economic oppression, of violent power transformed into consensual power. Organized racial terror sums up the singular predicament of blacks in America.

Seale, a member of the Panthers, was one of those arrested in the wake of the Democratic National Convention in Chicago in August 1968, but he alone was incarcerated. In 1970, he was still there and facing a death sentence on other charges. On April 14, 1970, Genet was present at Seale's trial when the latter asserted, "In my case in Chicago, I wasn't allowed to even defend myself, whereas in Nazi Germany in 1933 a Bulgarian Communist [Dimitroff] accused of setting the Reichstag fire was allowed to."[10] Genet made the Seale trial his "Dreyfus Affair."[11] Eldridge Cleaver maintained that being a black man judged by an all-white jury was "like being a Jew tried in Nazi Germany." Speaking of another trial involving the Black Panthers, Cleaver unequivocally stated that the "racist power structure in Oakland in California is going to try to *railroad Huey P. Newton* to the gas chamber and kill him."[12]

Hitler, Nazi Germany, and Jews on trial in Germany: both the black movement in the US and Genet knew this story. But for them, genocide was black.

In late May 1971, a year after his return from the US, Genet wrote his first text on the Palestinians. "Long before that," he wrote, "but especially between 1880 and 1940, in both secular and Christian Europe, anti-Semitism will go from relatively small-scale pogroms all the way to Dachau and Auschwitz. Europe massacres or threatens the Jews, while at the same time the Jews who have been spared are massacring or threatening the Arabs, with the help of English soldiers." He added, "They now know the cunning of those who were their masters [...]. The counterpart of these vexations is a knowledge of the powerful."[13] The same words kept coming back: pogrom, massacres and, soon, victimizer. We must take a moment to study what Genet meant by these words. He spoke best of the Palestinians when he failed to mention the enemy. The Hitler paradox, such as it was used by black Americans, found an echo in the complex irony of its victims in relation to the Palestinians: "Expert commentators [...] have argued that the Palestinians owe their new relative prominence in Western consciousness to the fact that their opponents were Israeli Jews."[14] This is how Edward Saïd, a Palestinian American whom Genet had met, returned to Genet's other debate. Saïd didn't claim this assertion was his; he even added that the change also had to do with constructive measures taken by the Palestinians to change their status along with the Israeli response. Yet Saïd's other paradox remained: "The classic victims of years of anti-Semitic persecution and holocaust have in their new nation become the victimizers of another people, who have become the victims of the victims."[15] During the timely debate, Hitler's name again surfaced, though not overtly, in the expression used to describe the Palestinians: "victims of the victims." The irony is fearsome if we're not careful. It seems to imply that for those who support the Palestinian struggle, acknowledging the suffering of the Jews—victims of the *Shoah*—likens, by the same token, the Israelis to the Nazis.

The history of the Jewish people reflected in the eyes of the Palestinians is a long story. It is possible to go back to the early stages of the twentieth century, before Israel existed and before the inhabitants of Palestine were said to have become victims. Their increased visibility at the time that Genet met them was part of the irony of the Palestinian situation; we must outline the relation between Israelis and genocide. According to David Ben-Gurion's political compass, near the end of the war of 1947, "[Another] million Jews—[and] the conflict will be over."[16] Of the Israel-Palestine situation, writer Yehudit Hendel declared, "To put it bluntly, there were almost two races in this country." On one side, in 1945, stood the Zionists who'd been there before the war—those "who thought they were gods"—and on the other, the survivors of the Holocaust, who arrived during and after the war, "the ugliest, basest thing."[17] Historian Tom Segev, who cited these statements, could make the following bizarre claim, as if they were ghosts: "Then the War of Independence broke out, and tens of thousands of homes were suddenly available." Neither Ben-Gurion, Hendel, nor Segev had anything to say about the Palestinians. After all, the consequences of the genocide against the Jews for Palestinians were not part of their discussions. The burden of one's ghosts is one thing, but who would want the burden of the ghosts of ghosts? Yet Segev had to acknowledge the irony when he wrote, "Free people—Arabs—had gone into exile and become destitute refugees; destitute refugees—Jews—took the exiles' places as a first step in their new lives."[18]

During the first Cabinet meeting in Israel's history, Minister of Agriculture Aharon Zisling spoke out about the atrocities committed by Israeli soldiers against Palestinians during and after the War of Independence: "I have not always agreed when the term Nazi was applied to the British. I would not want to use that expression with regard to them, even though they committed Nazi acts. But Nazi acts have been committed by Jews as well, and I am deeply shocked."[19] This irony took shape at a precise moment: the 1960 trial of Lieutenant-Colonel Eichmann in Jerusalem. Many questioned the wisdom of trying one of the heads of the Nazi Gestapo and police in Israel rather than elsewhere by an international court. Ben-Gurion addressed this issue in an effort to allay doubt and legitimize the trial being held in Israel: "The Jewish State (which is called Israel) is the heir of the six million who were murdered."[20] This statement had major repercussions. At once, it turned genocide victims into Zionists and implied that Zionist and Jewish were synonymous, meaning that the enemies of the State of Israel and the Jews were one and the same; therefore, supporting Israel meant fighting anti-Semitism. Ben-Gurion couldn't be sure that the victims would have made their way to Israel. Most Jews had been killed because they'd preferred to stay in their country rather than go to Palestine. We don't know how many of them were Zionists and were killed regardless of how they labeled themselves: Zionists, anti-Zionists, or even Jews. These differences have since been forgotten. The trial imposed by Ben-Gurion usurped the memory of the genocide in order to consolidate the state.

So when Genet wrote that Jews who'd been "spared" became victimizers, it favored one part of the reality—the ghosts of wars of independence chasing each other—and a national legend. The writer's words were a shortcut that, on one hand, picked up on an Israeli myth (the victims of the genocide had become Zionists or Israelis) and on the other, the reversal of victims and victimizers; it belonged to an unacceptable logic. By adopting the vulgate, Genet prevented anything new from arising. In other words, he stemmed the possibility of creating legacy. In his 1987 book *Memory for Forgetfulness*—whose subtitle, *August, Beirut, 1982*, could draw comparisons to Genet's last book—Palestinian poet Mahmoud Darwish wove together the different threads of this story. He wrote about a Palestinian: "He has to catch tuberculosis not to forget he has lungs, and he must sleep in open country not to forget he has another sky. He has to work as a servant not to forget he has a national duty, and he must be denied the privilege of settling down so that he won't forget Palestine."[21]

There is little difference between the Israeli, Palestinian, and European vulgates. According to the logic of exemplary nature, it's all the same in the end. The infamous men, however, wanted to change things forever. The Jews' future as Israel was real, brimming with promise and peril. The comparison to the Nazis is a joke indulged in at times by citizens of Israel, and also at other times by non-Jews; this is something that must be watched. As for the assimilation of the Palestinians as victims of victims, we might well say, in this case, that there were no victims.

Genet went to the Middle East in October 1970. Not long after, he wrote, "The origins of anti-Semitism in the Christian West are extremely complex. Perhaps one of them has to do with the Christians drawing the basis of their doctrines from Jewish sacred texts. However, this would require the kind of in-depth study I'm incapable of doing."[22] Let's not undertake this study, but instead ask what linked the Black Panthers to the Palestinians and those movements to Genet? Was it hardship, violence, or something else altogether? Was it anti-Zionism? Could the Black Panthers and Palestinians have been the two most anti-Semitic movements in the world?

When David Hilliard, proclaimed father and friend of Genet, named his daughter Dassine, he was "honoring the Palestinian rebellion."[23] On a less joyful note (if we can put it that way), he was remembering the name of the judge who sentenced Bobby Seale. In a February 1970 article in the *Black Panther Newspaper*, Hilliard launched an unexpected attack. Bear in mind, though, that it was cited in a text on the Black Panthers commissioned by the US government. Hilliard wrote, "We don't have to go all the way to Palestine or Israel to condemn Zionism. You have your own Zionists right here in this country manifested in Julius J. Hoffman, the Zionist that sentenced our Chairman Bobby Seale to four years in jail for merely trying to stand up and represent himself in a fascist court."[24] The will to trial of infamous men is foremost. Against power in general and in the name of blacks' historical fight for equal rights in particular, political expediency was satisfied by fighting under the polemic banner of black genocide. Genet was witness to the political, judicial, and financial reality of the segregation of visible minorities in the United States. But along the way, the criticism of Israel attached itself to the rhetoric of the Black Panthers. This prompted the American Jewish Committee to declare, "While we do not necessarily equate anti-Israel or anti-Zionist sentiment with anti-Semitism, the Panthers' expression of support for Al Fatah has been so strident and distorted as to make it impossible to make the distinction."[25] The members of the Black Panthers grew interested in the Palestinian issue following Eldridge Cleaver's flight from the American authorities to Algeria. A statement in the November 1, 1969 edition of the *Black Panther Newspaper* read: "The Black Panther Party supports Fat'h and the Palestinian people in regaining their occupied territory." No more, no less.

As early as 1948, the singular question of Palestinian anti-Zionism was raised independently of the general question of Western or Arab anti-Semitism. In 1969, the Seven Points of Fatah were issued. Article 2 stated: "Fatah, the Palestine National Liberation Movement, is not struggling against the Jews as an ethnic and religious community. It is struggling against Israel as the expression of colonization based on a theocratic, racist and expansionist system and of Zionism and colonialism."[26] The Palestinians started referring to their adversary as Zionists in 1971, a year after Genet arrived in Jordan. Historian Bernard Lewis argued: "But this is not racial, nor does it resemble Christian anti-Semitism. It rests on no theology of guilt, no scriptural condemnation, no assumption of racial distinctness and inferiority." Lewis drew a line between European anti-Semitism and "Arab hostility"[27] Enmity or hostility; an improvement, yet still not a policy. Much later: on November 13, 1988, the Palestinians nullified its first Charter (that denied the State of Israel's right to exist) and then recognized Resolution 242 of the United Nations and, with it, the right of Israel to exist. However, in its 1974 Palestine National Council Resolutions, the PLO stated that it would accept "every part of the Palestinian territory which will be liberated."[28] In so doing, they rejected the myth and improved their chances for true political liberation.

In his book (in which he cited Genet), Pierre-André Taguieff pointed out, "Apparently, Palestinian propaganda did not resort to negationist theories." According to him, there are two reasons for this refusal. "First, Palestinian propaganda frequently compared the Jewish victims of Nazism and Palestinian victims of Zionism. Second, Palestinian propaganda directed at a Western audience has always sought political recognition, which grants a certain respectability."[29] I have pointed to the irony of this analogy and what infamous men think of images. The disinherited refuse to be cast as victims. Through actions (acceptable or not) that are always violent, theatrical gestures, and political signs, they display the will to another trial.[30] Taguieff later spoke again of a "self-legitimizing victimizing myth," and unequivocally of "anti-Zionist Nazification of Zionists." I won't try to follow the slant of a language that is foreign to me. By its logic, the young men who fought (*intifada*) in Gaza and on the West Bank from December 1986 onward were "children cynically sent to die in order to create martyrs, sacrificed to an ideology of combat."[31] Taguieff admitted—albeit reluctantly, no doubt—that Palestinians were not anti-Semitic in the Christian and European sense of the term. Like others before him, he also drew attention to the irony of the victims of victims. However, the terms he used are reminiscent of Saïd's expert testimony. Invoking propaganda, myth, and sacrifice to argue for a history of anti-Semitism was hardly original, but he also neglected an event, such as the creation of a people through liberation.

Last, Taguieff came to recognize the necessity by which "anti-Jewish statements can function without any empirical foundation, without any contact with the vilified enemy—unlike, for instance, the Palestinians in 'occupied' territories whose anti-Jewish mythology is fueled by direct experiences such as 'humiliations,' expropriations, etc."[32] Let's skip over the word "mythology" and the quotation marks; the salient point is the ghost argument. At play here is the old structure that makes all racism possible, renders the enemy indistinguishable, at once omnipresent, elusive, and easily symbolized, both fleeing and dangerous. The Palestinians couldn't resort to myth or phantasmagoria because of their direct experience with Israel, whose political aims were achieved through practical means that led to the negation—but not the destruction—of another people.

Why insist so ardently that the two movements Genet was close to—the Black Panthers and the Palestinians—were in no way revisionist? And that, like all governed people, they were fighting there and then, so their hardships—or the reflection of their hardship, as was the case with the blacks supporting the Palestinians—would not remain a mere mute consequence of power, in this case of the State of Israel? If Genet was anti-Semitic, he and he alone will have to answer that charge.

If, as Leon Poliakov wrote, there's "less than a hair's difference"[33] between anti-Zionism and anti-Semitism, then patience and vigilance are in order.

SHADOWS

In 1986, in his last book, Genet is probably being self-referential when he writes: "[France] was invaded [...] by a few battalions of handsome fair-haired soldiers. Whether it was because they had too much beauty, too much fairness, or too much youth, France cringed before them."[34] In his novel *Our Lady of the Flowers*, which he'd begun to write in 1942 and clandestinely published in 1944 (before having it reappear, expunged, in 1951) he draws a comparison. Mignon penetrates Divine: "He rams it in. So hard and calmly that his virility, observed by the heavens, has the penetrating force of the battalions of blond warriors who on June 14, 1940, buggered us soberly and seriously, though their eyes were elsewhere as they marched in the dust and sun."[35] This old comparison can be seen again later, in a barely changed form; it is a mark of the past. If it reappears now, it means that other problems are on the horizon.

In 1940, the writer had not yet exited the prison of himself for the real world; his eyes were closed. Genet's official arrival in the literary world took place on May 29, 1943, after he was arrested in Paris. Arrested on the Place de l'Opéra and brought to the Chaussée-d'Antin police station, he claimed in the interrogation room, "I'm an electrician, I don't work. I write books." He then added, an obligation under the Vichy regime: "Unmarried. French nationality. Non-Jewish." He was freed. Locked up in the Tourelles camp for repeated book theft with his co-inmates who were political prisoners, he risked being sent to the concentration camps.[36] He wrote to Marc Barbezat, publisher of Genet's early works, on December 28, 1943: "I'm worried sick. [...] I'm consigned to the warehouse, waiting until the Chief of Police sends me to a concentration camp, as an undesirable."[37] In passing, his biographer quoted a deleted page from *The Thief's Journal* (1946) about deported men. Genet wrote: "Just think of my happiness when I saw these types, who didn't give a damn when I was behind walls three yards thick, suddenly at the mercy of an idiotic guard, riddled with bullets, starved to death, behind barb wire."[38] Through juxtaposition, Genet mixes up the Tourelles camp in Paris with one like Auschwitz. Through the sentence construction, the confusion turns the author into a deportee, or even a murdered Jew. But not a gassed Jew, for no one could know that reality in France at that time. Through numerous intercessions, Genet was freed, and *Our Lady of the Flowers*, his first book, was published, his eyes still closed. The last book, coming less from a long silence than a shared question to both the imprisoned man and the writer, will attempt to tell the disenfranchised that to drag oneself out of shame, through a book or otherwise, is easy. Genet knew: he knows he is a non-Jew, he knows the existence of concentration camps. He did not know the gas chambers. He sees himself as a ghostly presence, stuck dead in the barbed wire, in a camp. The writer's joy comes from the collapse of the French military *and* the death of others in his stead.

In the novel *Funeral Rites*, which was finished in 1945 and clandestinely published in 1947, a situation intertwines France, Hitler, and shame: "If I were told that I was risking death in refusing to cry '*Vive la France*,' I would cry it in order to save my hide, but I would cry it softly. [...] And if I had to believe in it, I would; then I would immediately die of shame." Of Riton, the book's lover, Genet claims that he feels "an evil joy, the joy of being joyous and handsome in a desperate situation which he had evilly got himself into, out of hatred for France (which he rightly confused with Society), the day he signed up for the Militia [...]." At a time of a Liberation unanimously celebrated, even if only a few had participated in it, Genet brings attention to France's shameful actions: had not the French, more liberated than the liberators, on the same day of their Liberation, committed under De Gaulle's orders the Sétif massacre, in which between 1,500 and 40,000 Algerians died?[39] He mourns the dead lover (a resistance fighter) and the war. He is already trying to understand the legacy of these atrocities: "Hitler's gracious and simple life was going to unleash terrible acts on the world, acts that would give rise to the most prodigious flowering of nightmares that a man has ever generated all by himself." Yet the writer remains a prisoner of a game itself trapped in fiction—"I'm amused by this game of recording here the shame of a country"—that belongs, to summarize, to provocation rather than quarreling; it does not allow the escape from shame. Then he can call Hitler a "poet."[40] These types of statements always come back every time we try to remove the political aspect from Genet's views, when we do not take the time, if at all possible, to separate the old refrains from the creative ritornellos. This one is certainly part of the dead-end phrases. He wrote it in the forties, and never wrote it again, he remembers that.

During two interviews before and after Christmas, in December of 1975, followed by one on the second of January, 1982, the author, sixty-five then seventy-two years old, recalls the Occupation, his old age, his sickness, and his stories; Nazism and death. During the December interview in Paris, his interlocutor is German. Hubert Fichte declares that he is taken aback by Genet's former admiration of Hitler, the elegant brutality, the concentration camps. Genet says, "Yes, but I was thirty years old when I wrote my books, and now I'm sixty-five." After that joke, he clarifies:

> Yes and no. It has drained away, but the space has not been
> occupied by anything else, it's a void. It's quite strange
> for someone who lives this void. What did it mean, this
> fascination for brutes or assassins or Hitler? In more direct
> and perhaps also simpler terms, I remind you that I was an
> orphan, I was raised by Public Welfare, I found out very
> early on that I wasn't French and that I didn't belong to
> the village—I was raised in the Massif Central. I found
> this out in a very stupid, silly way: the teacher asked us to
> write a little essay in which each student would describe
> his house. I described mine; it happened that the teacher
> thought my description was the prettiest. He read it out, and

everyone made fun of me, saying, "That's not his house, he's
a foundling!" and then there was such an emptiness, such a
degradation. I immediately became such a stranger ... oh!
The word isn't too strong, to hate France is nothing, you
have to do more than hate, more than loathe France, finally
... The fact that the French army, the most prestigious
thing in the world thirty years ago, that they surrendered
to the troops of an Austrian corporal, well, to me, that was
absolutely thrilling. I was avenged. But I'm well aware that
it wasn't me who wrought this vengeance, I am not the
maker of my vengeance. It was brought about by others, by
a whole system, and I'm aware, too, that it was a conflict
within the white world that went far beyond me; but when it
comes down to it, French society suffered a real blow, and I
could only love someone who had dealt such a serious blow
to French society. [...] On top of all this, I could only place
myself among the oppressed people of color and among the
oppressed revolting against the Whites.[41]

He concludes with this now famous comment: "Perhaps I'm a black
whose color is white or pink, but black. I don't know my family."[42] Now
we see where he is coming from. He goes on to speak about Bobby Seale's
trial. Later, during the January interview, he answers the same questions:

I believe that in the end my whole life has been against
white rules. [The rules of] White people. I mean that,
even now—and I'm seventy-two years old!—I can't vote.
Even if you think it's not very important, I am not fully a
French citizen. [Soon after] Just think, when Hitler gave a
thrashing to the French, well yes! I was glad, this thrashing
made me happy. Yes, the French were cowards. [He is asked
whether the extermination camps were also "amusing."] At
first, really, I didn't know about that. But what I'm talking
about is France, not the German people or the Jewish
people, or the communist people that Hitler massacred. It
was a question of the corrective the German army gave to
the French army.[43]

He then begins to talk of Arab people. Emptiness then joy, joy then emptiness: a moment of this story has passed. *All of Genet's spectacular political claims refer back to the origins of the writer*: the anacoluthon, the violent syntactic rupture that juxtaposes Hitler's name and a classroom in Morvan, the claim to being black and the status of an orphan. The violence to which he testifies may be small in grammar yet is huge in this vast and terrible world. The foundling child's status is simultaneously subjective (neither father nor mother), political (non-citizenship), and historical (Hitler). As a ward of the state and a one-time thief, the writer is deprived of his civil rights. He is thus not entirely French. He is foreign, and to say it, as he does, is not an empty act but a way of insisting on a political reality. In the French school system, the children laughed at this runt of a poet: without a home, without rights, he is stateless. An outsider. Hitler avenges the political affront Genet suffered from the children's teasing: this isn't his house. *The writer's life and work are found fully formed in this meeting between a childhood with political consequences and a political view that fills childhood's vacuum.*

Here we find a turning point. Genet mentions that he is not responsible. Hitler has taken his place. He knows as much: "[...] I am not the architect of my own revenge." At the time of George Jackson's trial, we saw how Genet moved away from the logic of the avenged. Here, rather than testify in his own name, he prefers to fill the void with someone else's. Hence, he is no longer *responsible*. Rather than accepting vengeance and the act of vengeance committed by another, he could stand up and say, All I ask is to be able to answer; I must be offered what should have been mine by obligation. His last book's tonality is the will to a trial. To absolutely refuse Hitler's name—reactive politics, reparations, racism—but to recover speech again. Not to wreak vengeance, but to speak his truth. This is already revenge, soon to be hatred, the joy that stems from these emotions; these are the dispositions of the child before his father and mother, or their absence. In this situation, no politics are possible. This is the hope of emerging from shame: to work, to invent, to love without need of a father or mother. Submission to reality, whether it is successful or not, is the writer's act of resistance.

Genet sees the reflection of the disinherited in the old concern for the French defeat at the hands of the Nazis. Twice, during interviews in Paris and Rambouillet, Hitler gives way to Genet's childhood concerns: Bobby Seale's trial and his support for the Black Panthers first, followed by the Arab people and the Palestinian cause. He never hesitates to link the two: "followed by" are the words linking Hitler's name and the causes he has at heart. To understand this, let's turn to a Palestinian's testimony: Afnan el Kasm, who translated passages of *Prisoner of Love* for *El Talia'a Arabia*'s July 1986 edition. With his name also comes Ezra Pound's, meaning the return of the cause, more precisely the reflection of the fascist cause espoused by the American poet seen through the French writer's eyes. The bridge between Genet and Pound comes from these pages:

> One cannot be a great poet without having a cause, and making that cause the principal concern of one's interests. We publish Pound's poems while insisting on the fact that being a great poet and supporting Mussolini have nothing in common. Seeing the poems in this light is a mistake. Under which criterion can we judge the worthiness of cause? Is language a sufficient criterion? No. A noble cause is not enough without language to back it up. In the opinion of some, Pound was not a great poet since he lacked a great cause. A poet cannot be great without a cause, even if he makes language his cause. There are many writers whose cause is the limit of their poem: they fall into trap of a false greatness.
>
> Conscience, content, and commitment to language are the causes of poetry, the homeland and humanity. It is thus that just causes form the poet's and artist's universe, whatever their origin or form, personal or otherwise. This is what Genet accomplished in writing about the Palestinian revolution. Genet was happy seeing Nazis walking through

Paris, not because he was a pro-fascist like Pound, but because he was against a system that had lost the war, as our systems lost the war of 1967, a war that made French people suffer as the war of 1967 did to the Arabs. Genet—a Frenchman—was not for the French cause because it was not just. Yet he was for the justice of the Palestinian cause like any other Arab, perhaps even more so.

Why do Zionists and pro-Zionists among French writers try to muddle Pound's and Genet's positions while being unable to properly read miraculous Palestinian writings? There is not a single Arab writer who believes himself universal who dared speak out in defense of Genet [the writer refers here to the show *Droit de Réponse* devoted to the writer, and the attacks made against him on that occasion]. Genet stayed close to Palestine for fifteen years, he lived with her, he made her the star of his writings—but where were these writers?[44]

Rough words, unexpected speech of resistance: let him speak his truth for once, for no doubt these are the words of the disinherited. The implicit comparison between two battles—the one that pitted France against the Nazis, the other the Arab people's against Israel in 1967—echoes the dubious irony we've already seen; irony of the Palestinians as victims of victims, becoming Nazis to the Israelis. But this irony is accompanied by a distinction between an unjust and a just cause, making the fight against the Nazis an unjust one, while judging the Palestinians' struggles against Israel to be just. This exemplary and comparative logic quickly displays its limits. As exemplary as it is, for the very reason identified here, it is possible to get rid of it, and refuse it.

Yet a transverse logic and a difference appear here. Pound's quarrel espoused fascism; Genet's is not the Nazi cause. Genet wrote in support of those who have nothing and the Palestinian cause. Despite the temptation to turn irony on its head and make the Palestinians into Nazis—and in virtue of the fact that they do or do not attack Israel's existence itself, but fight to recover all land that was occupied then liberated—must I point out that the Palestinian cause can never be confused with the Nazis? Genet was not pro-Nazi, if that must be said. He never wrote anti-Semitic pamphlets (like Céline), nor letters to the Fuhrer (like Artaud),[45] and neither did he want to meet Hitler or Mussolini (like Pound). Despite a proximity with these writers that this book has mentioned every time it was pertinent, the last Genet is not part of this constellation. Refusing to confuse the causes, understanding each situation based on a precise point in a struggle, refusing, in conclusion, to let enemies become ghosts, this is not the way to defend Genet—and it's not my goal—but the necessary preamble to let the words of men of infamy speak for themselves.

April 14, 1970. Genet is in a small courtroom in New Haven, in the United States. A month earlier, in March, he had called upon American students to prevent the "brutal genocide" of black people and the Black Panthers. I have already described this. As noted earlier, his appeal rests on a precise point of the Panthers' and Genet's experience: Bobby Seale's trial. At best he is looking at prison, at worst the death penalty. This is Genet's "Dreyfus affair." A new constellation is being drawn: Dreyfus, but also Hoffman, and soon the Rosenbergs. His aim is this: "And here everything seems to indicate that there is no interest in Bobby Seale because he is black. In the same way, Dreyfus was guilty because he was Jewish." And then: "It used to be that, in France, the guilty man was the Jew. Here the guilty man was, and still is, the Negro." Guilt, racism, a single name, intertwining Dreyfus and Seale, the Jew and the black man. We return to a certain exemplary logic, repeated many times in the black movement's discourse, but also in the writer's words. This first comparison has its limits: "Of course this parallel with the Dreyfus affair cannot be maintained at every point." Yet, Genet reminds us, there is neither a Jaurès nor Zola to write a "*J' accuse*." But this is not the main problem. The paradox of the exemplary is found in the name of Bobby Seale's judge. In Genet's article, published in the *Nouvel Observateur* on August 31, 1970 and reprinted in *The Declared Enemy*, he writes of those times, "Bobby Seale, who together with Newton founded the Panthers, was tried (and gagged, an unprecedented event) in Chicago, and transferred to the prison in New Haven: he's still there." In an article published in June 1970 which he sent to *Ramparts* magazine under the title "Here and Now for Bobby Seale," he continues the parenthesis: "Because of Chairman Bobby Seale's exceptional political stature, his trial is in fact [...] a race trial held against all of America's blacks." In Dreyfus' shadow, guilty because he is Jewish, we find Hoffman, a Jewish judge, and in the shadow of this shadow, Bobby Seale, guilty because he is black: a black man gagged and soon found guilty by the Jewish judge. It's already complex enough.[46]

The comparison soon becomes perilous, as does the collusion of these three names—especially when we read in the French version of the same series of articles written between March and June 1970—established after the speech given in the United States on March 18, 1970: "Because of the very fact that the Black Panther Party and we ourselves, white people, have the same enemy, meaning the police, and beyond the White House Administration, High Finance, we know that our struggle is a class struggle."[47] Nothing is said, but everything is there.

The enemy, the guilty party; they are the orientation of these comments. The end of the sentence that makes the struggle against the enemy a class struggle was at the time a concern for the black movement, leading the fight under Marxist ideology instead of a racial one. The attack on high finance is linked to this economic and racist (against blacks) practice: "I've seen many bails set at a hundred thousand dollars for blacks,"[48] Genet adds. Yet, by calling for the prevention of black genocide, by comparing Seale and Dreyfus, by naming the judge who gagged him, he identifies the enemy. Negatively, Hoffman, then positively; he is, all in all, what Genet names high finance. What Genet is pointing to here is the equation in his vocabulary: a judge, a Jew, finance.

The conclusion of this dangerous rambling remains unwritten. I would like to reflect for a moment on it, since I will most likely not return to it or, more likely, I will return to it but in a different form. After all, it is concerned with money, debt, value, or the capital of the possibility of asking, if not solving, the issue of legacy. Let us not allow banality to endure, and let's not believe that the author puts much importance on it either. In the bail that the Panthers were forced to pay during their various trials, we can see the emergence of a Christian-European anti-Semitic cliché: Jews and money. Christian, because Christians are the ones who pushed Jews into the financial sector in the Middle Ages, then blamed them for being there. Although the financial cliché is sometimes fact, we must put it aside in this trial's paradigm. Yet we can find these banalities in Genet's writing. Speaking of Palestine after Israel's creation, we read "[...] that where there had been a barley field now there was a bank, that the power plant had taken the place of the creeping vine."[49] Yet this anti-Semitic cliché is used to undo another one, Zionist: before the Jews' arrival, Palestine was a swamp; better yet, a desert. No, there was a field: gold, certainly, but also barley. In Genet's last book, this type of statement is reinvented in a series of other declarations that attack Jordanians' relationship with money: "Amman can be described in these terms. It's made up of seven hills and nine valleys, the latter consisting of deep crevasses that the banks and mosques can never fill." Then there is the Lebanese Phalangists' use of gold: "So I was getting to know them better, these Phalangists who kissed gold crosses between girls' breasts [...]"—and big Palestinian families' relation to money and particularly the PLO's to dollars.[50] Genet attacks the millions that burn in the avid eye of the fedayeen. No one is spared. Dollar, dirham, or shekel, golden crowns even, are all characters circulating through Genet's book. These currencies appear less as representations of racist ideology than poetic expressions of class struggle.

Meanwhile, a sense of urgency drives him to write not only in hopes of freeing Bobby Seale, but also another imprisoned Panther, George

Jackson. In his manifesto "For George Jackson," written in March 1971, and aimed at the French public, Genet's tone hardens. The same names return, with one addition: "We're now asking you to speak out for the release of Jackson, of Seale, of Angela Davis, as you did, with the means at your disposal, for the Rosenbergs." A new location, a new comparison: in America, Genet offers the Bobby Seale trial in comparison with the Dreyfus affair; in France, he draws a comparison with the case involving Julius and Ethel Rosenberg, the American communist couple accused of conspiracy to commit espionage: "At that time, you didn't have your asses glued to your armchairs. You were sharp and angry. What happened? Have you gotten old?"[51] In the first series of interventions, two men are compared, both guilty for racist reasons. Now the comment is different, a change is felt: the comparison between Jackson, Seale, Davis, and the Rosenbergs is drawn around the difference in the public zeal to defend them. An imbalance appears: for the Rosenbergs, the whole world showed its anger. Today, for Seale and the others, everyone is sitting on their thumbs: "Of course, although they were Jewish, the Rosenbergs were white." This comment states the obvious ("of course"), and makes a concession ("although"). This rhetorical trick displays the limits of the old comparison: Jews and blacks cannot be compared because Jews are white. The omission in this second comparison that tries to appear unrelenting in denouncing the difference in the public's treatment of the accused blacks and Jews is that the Rosenbergs were judged. (Found guilty of treason, they were executed in 1953.) Genet asks the question again: "[...] what are you going to do for Jackson, Seale, Clutchette, Drumgo, the New York 21? What are you going to do, they're black?" The public is up against the wall, but what about Genet?

The last element of this constellation is found after George Jackson's death in prison in August 1971. "After the Assassination" is responding to a more precise circumstance: a possibility, the liberation and life of George Jackson, is no more; he is dead. Then and there, against all odds, Genet praises the Rosenbergs: "To return to Jackson's assassination, and to the imbecilic and transparent fable put forth by the warden of San Quentin [covering up the murder: "there was too much wind"], I will say that the only way to refuse the goals of the white administration is to combat it head on, or to betray it."[52] The syntax is broken, in the same way a heart might be. To lend weight to this advice, he gives an example, the same as always: "We do not know whether the Rosenbergs committed treason or not—if they did, their treason was noble, even in the medieval sense of the word." A Jew may be beautiful if he betrays: an almost racist comment, insofar as it tries to make the traitor appear behind the Jew, or use treason to make the Jew disappear.

In his last book, in 1986, this logic reappears when Genet speaks of Illan Halévy: "There's only one Jew, a former Israeli, among the leaders of the PLO: Illan Halery [*sic*]. The PLO and the Palestinians trust him because he's completely rejected Zionism."[53] In the manuscript, Genet returned three times to the singularity of this name: it was important to him. In the same way, Genet must name, in *Prisoner of Love*, "Élie Cohen," a Jew who infiltrated the Palestinians, and was hanged in Damascus for treason in 1965: "[...] every Palestinian, every Arab even, felt threatened by Jewish espionage."[54] Cohen appeared in the 1971 text devoted to the Palestinians[55]: this is also important to him. With Cohen and Halévy, it is less about the fear of treason than the risk, or the chance, of becoming another, the question of limits. Treason's logic, fueled by the fear of separation and legacy, the invention of a heritage never bequeathed, demands that Genet cannot wish for the disappearance of a single Jew. He would prefer for everyone to definitively separate himself from what he was before. Except that the transformation is a one-way street.

Genet never explicitly expressed what we have been able to clear up here, but without him, we could not say it. It is about methodology: comparison, transfer, what is exemplary. Seale through Dreyfus' eye in America, Jackson through the Rosenbergs' in France: the point of comparison is always Jewish. Better yet, the logic of Genet's discourse is binary. According to that logic, blacks are victims, Jews are beautiful when treasonous, and whites are sitting on their asses, most of the time on gold. On one side, the black man is alone. On the other stand the rest: whites since they're American, Jews since they are white, and a judge, Julius J. Hoffman, who has found Bobby Seale guilty. The fight against racism (black genocide) in the name of another racism (anti-white); the logic of sameness or the exemplary (Hoffman standing in for the Jews)—this is the conclusion of this rather blunt political view. It is the imbecilic side of the fable, and it concerns racism. Another logic is at work in the same process. Seale and the Rosenbergs are temporarily on the same side. They struggle, in different circumstances and by various means—treason, the will to trial, and the translation of a legacy—against intolerable governments and war. The intolerable itself does not possess an immutable definition; it must be fought wherever it arises. This other logic, the struggle for independence and bursting forth, is mobile, tactical, it allows events to surface.

The Black Panthers and the Palestinians—while Genet was with them and before and after him as well—all have fought windmills: windmills of racist language and the fear that follows it. Petitions have no effect on them. These mills of language have been mills of death for more than one man since the beginning of time.

In Beirut, in the Shatila camp, on Sunday, September 19, 1982, and within the lines of "Four Hours in Shatila" published in January 1983 in the *Revue d'études palestiniennes*—Genet can be found there. He briefly turns himself into a Palestinian, then a *Muslim brother*, perhaps even a man capable of hate speech.

Yet Genet refuses the possibility of becoming Palestinian in his last book: "It was quite easy to help the revolutionaries, but impossible to become a Palestinian."[56] A first reading of "Four Hours in Shatila" can be seen as a critique of violence.[57] Then we must understand the achievement of this impossibility, a new reading of the events at Shatila as the poet's passage toward the collapse of his vocabulary. On

Saturday, September 18, 1982, after a thirty-six-hour massacre, more than 1,000 Palestinians were left dead in the Sabra and Shatila camps. The carnage was committed by Christian militias, the Phalangists, as Israeli soldiers looked on, after Israel's army occupied Southern Lebanon.[58] Genet became a witness, or more to the point, he testifies about the fate of the dead left without a prayer in a massacre that he saw as being "the thousandth and first injury of human history":[59] "After the roads were cut off and the telephone silenced, unable to communicate with the rest of the world, for the first time in my life I felt myself becoming Palestinian and hating Israel."[60]

This is, simply, an impossible possibility of Genet's life that has come to pass. A series of events inexorably led there: removal from the world (cut-off communications and roads), the appearance of a possible and impossible event (the first time), subjective feeling with no political solution (hate). First he is isolated for good from the rest of the world and so, among other things, from Judeo-Christian morals, but also from Europe's history and the Jews' history in Europe, of the memory of the *Shoah*. Isolated from the objective truth of the Jews' suffering, isolated from a certain culture and responsibility, he can freely feel hatred. It is his right, one that is possible only through absolute isolation. The writer takes on the life, the past, the claims, and the language of a nationality that is not his. The isolation is only relative; it is not a decision to hate made in absolute solitude. Hatred takes form in that brief instant between isolation from all identity but one's own and the acceptance of another's nationality: the impossibility of remaining in a desert, growing fat off the identity, the homeland, and the name from which one can hate the foreigner. It is only possible if you forget three conditions: it is impossible to become a Palestinian; the sudden isolation due to the war cannot subsume the solitude to which the writer aspires (for example, "It is in solitude that I accept being with the Palestinians"); and revolution, resistance, and liberation must not be locked into a nationalistic frame. Neither vengeance nor hatred, and especially not the belief in the correct origin, can cast a shadow upon the legitimate will to trial of those who have nothing. The past event (war, occupation, massacres of Sabra and Shatila), the existing circumstance (hate): *temporarily, the disposition of this hatred is not the eternal world of anti-Semitism but the real world of the struggle against Israel.*

Now—"I am writing from Beirut," he will add before writing what follows—but only after forgetting those three conditions, appear three statements—anti-Judaic, anti-Zionist, and anti-Semitic—combined into one. It was written, then partly cut; not at his request, it seems,[61] but probably by the Palestinian Elias Sanbar, director of the magazine that published "Four Hours in Shatila." From it, the irreparable breaks through (between square brackets, read the censured passage):

[The Jewish people, far from being the most unfortunate on earth—the Indians of the Andes have gone deeper into misery and abandonment—as it would have us believe from the genocide, whereas in America, Jews rich and poor had reserves of sperm for procreation, for the continuation of the "chosen" people,] in short, thanks to a skillful yet predictable metamorphosis, it is now what it has long been in the process of becoming: a loathsome temporal power, a colonizer in a way that no one can any longer dare to be, the Definitive Authority that it owes both to its long malediction and to its status as chosen.

[It is taking this loathsome power so far that one may wonder whether, at yet another point in its history, by bringing unanimous condemnation on itself, it does not want to regain its destiny as a wandering, humbled people whose power remains underground. It has now shown itself too much in the terrible light of the massacres it no longer undergoes but inflicts, and it wants to regain the shadows of the past to become once again—supposing it ever was—the "salt of the earth."

But then what a way to behave!

Could it be that the Soviet Union and the Arab countries,

however spineless they may be, by refusing to intervene
in this war, would therefore have allowed Israel finally to
appear before the world and in broad daylight as a madman
among nations?]

Many questions remain.[62]

The appearance of the collapsed vocabulary: in this statement, we can make the distinction between what arises from the irony of the victims' victims (massacres they no longer suffer), to the European, Christian anti-Semitism (underground power, money), to revisionism (they made us believe in genocide), to the racist condemnation of an entire people (Jews). These statements have been pushed aside by the disinherited—Panthers and Palestinians in particular—as long as they refuse the logic of ghosts; what still belongs to the critique of the fable (chosenness). All this has to be considered as a single intolerable block.

Genet removes these statements he made in 1982 from his last book. In the draft of *Prisoner of Love*, Genet added, then removed, a page discussing Palestinian guerrillas and terrorism. In this section of the manuscript, he wonders why the USSR, with the "free world," refused to seriously consider these war phenomena. He hypothesizes that the USSR's Jews are the reason for this refusal: peace and territory had to be kept for these people in a region of the world where the USSR no longer had any reason to be. Then, Genet asks himself, "But against who were the Palestinians fighting, shadow people, hidden by the mists and shadows?" If the question is asked this way, Genet must already know the answer. "The Soviet Union also refused to take it seriously and referred to it as terrorism,"[63] and in answering the question he himself has asked, he writes what we cannot read, having scratched out the lines from the last book so they disappear:

There was a certain fear, a frightening grandeur, to walk
out of the gas chambers, to [unreadable], climb out from
among the dead, and through ruse settle down in a beautiful
country, to carry once again the tools of the peasant and the

habits of the burnt land, even if promised. When shadows
return from the grave and become soldiers they give
themselves the right to use any means to send others into
the land of the dead. More ferocious than all were not the
Jews but the American Jews. They would not have ...[64]

These last lines are written at the bottom of the page; the text stops.
No more students' notebooks that should logically follow this one.
The text probably continues elsewhere.

In truth, in his last book Genet retained this fear of ghosts and
shadows, but dispersed. In "One," he came back to these thoughts:
"We should always remember that the Palestinians have nothing, neither passport nor territory nor nation, and if they laud and long for all
those things it's because they see only ghosts of them." He used the
word "dream" originally, which he changed to "ghosts." In "Two," he
came back twice to what "[...] prevented the Palestinians from seem-
ing quite real. An Israeli seeing them as a people of dream, of shadows rather than flesh and blood." He also wrote: "It seemed to me the
distance between the two lots of recalcitrants was infinite [...]"[65] The
link between these two sets of ghosts is due to a certain Mr Mustapha: a Muslim man married to a German woman. He appears rather
quickly after the first statement, whereas the second is directly placed
in his mouth, quotation marks and all.[66] Genet transforms himself into
a *Muslim brother*; that is to say, in his own words, capable of things like
those we have just read, even if he states he, "never [having] gained
access to their infernal secrets, as a reader in the old days might be
admitted to the forbidden books in the Enfer of the Bibliothèque Nationale," was capable of "heinous statements."[67]

The question of the other haunts Genet. It finds its form within a
terrifying connection that links the enemy and his shadow. The same
expression describes ancient enemies: "shadow people." Palestinians
and Israelis are reflected in the author's eyes, but the Israeli shadows
come from far, far way. What is forgotten? Between the self and the
other, the right distance—so that all these men are not thrown to-

gether, carried off in the same inhuman disappearance, the same fire. In other words, to reflect on the enemy is to seek the invention of the other, to understand the link to the other and the question of limits. We will look at this question as a conclusion to this story.

The hatred for France and provisional admiration for Hitler are intertwined in the same way as the love for the Palestinians and the circumstantial hate for Israel. Yet the defeat of France was also the massacre of Jews, if the Palestinian victory is won politically over the Israelis; an astounding collusion on Genet's part. The child become old stands with legs spread, one foot on a little mound of mud (France), the other in Beirut. Genet as Gulliver, great or small, it depends. Here, only his smallness remains.

A moment of folly—"if not crazy," I wrote of this testimony, "Four Hours in Shatila." And now the scratched-out page of his last book, for which Genet is responsible.

ENEMIES

"What language had they spoken there? None of them knew Arabic. Greek and Latin, perhaps?"[68] Less of a question than an address to the first Jews to arrive in Palestine, the answer must be found in Genet's language. The language war is not the final word in the *Querela Pacis*, but its foundation: here, it produces a collapse of vocabulary. Fables, history, and language today are carried in the same hand: the seam between the world and the writer, where the rules of the grammatical world and the law of exterior reality join together:

> In other days I think I'd have avoided words like heroes,
> martyrs, struggle, revolution liberation, resistance, courage
> and such-like. I probably have avoided the words homeland
> and fraternity, which still repel me. But there's no doubt that
> the Palestinians caused a kind of collapse in my vocabulary.
> I accept it in order to put first things first, but I know there's
> nothing behind such words. And precious little behind all
> the others.[69]

The writer is also subject to collapse. Between these two moments of this argument with the self and language appears a transformation. The first time he introduces the question of collapse, Genet tells us he wishes to rethink a choice. The second time, he speaks of a friendship as the source of this collapse. In other words, collapse is the consequence of a meeting. Genet is not alone with language.

Very little has been written on the war between the Palestinians and Israelis in regards to language. It's not unexpected that Genet decided to pick up the task. He now observes the glint of Hebrew in the Palestinians' eye: first in Paris, then in occupied Beirut, ending in his last book. Genet provides an episode from this war as he himself saw it on the occasion of King Hussein's visit to Paris, at the Opera: a minor episode in which two slogans had been spray-painted on the monument, from which the markings have no doubt been erased, yet still a reminder of a terrible war. In "Two," as Genet speaks of his long military service in Damascus, Syria, in 1930, he is overwhelmed by the word "memory" and writes: "The distance between 'Palestine shall conquer' and 'Israel shall live' is that between a sword blow and a bud. And that chance metaphor, though only a figure of speech, makes me fear military defeat."[70] The two slogans illustrate the fight for the same territory, which is vocabulary. Yet the one used at the end of the twentieth century—"Israel shall live"—obliterates another that appeared at the beginning of the same century. Apocryphal, who remembers it now? "A land without people for a people without land:" another slogan, by Theodore Herzl, the father of Zionism.[71] Between the two, and on the occasion of his own language war, Genet darkens his discourse. The expression "simple rhetoric device" is an understatement that hides a dreadful abyss.

In 1986, the episode about slogans is at first sight the foundation of the larger war on vocabulary: the apparent praise for Israeli rhetoric. In truth, under the guise of detached and disseminated formulas in his last book, the war continues, always present, word after word in

Genet's vocabulary. In 1973, in the quite singular context of the seventies, in the critique of violence and the will to trial of infamous men, Genet gave a description of the master: "to be the master: determining the meaning of words, bestowing them with a morality, or, to the contrary, take away this meaning to replace it with a vile weight." He then writes, during the Munich attacks and the increased visibility of the Palestinians, "The choice of words made the Palestinians outlaws." From there, in the day's vocabulary, "since imperialism and its outgrowth, Zionism, are the most recent incarnations of Judeo-Christian morality, itself master of defining its lexicon."[72] In *Prisoner of Love*, at a crucial moment of his adventure, he concentrates his attack: "Words are terrible, and Israel is a terrifying manipulator of signs." Better yet, and still in 1986: "Israel, imposing its morals and myths on the whole world, saw itself as identical with power."[73] Identical to the point of confusion, Genet tells us.

He does not restrain himself from using, in 1973, the argument that states that Jews manipulate the press. Again in 1986, telling the story of the assassination of three Palestinians committed by the Mossad in Beirut, Genet, in a trembling voice, writes about Israel's tendency to magnify its successes: "You may suppose Israel praised the exploit in its newspapers in Jerusalem and other cities."[74] "Jerusalem and other cities" seems miniscule perhaps, but we cannot ignore the posterity of the statement. The logic of this sort of comment has been explained beforehand: the Jew, in the same way as man, does not exist. This comment akin to conspiracy theory must not go uncriticized. Pushed further still than the praise of Israel's rhetoric, the writer must not let himself be carried away by European anti-Semitic clichés. This type of discourse begins with statements about the press, and ends with the inquisitors' judgments of books, if not men. In this sense, the vocabulary of the will to trial—the Panthers' trial, the Palestinians,' or the writer's—embraces this political language that soon turns religious. It confuses earth and heaven, the particular and the universal; it announces a war of the eternal, *against* the eternal, the single country of Israel. This connection makes the language of trial and the will to trial one and the same, something messianic, and causes the collapse of vocabulary. Each time Genet praises Israel or the Jews, his statements must be identified as *sarcastic praise*. In this sense, it reveals a secret. In 1973, Genet dashed this off: "There appears censure whenever it is time to question the origins of the Jewish state."[75] And he followed up in 1986 with: "My friendship with the Palestinians is at the origin of the collapse of my vocabulary." The writer's past must be the bridge between these two statements. But in a definitive manner, very early on, *the "master's language" is identified with the Jew's language.*

Lebanon, 1982. As the hegemonic policy begins to take effect in the city's streets, writing under the occupation becomes an urgent and necessary act. Genet's relation with the enemy's language moves him to write these lines: "Arriving in Beirut from Damascus and seeing those signposts at the crossroads was as painful as seeing Gothic lettering in Paris during the occupation. The trilingual road signs reminded you of the Rosetta stone, but the languages were English, Arabic, and Hebrew."[76]

For the third time he finds himself in an occupied city. In 1930, Genet was in Damascus, Syria. In his last book he looks back: "[...] for the first time in my life I saw a city in the power of young soldiers. For me Damascus meant three things: exoticism, freedom and the army."[77] The occupying army is the colonial French one, the occupied are Syrian Arabs, the writer a soldier. He thinks of himself at that time as a "janissary" for the colonizer; more than a colonizer, he feels Turkish. The second time is in 1940, in Paris, as a prisoner of the German army. In the Tourelles camp, he risks death but is freed. He then writes his first book and is delighted by the French army's defeat at the hands of the Germans. I have said this. Yet in his last book, to a certain extent, he revises what had become his vulgate: the shame of the French, his joy, the Nazi triumph. Describing the fantastic transformation (in his eyes) of the French into their own immigrant labor, following the Exodus, he writes: "I watched the metamorphosis with jubilation, but with the carefully hidden distress of being excluded from it."[78] Instead of being part of the friendship born of flight or collaboration, the writer feels excluded.

The third time is Beirut in 1982. The occupying army belongs to Israel, and the occupied are Arabs, Lebanese, or Palestinian. For the first time, and provisionally, Genet feels himself "becoming Palestinian": a player in 1930, jubilant but separate in 1940, has he become a jubilant Palestinian in 1982?

Genet sees the reflection of the Paris occupation by German troops in Beirut's occupation by Israel's. He compares two of the three occupations he's experienced; a comparison we've heard before, and one we have to watch out for in case it returns. Genet feels sadness in 1986. Yet he was joyous in 1940. A contradiction? Excluded from the Parisian metamorphosis, Genet in Beirut has become provisionally Palestinian. Like the languages on the signpost and the armies in the streets, Genet's position has changed: occupier (Damascus), occupied (Paris, Beirut). Except for the relation to Hitler, Nazism, and genocide: it remains fixed, does not allow metamorphosis or resistance. If Genet wishes to become a partisan now, for the first time, he can't give in to a former comparison that won't allow him to resist. Real resistance would mean renouncing this comparison: Hitler, the hyperbole of the remembrance of occupation.

"Fire came down from the sky": a sequence from his last book opens on the gap between sky and earth, and it ends with the expression of peace recovered. This abyss tears the book in two. One last time, on the road to Beirut, retracing his footsteps, the writer looks at Hebrew letters. This look back on these inscriptions is a response to the ugly passages from 1982 seen before. More than that, it offers a response not to Israel, not even to Hebrew, but to a *dead language* inside him that he recognizes and wishes to understand, if only to get rid of it: the moral tongues of Judaism and Christianity, languages of power, of law even, since Genet feels the will to trial. The refrain of the times, the old comparison with Hitler, gives way to another, the appearance of a prehistoric animal with a huge body and tail. Its name, from the Greek *deînos*, means terrible:

> The Hebrew characters, drawn rather than written and carved rather than drawn, induced a sense of unease, like a quiet herd of dinosaurs. Not only did this writing belong to the enemy, it was also an armed sentry standing over the people of Lebanon. I had a childhood memory of seeing these incomprehensible characters carved on two oblong stones joined together lengthwise and called the Tables of Law. I say "carved" because the illusion of relief was given by alternations of light and shade. Most of the letters were squat and rectangular; they read from right to left in a broken horizontal line. One or two had a crane-like plum on top: three slim pistils bearing three stigmata and waiting for the bees who'd scatter their age-old, nay primeval, pollen all over the world. But the feathers—they belonged to a letter that sounded rather like sh—didn't add a touch of lightness. They expressed the cynical triumph of *Tsahal*, and had the slightly foolish grandeur of a peacock's head or of a dumb girl waiting to be serviced. [...] That writing hadn't only surged up from childhood. Though it had been presented to the world on top of a mountain, it came from the cave, dark and deep, in which God, Moses, Abraham, the Tables, the Torah and the Commandments had been imprisoned.
>
> Now back at the crossroads belonging to a prehistory before prehistory, and even if we didn't know much about Freud, we felt the enormous pressure which after two thousand years had brought about the Return of the Repressed.
>
> But above all we were surprised and repelled by the terrifying discontinuity: the letters were separated by immeasurable spaces filled with several layers of time—a time as dead and incalculable as the space between a corpse and a living eye looking at it. In the space between each Hebrew letter, generations have been born and spread

abroad, and its silence shattered us worse than bullets and bombs.

Ajloun, my favorite place, at peace again, was mine.[79]

The writer's time is superimposed on the time of the occupation, and immediately we return to the beginning of time. The two remembrances coexist in occupation and in law: Genet now ascertains what he believes to be the language of origins. It births a bestiary.

An adventure took place. It concerns language, the invention of Modern Hebrew. Genet remembers it. Israel's varying political projects depended on the choice of tongue. Members of the Jewish diaspora spoke the various languages of the countries in which they resided, as well as Yiddish. Genet read Herzl, he says as much in 1972 while writing of the Palestinians, about the "massacring [of] phantoms."[80] Herzl was against the use of Hebrew: "It is unimaginable for us to speak Hebrew among ourselves. Who among us speaks Hebrew enough to buy a railway ticket in that language?"[81] For Herzl, German would become the Jews' language in Palestine. Hebrew triumphed for historical reasons: the refusal to speak the language of the ghettos (Yiddish), then the refusal to speak the language of the destruction of the ghettos (German). But what Hebrew? Eliezer Ben Yehuda (1858–1922) was the creator of the language. He wrote a dictionary and made his wife use the new words, so that "the first children would be born whose babblings would be in Hebrew."[82] Ben Yehuda's son, Itamar Ben Avi, wished to perfect his father's work: he proposed Latinizing the Hebrew alphabet. This would have secularized the language by separating it from its religious past. He would have no success. If he had, Genet would not have been able to write his page on the Beirut signposts. This language is a volcano.

Trying to untangle the determinations of the Hebrew vocabulary is far from easy, as Genet well understood, having tried. The historian Alain Dieckhoff, in a chapter focusing on Israel's birth, entitled "Hebrew, the Language of a Nation," skips a step in his analysis. "Even though Israeli Hebrew uses the language base of classical Hebrew, in reality it is a new language [...]." It would seem that Hebrew is a modern language. Then, later, "Although modern Hebrew became a language for secular use, it retained because of its origin and its relation to liturgical Hebrew, a sort of holy status [...]." Thus, modern Hebrew has become a profane language, although it has kept, by its relationship with liturgical Hebrew, a certain religious character. From this stems the conjuring trick: "Hebrew, the sacred language of the religious congregation, became that of the national community. It had once been in the service of God, now it was in the service of the nation."[83] In this last statement, we do not know of which Hebrew we are speaking, whether ancient or modern, religious or secular. Concluding these confusions—appearance/reality, although/because—the modern profane tongue and the dead sacred language have become one: Hebrew. God's Hebrew and the nation's Hebrew, fused into one. Immediately recognized as one of Palestine's official languages with English and Arabic, Dieckhoff can conclude by saying, "Accepting Hebrew in the conduct of the Mandatory government administration was to impose it as a language of authority, as had been done with French by François I with the Villers Cotterêts Ordinance of 1539."[84] Faced with the language of power—not power in general but specifically, geographically, and historically located power, the power of the Israeli State as it wages a war of occupation with nationalistic motivation—Genet refuses the enemy's language. Up until then, the scene of signposts is one of resistance.

Now he begins to transcribe Mustapha's words: "If it isn't certain the Palestinians are direct descendants of the Canaanites, it's even less sure Miss Golda Meir was the great-granddaughter of Moses, David and Solomon."[85] Genet doesn't entirely buy into this statement. Yet Dieckhoff, who earlier described the history of the promotion of a mother tongue—idiom of the Jewish nation and then official language—judges the question to be crucial. We will look attentively, once again, at Genet's surprising sympathy to linguistic struggles, to the exact correspondence between the *Prisoner of Love*'s vocabulary and the historical question brought forward by Dieckhoff. In this quarrel of languages, Genet swims comfortably, although drowning awaits, or even collapse. Here is, in Dieckhoff's words, an outcrop of this adventure: "Was not the fact that [David] Ben Gurion apparently spoke the same language as Moses the best guarantee of legitimacy of Zionism?"[86] As such, Genet asks the right question: "What language had they spoken there? None of them knew Arabic. Greek and Latin, perhaps?" In a handwritten note, this question is revisited through this comment in his last book: "If I were a Jew ..."[87] His memories now confuse the origin of his friendship, his passion for the origins themselves, and the religious and political fable of the origin of the Laws.

Due to Genet's historical confusion—identification between ancient and modern Hebrew—and his subjective collusion, he mistakes Hebrew signposts in Beirut for the Tables of Covenant. He condemns what he believes to be the language of origins. In the terrible discontinuity of the letter (Hebrew), he sees the frightful continuity of a people (Chosen): procreation, birth, ejaculate. If a bird has attached itself to the writer's neck, what does he fear? Memory, transmission, and legacy. Fastened on the single letter *ch*, the letter we find in the first word of the first book of the Old Testament (Genesis, 1, *berechit*, in the beginning), the scene in Beirut is transformed into a war against the Verb. By sending poetic aggression against the "terrifying discontinuity," the first and second parts of *Prisoner of Love*, Genet eliminates war and anarchy, but *through* war; he creates order through disorder. This page, and the following parts of the book, are thus less a mythological questioning of the languages of heaven than a political statement that does not declare the end of the war, but continues stirring up the quarrel of peace. As such, *the entirety of Genet's last book, if this page is read as beginning and end, is an act of anarchy.*

Judgment, fire, and heaven, Genet's last book can be read as a growing sense of dread. The fixation on war and origins forces the author to look far behind him, to his childhood, and gives birth to a prehistoric bestiary. They are fastened to a single signpost, or a letter, a book. Judgment is what distinguishes us, separates, splits. The Tables of the Covenant are also split, before Moses broke them. Through this story, the writer repeats the very ancient act of judgment, of separation—in the end, bursting forth. Will we judge that it is still wanting? He is stopped by the letter, but as a sign of Law: the rules of the exterior world, and grammatical rules. Have we come forth to receive the law, or is it because we have come forth that we received it? What of Genet's coming out if he wishes to break the law?

The assault on the verb, in other words, the war against a certain legacy lodged in language, this is the foundation of Genet's adventure. It is the mark of collapse, it drags truth into a bottomless hole, builds it into an edifice without foundation that is not one of falsity, stupidity, or confusion. Genet's statements on language, on the master's language, on mastery as an imposition of language—assigning to a word a moral or infamous charge—are partly true, without a doubt, but what truth and to what extent? The logic of this blindness is more one of blinding lucidity, of insanity or gravity that must speak of our time, our wars, perhaps even our wars of religion.

The writer who recognizes himself in the fable of race, the one who feels the myth of origins, seems to be the heir who does not refuse his inheritance, no matter the indecency of its origin, born of the clearest imposture: the use of the fable by power, moralizing through politics. *He carries the weight of legacy, in language, of all power, religion, infamy.* Although his point of departure is his friendship with a Palestinian, the acceptance of this legacy makes of Genet the lowest, in the sense of the worst.

Religious fable and the myth of race are tied together in Genet's mind as an issue of origins. The verb is the rock on which he founders and the sea in which he drowns. The question of language, the question of origins, this is what the writer discovers. Within language, the intuition that through language origin is brought down—he feels a terrible sadness, one of historical size. This sadness is political since the questions it carries are the foundation of all nations, of all societies, of man.

ENDNOTES

1. M. Olender, *The Languages of Paradise: Race, Religion, and Philology in the Nineteenth Century*, trans. Arthur Goldhammer (Cambridge: Harvard University Press, 2008).
2. *CCNY Observation Post*, March 13, 1970; quoted in R. Sandarg, "Jean Genet and the Black Panther Party," *Journal of Black Studies*, March 1986, 272.
3. Malcolm X, A. Haley, *The Autobiography of Malcolm X: As Told to Alex Haley* (New York: Ballantine, 1992), 247.
4. Malcolm X, *The Speeches at Harvard* (New York: W. Morrow, 1968), 169–170.
5. *The Autobiography of Malcolm X*, 347–348.
6. P.S. Foner, *Black Panthers Speak* (Da Capo Press, 2002), 254–255.
7. Foner, *Black Panthers Speak*, 80.
8. C. Garry in *Black Panthers Speak*, 257.
9. B. Seale in *Black Panthers Speak*, 83.
10. Ibid., 84.
11. "May Day Speech" (speech given in New Haven, May 1, 1970); *DE*, 37.
12. In H.E. Weinstein, "Conversation with Cleaver," *The Nation*, January 20, 1969.
13. "Les Palestiniens" (I), *Zoom* 4, August 1971; *DE*, 71–72.
14. E. Saïd, "Reflections on Twenty Years of Palestinian History," *Journal of Palestine Studies* 20, no. 4 (Summer 1991): 12.
15. Ibid., 15.
16. Quoted in T. Segev, *The Seventh Million: the Israelis and the Holocaust*, trans. H. Watzman (New York: Holt Paperbacks, 2000), 113.
17. Ibid., 179.
18. T. Segev, *The Seventh Million*, 161.
19. Quoted by T. Segev in *The Seventh Million*, 293-294.
20. Ibid., 322.
21. M. Darwish, *Memory for Forgetfulness: August, Beirut, 1982*, trans. I. Muhawi (Berkeley and Los Angeles: University of California Press, 1995), 16.
22. "Les Palestiniens" (II), *Shoun Falestine*, 1973: *GC*, 157.
23. D. Hilliard and L. Cole, *This Side of Glory* (Boston, New York: Little Brown and Co., Back Bay Books, 1993), 305.
24. D. Hilliard, *Black Panther Newspaper*, February 17, 1970, in Committee

on International Security, *The Black Panther Party, its origin...* (Washington: US Government Printing, 1970), 17.

25. P.S. Foner, *Black Panthers Speak*, xxi.

26. W. Laquer and B. Rubin, eds., *The Israel-Arab Reader: A Documentary History of the Middle East Conflict* (New York: Penguin, 2008), 130.

27. B. Lewis, *Islam in History: Ideas, Men and Events in the Middle East* (London: Alcove Press, 1973), 146.

28. Laquer and Rubin, *The Israel-Arab Reader*, 162.

29. P.-A. Taguieff, *Les Protocoles des Sages de Sion: Introduction à l'étude des Protocoles, un faux et ses usages dans le siècle* (Paris: Gallimard, 1992), 283, 320.

30. See chapter 6.

31. P.-A. Taguieff, *Les Protocoles des Sages de Sion*, 329, 331, 335.

32. Ibid., 344.

33. L. Poliakov, quoted by S. Kassir and F. Mardam-Bey, *Itinéraires de Paris à Jérusalem: la France et le conflit israélo-arabe* (Paris: Les livres de la *Revue d'études palestiniennes*, t. II, 1993), 205.

34. *PL*, 392.

35. *Our Lady of the Flowers* (New York: Grove Press, 1994), 106.

36. Quoted by E. White, *Genet: A Biography* (New York: Vintage Books, 1994).

37. *Lettres à Olga et Marc Barbezat* (Décines: L'Arbalète, 1988), 22.

38. E. White, *Genet: A Biography*, 244.

39. M. Ferro, *Colonization: a Global History*, 323.

40. *Funeral Rites* (New York: Grove Press, 1994), 32, 116, 160, 177.

41. "Interview with Hubert Fichte," *Die Zeit*, February 13, 1976: *DE*, 125–126.

42. In the interim, we have learned Jean Genet's other name: his father was called "Fréderic Blanc," or White (see Albert Dichy, *Jean Genet, essai de chronologie*, Paris: Gallimard, 2010).

43. "Interview with Bertrand Poirot-Delpech," *Le Monde aujourd'hui*, April 20, 1986; *DE*, 198–200.

44. Afnan el Kasm, "Between Pound and Genet, Palestine," in *El Talia'a Arabia* ["Arab avant-garde"] (July 21, 1986); English translation based on the French translation by Basma el Omar and Hadrien Laroche.

45. A. Artaud, "Révélations" (December 1943), *La Tour de feu*, no. 63–64 (June 1948): p. 32.

46. "Here and now for Bobby Seale," *Ramparts* 8, no. 12 (June 1970): 30–31,47.

47. "Letter to American Intellectuals," (speech, University of Connecticut, March 18, 1970); *DE*, 32.

48. "Interview with Michèle Manceaux," *Le Nouvel Observateur*, May 25, 1970; *DE*, 46.

49. "Four Hours in Shatila," *Revue d'études palestiniennes*, n. 6, January 1, 1983; *DE*, 220.

50. *PL*, 19, 45, 151.

51. "For George Jackson" (manifesto mailed in July 1971); *DE*, 68.

52. "After the Assassination" (unpublished writings, August 1971); *DE*, 86.

53. *PL*, 65.

54. *PL*, 167.

55. "The Palestinians" (I); *PL*, 73.

56. *PL*, 230.

57. See chapter 6.

58. A. Kapeliouk, *Sabra and Shatila: Inquiry into a Massacre* (London: Five Leaves, 1984), 89.

59. Interview: "The Thousand and First Injury of Human History," *Palestine al-thawra* [Palestine of the Revolution], no. 560 (June 1985): 46; English translation based on the French translation by Basma el Omari and Hadrien Laroche.

60. "Four Hours in Shatila"; *DE*, 215.

61. *DE*, notes on page 370.

62. "Four Hours in Shatila"; *DE*, 221, 372–373.

63. *PL*, 126.

64. "Un captif amoureux, volume I, Souvenirs I, Souvenirs II" (manuscript, yellow labeled student notebook, Gallimard Collection), 143; *PL*, 125–126.

65. *PL*, 84, 321.

66. Ibid., 89, 322.

67. Ibid., 89–90.

68. Ibid., 323–324.

69. Ibid., 312–313.

70. Ibid., 386–387.

71. I. Halévy, *Arab Studies Quarterly*, Spring–Summer 1983, 6; M. Darwish, *Une mémoire pour l'oubli*, 95.

72. "Les Palestiniens" (II); *GC*, 147–150.

73. *PL*, 166, 374.

74. *PL*, 185.

75. "Les Palestiniens" (II); *GC*, 152.

76. *PL*, 310.

77. *PL*, 382.

78. *PL*, 387.

79. *PL*, 310–311.

80. "Les Palestiniens" (I); *DE*, 71, 2n.

81. T. Herzl, *The State of the Jews*, quoted in A. Dieckhoff, *The Invention of a Nation* (New York: Columbia University Press), 103, 9n.

82. Yehouda, *Le Rêve traversé*, quoted in Dieckhoff, *The Invention of a Nation*, 136.

83. A. Dieckhoff, *The Invention of a Nation*, 104–105.

84. Ibid., 105.

85. *PL*, 323.

86. A. Dieckhoff, *The Invention of a Nation*, 104.

87. *PL*, 324.

10 | The Man Who Gave Birth to Humanism

How does one escape fratricide? Is it possible to forgo nationalism while affirming one's allegiance to a homeland? How does one *belong* to a place without taking part in the worst aspects of this belonging? What vigilance is necessary to need a homeland, a nationality, and a language while keeping intact the desire for constant metamorphosis? What work must one undertake in order not to succumb to the frigid trinity of the nation, the territory, and the language, while avoiding an artistic, erotic, and esthetic brand of politics open to all sorts of abjections? What art must one create to affirm the necessity of politics, of the subjective, of the imperative truth of revolt? What kind of man must one be to tell the story of this immense pain through immense desire?

Not much remains to be said, nothing definitive. There is no system to Genet, perhaps only a *Micro-Treatise on a Mini-Politics*.[1]

LIMITS

"One day in a train compartment while looking at the traveler seated across from me I had the revelation that every man is *worth* every other."[2] A train runs between Salon and Saint-Rambert-d'Albon. Genet was in one of its carriages in 1953. He describes his experience in 1967. This event is an example of what is called the spiritual crisis of the writer.[3] Genet gives two formulaic versions of this revelation: "Every man is every other man and I as much as the others." He still feels "the solitude of being exactly the same as all the others." The sadness, the profound despair, call it "disintegration" even, this is his disposition.

In this same passage on the train and on sadness, Genet feels two other dispositions; he recognizes a belief and feels it is possible to escape this belief: "[...] I knew that I was identical to every man [...] I quickly came to believe that it was this identity which allows every man to be loved, no more and no less than any other [...] identity (a word that keeps coming back, but perhaps only because at the time I didn't have a very rich vocabulary)." He recognizes that his belief in the identity of man may abandon him, that this possibility exists. This first intimate revolution, or perhaps the translation of the writer's thoughts in this train, without beginning, without direction, without end—this is often missed. Yet the parenthesis is a correction of a word, a thought. Now he must not sacrifice "a sort of common identity between all men" to this belief.

The author's interior monologue continues. He returns in 1973 to an event—felt first in 1953, written down in 1967—that combines men, love, and language. On the occasion of his first trip to Jordan, he feels both this same experience and its opposite. The same words return. Perhaps Genet is thinking back to his experience on the French train. Better yet, he corrects this sadness with joy, a dance of revolutionary movements that he is now partaking in. As a witness, he looks back on his trip to Jordan: "In the Palestinian camps, I dealt with the opposite: I changed in the sense that my relationships with others changed, since every relationship was different. No man is interchangeable with another."[4] While in Europe, due to innate laziness, he had gotten used to considering the function of men rather than men themselves. Now, "we only noticed the man, independently of his function, and this function did not serve to maintain in place a system, but rather to destroy one." In other words, he adds, the revolutionary desire had not only changed those who felt it, "but I with them." This second revolution, within the same experience, is a prelude to his liberation.

Yet we must be careful not to oppose 1953 Europe to 1973 Arabia. The experience in the camps cannot be substituted by the one in the train. No progress, no idealism, no teleology: the revolutionary experience would be destroyed if it imposed order. Genet's introspection, his changed vision of others, a change in the writer's conversation with himself and others that moves him to drop the word "identity" for "relationship": this is a true metamorphosis, no more, no less. Perhaps only a small one, but with the possibility all the same of a temporary accord with men, though changing, floating.

In his last book, a new movement within the same experience of identity and relationship begins: a generalized return to old identity, the uninterrupted travesty, permanent metamorphosis, depending on whether we choose a historical-religious, sexual, or political vocabulary. An immense tribe of men and women, at every moment, in countless places and perfectly determined circumstances—by their names, vocabularies, or sexes—is called into being, be it human, animal, or material. "Joy of the transsexual, [...] of the kamikaze,"[5] Genet writes. Between two worlds—the expression not only describes every man Genet meets, but it places him in every chapter of the story, at every age—this moment and this age describe both time and space— "every being becomes his own shadow, and thus something other than himself."[6] Genet writes this on September 8, 1985. He must act quickly now, the child become an old man will pass, never born. He will die, the ultimate change.

Yet the writer remains vigilant. The transformation of oneself into another demands much energy. He fears what he calls "logical reflection." On that same page from September 1985, he particularly fears the invisible metamorphosis of a fedayee into a Muslim brother. Genet wants neither his own ghostly presence, always dangerous since it allows racism, nor the grayness of death. What we see is a certain madness, the unreason between life and death. Madness of the day, madness of identity, madness of murder if the enemy is an other, madness now recognized for what it is: "[...] the young men would eat here just like Arabs, wiping the fingers on the thighs of their trousers. Maybe, in Tel Aviv, they ate like Jews."[7]

Identity, then relationship, affinity after, metamorphosis finally; slowly, the author is discovering a new vocabulary. He sketches out a political possibility: a constitution created by "men from everywhere."

BORDERS

The event that is the experience both on and off the train, this movement between the identity of men, among them Genet, leads the questioning about nations. The train crosses borders. The critique of identity, the basis of all nationalistic policy, becomes an attack on the notions of homeland, border, and territory. His questioning of limits is more than just a writer's concern: his history is already one of limits. Insurmountable walls or a simple chalk circle of language: the prisoner wishes to know them all.

His questioning of the notions of nation, country, and homeland give a rhythm to his political action. Genet must face these questions. There is an order, an imperative: he begins his penultimate text devoted to the Black Panthers in August 1971. Jackson is dead, he has written a book, Genet is distressed: "It is time now to ask to what extent a man belongs to a country in which, all things considered, he was born by chance."[8] He mentions the birth of an old idea that will later be picked up by others, notably on the occasion of the 1993 creation of the European parliament of writers in Strasbourg. Genet continues this imperative: "Whose compatriot, then—to go back to this question—was George Jackson if not ours, we who read, loved, and admired his book, and the people—I mean entire peoples, immense countries of men—for whom, from the depths of Soledad Prison, he wrote his book?" Solitude may be first, but it is felt late and decides whether men wish to belong to a people. A person's solitude opens him to the immensity of the masses. Belonging not to a nation or a country, but to a people of readers—not always the same book and not always the same people—is already something. A possible ramification of the question of nation may well produce a community of books to come, not the Book but books, disquiet, waiting, interrupted. This is just an idea, not a final thought. The idea of compatriots will not return. Belonging to a country demands detachment.

In a page devoted to the region—not the religion, although the ground is said to be sacred—of Chartres Cathedral, chosen for this occasion, Genet asks himself what the word "nation" means. In 1977, the article was completely overlooked or misunderstood by *L'Humanité* readers, who saw it as a petition for a new nationalism. "A country is not a fatherland." And then: "The fatherland is not a nation. At best, it can be a threatened nation, an ill nation, a wounded or troubled nation." Then more: "Each country has its own spirit, yes; so what? Each country, in fact, has 'its right to difference,' so what? And each region its own."[9] This dual negative definition that reciprocally separates homeland and nation is transformed into an escape from two credos, one ancient, one modern: genius and difference. Genius is idiocy, difference is a cliché: isolating someone within their genius or attempting to see what separates a man from another is but a single movement that Genet wishes to avoid. Hate is exacerbated when differences become formal and assimilation substantial. Love, soon transformed into hate, each time suggests at best an attempt at understanding the other that identifies him as what we believe we are; at worst, the war with the other based on what we believe he isn't. In fact, questioning identity has already put the problem in a new way: a man is and is not interchangeable with any other. Genius, difference? Solitude, more likely. In passing, Genet wishes to explore a new word: "Let us take up the old-fashioned word 'affinity.' Men who have the same affinities are not in the same chocolate egg."[10] Meaning in the same fatherland. Had not Tristan Tzara risen up against "the chocolate nationalism, the vanilla vanity and the almost Swiss stupidity of some of our more precise fellow citizens!"[11] Affinity is a word that will stick.

There will always be someone, in a country more real than imaginary, demanding "Your ID!" Nation, homeland, region, province, plot, workplace—territory can be broken down into a thousand scattered pieces, in which men "will go work and die anywhere."

In this same rough draft, Genet finally imagines a small homeland. More to the point, he dreams up a draft of a homeland. "We can imagine a fatherland consisting of the following: eight Moroccans, seven Japanese, eleven Germans, fifteen Cubans, a few French, a single Beauceron, etc."[12] The unfinished list is a composite, but necessary for the writer. It is built on the successive or simultaneous affinities of the writer with certain men. Five nationalities, one regional identity, and the foreign writer make seven. Genet lived in Morocco, in Japan a young woman welcomed him, Germany won't leave him alone, Cubans are still communists, the French are abhorred, a Beauceron—from northern France—is probably beautiful. His fatherland is without Palestinians; they shall have their own if they wish. This is an invitation, for each and in any circumstance, to continue yesterday's men in a new way, and invent a temporary and imaginary fatherland, then defend it.

The stones and stained glass of Chartres—archaeologists have recently discovered its clumsy imitation on a Sudanese gold coin, an Arab touch—give way to Shatila's ruins: the writer's monuments do not keep the nation compact. He underlines the fractures, shows the debris, is a witness to the ravages of the idea of nation. On this occasion, he explains not so much a belonging as a worrisome trend. In 1982, in "Four Hours in Shatila," he writes: "If someone chooses a particular community outside of his birth—whereas to belong to this people one must be born into it—this choice is based on an irrational affinity [adhésion]." He continues for those who are hard of hearing: "I am French, but I defend the Palestinians entirely, without judgment."[13] By writing this sentence, he does not renew the necessity of questioning one's belonging; neither does he imagine a community. He is answering his own twelve-year-old imperative about the meaning of nation. Without judgment, he decides to temporarily belong to what people hope will become a nation. He makes a political choice.

This remarkable choice of a particular community possesses the form and duration of a kept promise. Yet who wishes to hold a promise this way? In December 1983, Genet explains the limits of his belonging: "The day the Palestinians become a nation like other nations, I won't be there anymore." Will he have died or no longer be a partisan? So as not to leave the comment unclear, he adds: "I don't know if I'd be able, while alive, to adhere to a territorially whole Palestine. But is that what's important? I ask myself."[14] He does not deny the promise, but confirms the tenacity of the fidelity to himself.

Who are George Jackson's compatriots? All right: each nation has its genius and each country "its right to difference," but so what? What is the point in believing in a Palestinian homeland? Faced with these three important questions, Genet writes in his last book, "But now as then I'm fascinated by the comedy of hatred and the comedy of friendship, both of them often feigned, which still govern the drawing up of [borders]."[15] The tone is truly typical of *Prisoner of Love*: the quiet voice, speaking to himself, free with laughter. Borders are human. He goes on to give a definition: "A [border] is an ideal line that mustn't be tampered with except with the agreement of both the peoples concerned. Yet both sides keep a fierce watch over the boundary and the crossing of it. Hence the comedy of [border] agreements, where the negotiators' faces range from the darkly threatening to the charmingly meek." To see both sides of the line at the same time, meaning to see the faces that men make while drawing them, is a new event for Genet. "A border [*marche*] is where human personality expresses itself most fully, whether in harmony or in contradiction with itself." This *marche* (a march, a border district, especially in time of war) is a memento of the border, but ancient. Toward the end of the twelfth century, the game of family alliances, inheritances, and tribute breaks the limits of the kingdom into marches."[16] Because they are a place where men can express themselves freely, we must observe the consequences, for the movements that surround it, of the definition of homeland and its limits.

Genet ties himself to two movements, the Palestinians and Black Panthers, and what they share is a lack of territory. He wrote in his last book: "Their two situations [...] are not completely identical, but they are alike in that neither group has any territory of its own."[17] The first group looks for the liberation of part of the American territory, the second an independent nation in the Middle East. *Is the writer's questioning of identity and nation—two terms he wants to wear out—compatible with the wish of the disinherited to form a people and belong to a nation?* Does the question conclude with contradiction or laughter? It is the question I have tried to answer throughout these pages and again now with the example of the Palestinian homeland. For a moment let us put aside these movements' demands, the richness of Genet's disposition, and the break between himself and the movements.

The collapse of vocabulary is again the keystone of this political question. Heroes, martyrs, struggle, revolution, resistance, courage, and more so homeland and fraternity are words that provoke this collapse.[18] The political vocabulary affects the writer's language, but he attacks the statist rhetoric, sometimes democratic, as well as the revolutionary vulgate, sometimes anarchist. Genet stands, legs spread, over the border that separates these two ways of speaking polity. He observes the reflection of the misery of the government in the eyes of the governed. The logic behind this discourse, that takes aim at power, is criticized while being experienced. Political coming out is not the humanity-destroying process we believe it to be, but it does call for a new political vocabulary and creates a quarrel among men.

I repeat the question: is the critique of nation compatible with the will to territory among the disenfranchised? As a question of limits, certainly. Malcolm X wondered about that when it came to electoral fraud, but the question is valid for borders between countries, the protections that separate nations, the invisible lines that close Europe to all that is unlike her: "I haven't ever seen any Negro changing any lines. They don't let him get near the line. It's the white man who does this."[19] Let's take color for what it is, without importance now. Let's not draw any new borders now, "Which are [...] traps,"[20] Genet tells us. We must ask ourselves instead: who are the ones looking after limits? What does seeing a limit signify? What of the uncauterized limit between two eras?

The last definition of nation, appearing early but remaining in the 1977 draft, is this: "The true fatherland, every fatherland, is a wound."[21] The same examples return: occupied France, the Palestinian resistance. "Not long ago, the French fatherland was both sparse and unified during the Occupation. Today the Palestinian fatherland exists because it is bruised and wounded." The positive definition of nation is not new; it remains a variant of the national unity theme. Sacred, it is born when faced with peril. The examples shed a different light: Europe and the Middle East, resistance and collaboration, link, difference, and movement between a fatherland found in, and lasting only as long as, exile ("For the following five years, France was a nation for many less French"), and exile at the origin of a nation, that will perhaps not last much longer than the occupation that will be brought to an end. A wound, a hurt, and the scar that speaks for it. At the same time, following the temporality of a single movement that lasts for seventeen years, following the thread of his reflection on the borders that build nations, Genet summons a last wish. At the twilight of his life: "It might be a good thing to extend border areas indefinitely [...]."[22] A nation is a unit both permanent and transitory, if not necessary: a wound opened, then closed.

Genet's political standpoint is not a critical revisiting of colonization; it challenges its modern incarnations. In America, he sees a novel form of internal colonization, insofar as the separation between the mother country (the *metropole*) and the colony is geographically absent. Conversely, in the Middle East, Israelis and Palestinians must liberate themselves from territory: the same land for colonization and population, liberated or occupied, is inextricably bound up. In Europe in general and in France in particular, "Here and now, we can see that our colonized people, who perhaps appear to us like shadows in our midst, are about to become our adversaries in our own country."[23] The creation of men from everywhere into self-colonized people, prisoners of imaginary territories, from within limits imposed or desired, captives of a shadow they refuse to see—this is naked political truth.

To establish the limits of identity and of the nation is a difficult act. An act of solidarity would be to attempt its expression, the movement between the world and the universe of language. To feel the necessary separation, both these elements have to find the right distance.

The human wound, the identity wound, the wound of the nation now; today, the writer has managed to put his finger on it. Can he do any better?

MARGINS

Language is at the foundation of identity and homeland, but also at the heart of the writer. Language must carry the political questioning of the European trinity of values. With it, we must begin again. Genet's writings about the Black Panthers and the Palestinians reflect on the links between these movements and a national or mother tongue. Genet briefly calls for a separate language in the Panthers' case, yet for the Palestinians, he chooses, without abandoning the necessary separation, the simple practice of a concise language. It frees him from shame, and even allows beauty to appear.

In his Introduction to *Soledad Brother*, George Jackson's collected prison letters, a passage, isolated from the others, pertains to the war of languages. The issue of the languages of men from everywhere is a political question: the word "nation" appears again. In July of 1970, he writes: "Here again the prisoner must use the very language, the words, the syntax of his enemy, whereas he craves a separate language belonging only to his people."[24] Proposition, possibility, and promise: but a separate language remains a part of the nation, itself criticized.

In this implacable text, Genet understands the contradictions of an "unfortunate and hypocritical situation." He thus writes of the prisoner, saying: "[...] his hatred for the white man can be expressed only by means of the language belonging equally to blacks and whites. [...] If he writes a masterpiece, it is his enemy's language and treasure that will be enriched by this additional jewel [...]. He has then only one recourse: to accept this language but to corrupt it so skillfully that the whites will be caught in his trap." Hate and the refusal to contribute to the enemy's capital; this message of corruption of capital is not new. This necessary work remains difficult, perhaps even useless. Synchronically, Genet considers that Jackson's work is "contradicted by that of the revolutionary." And here is the second contradiction: the hypocritical situation is echoed by an unfortunate one: "The revolutionary enterprise [...] can be born only [...] by rejecting in disgust and rage, but radically, the values venerated by whites, although this enterprise can continue only on the basis of a common language, at first rejected, finally accepted, whose words will no longer serve the idea taught by whites, but new ones instead." The refusal tails into acceptance, which itself turns into refusal; it's a single enterprise: "[...] poetry contains both the possibility of a revolutionary morality and what seems to contradict it." The impossible possibility of revolution returns on the basis of language, or any other means. Once again, the writer marks the fact that the contradiction was not comprehended, still less resolved: *his unfortunate act attains the limits of this quarrel, his language clouds an unsolvable situation, and the last book finds this way out, even if the author never did.*

Genet and, with him, black Americans, remain on a battlefield not of their choosing. Yet the eye turns, and the retraction from this logic desired by those who govern shows its limits. The will of prisoners for a new tongue is legitimate. Now we must observe its political legitimacy. In this same passage, instead of underlining the link between the search for a national language and an unfortunate situation always susceptible to disappearance, Genet decides to consider the need for a separate language as an obsession: a sexual obsession that makes it so that every time a man sees a black man, he sees the image of "[...] *niggers* hanging[25] [...]." The desire for a separate language always shows its difference within the same gender, not color. Malcolm X expressed a situation that appears less like an unsolvable dilemma and more like a reality calling for struggle: "But since the white man, your 'friend,' took your language away from you during slavery, the only language you know is his language. You know, your friend's language. So you call for the same God he calls for. When he's putting a rope around your neck, you call for God and he calls for God."[26] The lynching, the choking, the fear; a violent end always speaks the truth. The language of the enemy is also the language of the friend. The language of revolutionaries, although separated, is tied to the idea of nation. The language of those who govern must be rejected since it always, as a last resort, calls on the name of God. Let's not forget that the hated language is grafted to the idea of God, black or white. Let's remember the link between the possibility of a separate language and the impossibility of the nation, a necessity and a refusal to avoid celebrating victory too soon. We feel the need to struggle against the language of power, but without recourse to the language of the nation, always liable to bring us to God's language. Without finding the correct way of saying it, we understand that the need for a separate tongue feeds on the fear of division in language. The possibility, even if necessary, of a separate language seems, for now, to be terribly difficult.

The need for a distinct tongue is not the anxiety of discovering a language able to describe a nation, an identity. It seems more like a desire to express a *flaw* of the identity and of the nation. Genet prolongs this reflection on the issue in three different accounts of the Palestinians in 1971, 1977, and 1982.

At the same time as he wrote the introduction to George Jackson's book in 1971, he says of the Palestinians: "The complexity of the poetic act, both within and outside of a revolution, forbids us from making or attempting an analysis of it here." Then: "The Palestinians, whether crushed or driven out, intended at first only to liberate a territory where their history was made. Through a play of forces that tipped in this direction, these attempts at liberation would eventually lead them, for a while, beyond the notion of a fatherland toward the notion, new to them, of a social revolution." Finally: "It is perhaps by way of a poetic art that each person, in the midst of a project undertaken in solidarity, can safeguard an intimacy and develop a sensibility in which new forms and new values are discovered."[27] Once again, the equation is presented between fatherland, revolution, and the need for a language now named as something new: poetic art. In those times when revolt was born, Genet felt the need to tie together an experience of solidarity and a solitary enterprise. This art consists again in the invention of a language that might make a distinction between the idea of homeland and that of revolt.

In the second part of this same search, Genet's particular issue meets the questioning specific to the Palestinians: the one that has to do with "Arab identity." The Palestinians have to rid themselves of this identity: "If the need to regain for themselves an Arab identity—one which perhaps used to exist—is not lived but mimicked, this need and identity will appear as nothing." The black prisoner feels the need for a separate language, a Palestinian feels the need to regain his identity. A similar need: language, identity, homeland, but how to invent new connections between these perhaps necessary notions? The Palestinians "live this emptiness [Arab identity], and in order to forget it, they have a sort of dance, an exaggeration of gestures and words. [...] After dispelling but not filling their emptiness, a very obvious economy of language leads them back into contact with the real."[28] Then follows the last word and the beginning of a political process: "Having reject-ed the slightly affected ancient nobility, their gestures are simple, ef-fective, ready for action. Their language is concise, indicating a desire not to continue the immemorial attitude, but to shatter the image the Arabs wanted to perpetuate."[29] Separate language is first the one that steers away from undesired identity. This will to separate from dead identity allows the emergence of beauty.

The last breath of this destructive and creative movement is simple. In 1982, he writes: "[...] is a revolution a revolution if it has not re-moved from faces and bodies the dead skin that distorted them? I'm not talking about an academic beauty, but rather the impalpable, un-able joy of bodies, faces, shouts, words that are no longer dead, I mean a sensual joy so strong that it tends to drive away all eroticism."[30] No doubt order looms.

Of the three major terms of the trinity—identity, language, na-tion—a fundamental political equation, the two outcrops have been blunted. Now, the language that holds this trinity together is also at-tacked. Immediately, the machine rumbles. The questioning by the Panthers about language remains haunted by the idea of a (black) na-tion; the Palestinian question of language is haunted by the question of (Arab) identity—what is to be done? *To make ourselves concise. Mean-ing not to hope to fill a void through language: emptiness of identity and emptiness of the nation.* In other words, we must refuse to fill emptiness with another emptiness, space between words and abyss of language. Language empties itself from imposed identity, the usurped nation and the collapsed vocabulary; this void is filled by nothing at all. The result is an economy, a very slight one.

What follows is only a suggestion. Before closing the chapter on the political trinity and ending, the critique that Genet made, I must dis-pose of the duo that has appeared before us: revolt and beauty. This step is necessary because we might believe that the author substituted this pair for the banished trinity of identity, homeland, and national language without further care. Genet spoke about exactly this subject in his penultimate interview in December 1983: "This beauty of which I speak, we must not insist too much on it, I fear we might be wrong."[31]

A page from the last book tells of the Panthers' poetic victory. The explanation, the demonstration of their success, starts with these words: "For every well-defined people—and even for nomads, for they don't visit their grazing areas at random—land is the necessary basis of nationhood. It is more."[32] The question that the Panthers, deprived of space, must ask is this one: "On what territory can these martyrs prepare their revolt?" The ghetto? Genet excludes this possibility since it would lead back to the logic of borders and limits, as well as their contradictions: ramparts, barricades, or bunkers. If these walls don't allow blacks to fall back, they will never make any border of any state airtight. The outside and the inside push against each other; they do not exist separately: the exterior is within the interior. Genet's answer is given in a curious syntax: "The Panthers' subversion would take place elsewhere and by other means: in people's consciences." Does he mean that the operations will be made within consciences, or that these conscious operations will be made elsewhere? The writer's syntax is separated. It does not obey the enemy's language, the use of which traces limits between the interior and the exterior. He calls this operation the "spectacle." On a small scale, it is visible in the vocabulary, and through it, he avoids false dualisms. On a larger scale it can be seen in the Panthers: "But spectacle is only spectacle, and it may lead to mere figment, no more than a colorful carnival; and that is a risk the Panthers ran. Did they have any choice?" Without further explanation on what this spectacle was, it allowed "physical terror and nervous dread [...]." Toward the end, Genet is able to conclude: "All those options happened [madness, metamorphosis, death], but the metamorphosis was by far the most important, and that is why the Panthers can be said to have overcome through poetry."[33] A total victory, but what about beauty? The spectacle is beautiful, this torrent of hair, drugs, and dance that he witnessed and that made revolution into a true pleasure. Blacks became visible, the writer has changed, the metamorphosis is immense. Beauty: the spectacle that calls forth physical terror and nervous dread. Politically, the spectacle is beautiful if it makes the ground something else than the foundation of a nation, through necessity.

The possibility of a Palestinian victory recalls another one; not the Panthers', but the metamorphosis of Arabs in France: "In France, before the Algerian War, the Arabs were not beautiful, they seemed odd and heavy, slow-walking, with skewed, oblique faces, and then almost all at once victory made them more beautiful; [...]." And then: "Working its way into the faces and bodies of Arab workers: something like the approach, the presentiment of a still fragile beauty that would dazzle us when the scales finally fell off from their skin and our eyes."[34] As in the case of black spectacle, the operation of which travels from mind to mind, the metamorphosis from which beauty springs, is shared by Arabs who see themselves as beautiful, and by those who watch. Laughter belongs to he who laughs; the scales of shame are visible on his face but also in the eyes of the man responsible for misery and shame, if he were able to laugh. He must rid himself of this shame. And so: "In the same way, having escaped at the same time from the refugee camps, from the morality and the order of the camps, from a morality imposed by the necessities of survival, having escaped at the same time from shame, the fedayeen were very beautiful [...]."[35] The political reality described here calls for vigilance: the refugee camps are contrasted with the military bases. Between the two, there is the distance between those who require assistance, encouraged by more or less charitable associations, and a burgeoning autonomy; the difference between a humanitarian situation and a political reality. To survive and to exist are certainly not synonymous. After his slight reservation on the question of beauty with which he began, Genet added this distinction: "I think in the act of revolt we assert existence."[36] What of beauty? "[...] by beauty we should understand a laughing insolence spurred by past misery, by the systems and men responsible for misery and shame, but a laughing insolence which realizes that, when shame has been left behind, the bursting forth of new life is easy."[37] Politically, the breakthrough represented by spectacle is beautiful yet delicate. The ugliness of the men in the camps cannot be judged—if the man who feels his freedom from shame renounces judgment, he will be beautiful through the necessity of living freely. The shame of which Genet speaks, the original disposition of his gesture that he wishes he could make vanish, does not arise from morality or judgment: it reflects a political decision about himself.

Let's look at the reflection of the beauty of the Panthers and Palestinians in the writer's eye. In his last book, Genet writes this page that he sees as conclusive: "The first two fedayeen were so handsome I was surprised at myself for not feeling any desire for them." The scales are now falling from his eyes. "The fedayeen didn't do as I told them, they didn't appear and disappear to suit my convenience. What for a long time I took to be a kind of limpidity, a total lack of eroticism, might have been due to the fact that each individual was completely autonomous. [...] That's how it had been with the Black Panthers in the United States."[38] This is the law of escape, the new rules, the submission to reality: if they are not yet independent, Genet at least understands the autonomy of each individual Palestinian and Panther. The metamorphosis is possible, "perhaps when you're lonely, when you're near death, when you risk nothing because all is lost?" This is what brought the end of youth, the becoming a man, the first step in a story without style.

With the Panthers, the Palestinians, and now Genet—in the eyes of those with nothing who wish to become other—we now see "all the beauty of the world tearing itself away from shame." Political beauty, if we can put it this way, seen by Genet; or rather the beauty that comes from understanding that coming out from behind shame is easy if the shame is that of a particular politics. The writer did not associate with

these imprisoned men because they were beautiful; they became beautiful because they were in revolt. The esthetic approach is neither a
goal nor a means, but a cause: the submission to a real world is part of
Genet's adventure, to the reality of the cause more than the dream of
an end. Beauty being perilous, it becomes a supplement on which we
must insist. The proximity between beauty and politics, even if this
intimacy seems to be the last word of his political view, comes from
further still: it arises from his meetings with these movements, born
of the reflection about the concept of violence, of patient, reasoned,
and precise criticism of the Western political trinity—identity, nation,
language. This political work is also erotic: an understanding of love
as the recognition of otherness and solidarity with men in revolt, who
are alone. On the subject of eroticism, Genet speaks his truth. Future,
ancient, fleeting, his concern for reality is coextensive with his will to
invent a new political space-time. The total, absolute, and definitive
submission of his political view to the real world can't be separated
from his desire for the poetic metamorphosis of reality. Between revolt
and beauty, Genet sees the same relation as between the weight of reality and the spaces between words, between poetry and politics: he sees
the necessary link and the legitimate distinction. Beauty, but without
desire. All men are free before being subjects of desire. The exit from
shame, tied to the submission to reality, makes burgeoning beauty a
political wave.

"They emancipated themselves politically so as to appear as we needed
to see them, very beautiful"—let us not, in these times, be offended too
quickly by the obvious nature of these lines. The Panthers, America,
black Americans? "Instead of seeking real independence—territorial,
political, administrative, and legal—which would mean a confrontation with white power, the Black underwent a metamorphosis in himself."[39] The fedayeen, the Arab world, the Palestinians? "Although they
have a goal which is the independence of their national territory, what
is most important is that on the road toward this goal they can retain

the liberty of existing within actions they see as fair."[40] The writer, France, Genet? He asserts once again in 1986 that he "didn't belong to, never really identified with, their nation or their movement."[41] To become visible, to act fairly, to remain non-aligned: this is a political worldview.

By attacking the vocabulary of identity, nation, and language—the national mother tongue—Genet questions the notion of nativity, as well as the Western political trinity founded on it. He underlines the irreconcilable space between birth and the nation. He points out a space full of holes. The critique of nativity is an answer to his phantasmagoria about Hamza's house; the critique of the founding trinity of the nation is a reply to Genet's ghost in the house of Hitler. Critique, answer, and reply are both political and poetic. The questioning of the subject of the three major terms of Western political vocabulary reflects the collapse of the writer's vocabulary; deprived of his civil rights, he wished to be judged on his political ideas.

If I mentioned earlier the spiritual crisis of the writer, or perhaps a broken movement of his syntax and thought, the reader—if only one—must now open his eyes and consider his movement's story as the possibility of a truly ethical political metamorphosis.

ENDNOTES

1. Alternative name for the article "Chartres Cathedral," in *L'Humanité*, June 30, 1977; *DE*, 344.

2. *Oeuvres completes* (Paris, 1951), 4:21–31 and 5:51.

3. E. White, *Genet: A Biography* (New York: Knopf, 1993), 401–403.

4. "Les Palestiniens" (II), *Shoun Falestine*, 1973; *GC*, 110.

5. *PL*, 62.

6. Ibid., 254.

7. Ibid., 171.

8. "America Is Afraid," *Le Nouvel Observateur*, August 20, 1971; *DE*, 89.

9. "Chartes Cathedral"; *DE*, 165, 167, 169.

10. Ibid; *DE*, 165.

11. T. Tzara, cited by M. Dachy in *Dada et les Dadaïsmes*, Paris, Gallimard, coll. "Folio," 250.

12. "Chartres Cathedral"; *DE*, 344, notes.

13. "Four Hours in Shatila," *Revue d'études palestiniennes* 6 (January 1, 1983); *DE* 218.

14. "Interview with Wischenbart and Barrada," *Revue d'études palestiniennes* 21 (Fall 1986); *DE*, 246–248.

15. *PL*, 169–70.

16. B. Guenée, "Des limites féodales aux frontières politiques," in P. Nora, *Les Lieux de mémoire, tome 2: La Nation* (Paris: Gallimard, 1986), 19.

17. *PL*, 99.

18. Ibid., 316.

19. Malcolm X, *Malcolm X Speaks: Selected Speeches and Statements* (New York: Grove Press, 1990), 30.

20. *PL*, 89.

21. "Chartres Cathedral"; *DE*, 344.

22. *PL*, 170.

23. "Letter to American Intellectuals" (speech at the University of Connecticut, March 18, 1970); *DE*, 31.

24. J. Genet, "Introduction" in G. Jackson, *Soledad Brother* (Chicago: Lawrence Hill Books, 1994), endnote; *DE*, 53–54.

25. *DE*, 55.

26. Malcolm X, *Malcolm X Speaks*, 162.

27. "*The Palestinians*" (I), *Zoom* 4 (August 1971); *DE*, 76–77.

28. "Près d'Ajloun," *in Per un Palestinese. Dediche a più voci a Waël Zouaiter*

(Milan: G. Mazzotta, 1979); *DE*, 152–153.

29. Ibid., *DE*, 156.
30. "Four Hours in Shatila"; *DE*, 225.
31. "Interview with Wischenbart and Barrada", *DE*, 250.
32. *PL*, 99.
33. Ibid., 99–100.
34. "Four Hours in Shatila"; *DE*, 225.
35. Ibid.
36. "Interview with Wischenbart and Barrada"; *DE*, 251.
37. "Four Hours in Shatila"; *DE*, 225.
38. *PL*, 205.
39. Ibid., 98.
40. "Interview with Wischenbart and Barrada"; *DE*, 251.
41. *PL*, 105.

Epilogue

11 | The River

On Jean Sauvage's instructions,[1] in 1517 Erasmus wrote *The Complaint of Peace Spurned and Rejected by the Whole World*, or *Querela Pacis*. As an epilogue to this study of Genet's politics, may we name the man who gave birth to humanism—Erasmus—and who is synonymous, at least in the Western tradition, with humanism itself? Without any assurances that Genet read *Querela*, may I begin a practical test of his criticisms of humanity by refusing the universalist abstraction known as the name of Man? Would you consider, for a moment, centuries later, Jean Genet rather than Jean le Sauvage with Erasmus, so as to end the untimely criticism of Genet over a certain evangelical slant in politics? I believe so, since the reading I propose wishes to keep its promise. It is a promise made at the beginning of this book, which was to hear Erasmus' concern and Genet's dispositions as a single movement toward *one* man. It begins like this: "When I hear the word 'man,' I run to him at once, as if to an animal specially created for me, confident that with him I shall be permitted to rest; [...]."[2] To read Erasmus is, in a way, to offer Genet's distinct political exclamation, his vision of man as "the basis of humanism,"[3] a more practical content here and now. After all, the word "quarrel" (*querela* in Latin, *querelle* in French) is one of the writer's names.[4] In a way, Genet substitutes the name "Querelle" for the word humanity in order to speak of the man who wages war against himself. To turn to Erasmus' work may give us an answer, though silent, to the question: is Genet's political worldview humanist?

We must travel back through time to follow the course of Genet's politics. From one steeple to another; the Catholic cemetery in Larache, Morocco, where he was buried, and the Chartres Cathedral where he first saw the debris of the European political trinity. It is buried deep in ancient soil, but one that is re-emerging: the humanist soil of the Beaucerons and Rhénans. *A Complaint of Peace Spurned and Rejected by the Whole World* (1517) is the *Querela Pacis* in Latin. This political work is the first part of a diptych, the second being *A Most Useful Discussion Concerning Proposals for War Against the Turks* (*Utilissima consultatio de bello Turcis inferendo*), signed in Fribourg-en-Breisgau on March 17, 1530. The Oriental Christian Empire is undone, the Turks have achieved victory in Hungary, a victory that will lead them to Vienna (Mohacs, 1527), the place where this story begins. At the beginning of the sixteenth century, the threat to Western Christendom is real.

Together, this diptych becomes a war and peace. It is interesting in more than one way: the two parts form a *De contemptu mundi*, a *Contempt for the World*—a style in which the same ideas are sometimes stated, sometimes denied, and in which praise and criticism seem akin.

Finally, the *Querela* is a personification. If we all, every time we think or speak, exclaim, Who, me, humanity? If peace is dead, we need to make the dead speak in a dialogue with the living. Isn't the dialogue between the dead and the living our main concern?

When we read Erasmus, we must remember he was one of the "great humanists," one of the few if not the only one, who did not learn Hebrew. In fact, a commentator once wrote: "He seems to have a mental block when it comes to Hebrew."[5] In *De recta pronuntiatione*, Erasmus indeed writes: "I would fear that by studying it [Hebrew], the child might be impregnated with Judaism."[6] The ideal of the *homo trilinguis* is not true with Erasmus; he thus turns to bilingualism. As much anti-Judaism as a profession of his faith, this concern with language is the expression of a political view.

From here, let us briefly look at what is said in this discourse on friendship, violence, and history—but on language also, if this triple questioning is brought together in a vocabulary.

The foundation of this long and double personification, to which I cannot hope to do justice, is friendship. Erasmus first examines the natural reasons for which we prefer harmony to quarrel: "You can find friendliness in trees and plants."[7] This universal friendship, also visible in celestial harmony, is the basis of the harmony between a man and himself: "And what can be so dissimilar as body and soul? Yet the closeness of the tie with which Nature has bound them together is indeed revealed when they are torn." And from there, the belief according to which "all which aims to the kindness that individuals practice toward one another is usually called human"; this would be where the word *humanitas* comes from.

In the name of friendship, affinity, or *humanitas*, Erasmus concludes with the necessity of peace: "Then there are ties of kinship and affinity, and similarity of disposition, interests, and appearance amongst several people which is certain to foster goodwill." He then adds: "Need created cities, need taught the value of alliance between them, so that with combined forces they could repeal the attacks of wild beasts and brigands."[8] The word "man" seems to already exclude thieves.

As such, what happens if one is a thief, or if the father and his teachings, especially of filial love, are absent? As of 1494, most wars had as origin a marriage contract or failed marriage. Later in his text, this reality makes Erasmus write: "A sound peace does not rest on alliances and treatises between men, which, as we see, can often lead to wars. The very sources from which the evil springs and the base passions which give rise to your conflicts must be cleansed."[9] From which we understand that the idea that "affinities [...are] certain to foster goodwill" does not hold up. In the *Querela*, the same arguments in favor of friendship can be used against peace. *Better yet, the sentence of peace causes war.* Friendships between men are built on quarrel. So that affection—that is far from love, and soon to be hate—not be destroyed, we must close our eyes, dream, forget reason or poetry.

A great violence now appears in this call for peace. Erasmus proposes a distinction: "I am speaking about the wars which Christians generally fight against Christians; I take a different view of men who repel the violent attacks of barbarian invaders by their wholehearted and loyal determination, and protect the peace and security of their country at their own peril."[10] Peace is thus presented with a dilemma: "Before that I must briefly take issue with two sets of opponents: those who, wrongly, are fired up for war on the Turk, and those who, also wrongly, argue against making war on the Turk."[11] Erasmus, or peace, seeing that war is everywhere, first attributes this situation to Satan: "[...it] amounts to the betrayal of Christendom to its most implacable foes [...]." The humanist replies immediately, wishing to distinguish between a people of war and a people of peace: "[...] for it is foolish to argue as some do that in the Old Testament God is called Lord of hosts (*Deus exercitum*) and of vengeance (*Deus ultionum*). There is a great difference between the God of the Jews and the God of the Christians even though by his very nature he is one and the same God."[12] The distinction is established within unity, itself the basis of this quarrel.

Erasmus can highlight these differences. After having mentioned in passing, "[...] bloody slaughters which fill the pages of the Hebrew Scriptures [...],"[13] (this being the Old Testament, he interprets these massacres literally), the humanist seems to ask himself: "When Christ was born, did the angels sound trumpets of war? The Jews heard the noise of the trumpet, for they were permitted to wage war, and this was the appropriate sound for men whose law told them to hate their enemies. [...] And (shameful to say) the cruelty of the fighting exceeds that of the Jews, of the heathen, of the wild beasts."[14] Following this comparison, we must ask whether, within these comparisons, the lowest word for Erasmus is the first one. Finally, the same logic of distinction and exemplarity observable here assembles, under the title of quarrel, both Christians and Jews since "[...] every Christian life is occupied with one thing: war [...]."[15]

In the *Consultatio*, war is in the air, and so Erasmus presses harder: "But when the ignorant mob hears the name of the Turks, they immediately fly into a rage and clamor for blood, calling them dogs and enemies of the Christian name; it does not occur to them that, first of all, they are human beings and, what is more, half-Christian. They never stop to consider that whether the *casus belli* is legitimate [...]."[16] Turks are seen as half-Christians since they are monotheistic. Their sympathy for Jews, he writes, should serve as an example for Christians who believe they have the right to kill a Turk, or a Jew. Redoubtable argument: "But the mass of Christians wrongly believes that anyone is allowed to kill a Turk, as one would a mad dog, for no better reason that he is a Turk. If this were true, then anyone would be allowed to kill a Jew."[17] Now Erasmus can compare Christians and Jews—thrown together as barbarian peoples, as opposed to the Turks—pacifists: "What is more, such was the clemency of the church's leaders in the days gone by that they were reluctant to see even relapsed Jews punished with death." He gives another example: "For King Sisemand had discovered that many Jews who, renouncing their former impiety, had professed the Christian faith had not only relapsed into their old blasphemy but were also practicing detestable Jewish rites and had circumcised their children and slaves [...]."[18] Despite these "monstrous crimes," Turks did not execute Jews. As such, he concludes: "It is thus clear that priests have no right to kill anyone." In this sense, it is only because the murder of Jews is, after all, impossible, that murder of Turks is not allowed. Erasmus sentences Christians to peace because he cannot condemn Jews to death, if even the Turks haven't done it. All that remains is the ash or the fire of this logic: *the sentence of peace leaves the sentence against the Jews intact.*

The reflection of the monstrosity of Jewish rites in the Christian eye remains alive. There is the fear of generalized backsliding: Jews might have disowned their fathers but still practice their faith. The same and the other are engaged in a fight even more terrible, for the other is lodged in the same. The possibility offered to each man to become his own shadow—meaning other than himself—calls for the murder of men. If Turks are half-Christians for their leniency, and Christians are akin to Jews for war, then Jews, Christians, and Turks are condemned to resemble each other. We can then say of these three people what Erasmus writes in the *Consultatio* about Turks: "They are a race debilitated by debauchery and fearsome only as brigands."[19] The people of war are also a feminine people. As a header to the *Quarrel of Peace* and the *Discussion for War*, titles that begin to speak truth, we find the three monotheistic religions—Judaism, Christianity, and Islam—resemble each other in a single monstrosity: "It would seem a strange portent demanding propitiation if branch warred on branch on the same vine[20] [...]." *The call for peace is haunted by a call for murder.*

The personification of peace finally shows how the division of the same, the monstrosity of the struggle of the same with the other on a same branch is found in language. Erasmus writes: "Furthermore, when there is no cause at hand they invent their own reasons for picking a quarrel and misuse names of places to feed animosities."[21] In the following invocation, the quarrel of peace is now found in the division of vocabulary; it drags friendship into war:

> What perversity—for the mere name of a place to divide
> people when there is so much which could bring them
> together! [...] Are we then to treat the common name of our
> country as a serious reason why one nation should be bent
> on exterminating another? Even that is not enough for some
> people, whose minds are avid for war; with perverted zeal
> they seek occasions for dissension, they tear France apart,
> and by mere words create divisions in areas not divided by
> seas, mountains, or genuine place-names. And just in case

> sharing a name may unite people in friendship, they make
> Germans out of the French.[22]

Names of places and names of people, constraint and condemnation, war and peace are necessarily swept away by the eternal quarrel found in language. The impossible end to this quarrel is found only in the name of the Father. At this precise spot, after having identified the "division by the constraints of vocabulary," Erasmus finds a way of joining with the beginning of his text, by writing, "Surely lawyers should rather look at the facts and reflect that this common world of ours is the homeland to which we all belong, assuming that the name of homeland is [a] unifying influence; that we are all descended from the same forbears, if consanguinity makes men friends [...]. Do you forgive much where there is a family relationship and nothing where there is a union in religion?"[23] What is this law common to all men—consanguinity before God—in the name of which we can find peace? "If you believe that fornication, incest, and worse are loathsome evils, war is the school where they are taught."[24] In the end, peace sighs: "It has thus been impossible to find among these men a place to sit in which they are not responsible for these wars." The contempt for the world leaves no place for peace. "The man I speak of wages war against himself"[25] is his last breath. The sigh of dying peace, though not the end of humanism. *To become monstrous; this is perhaps the wish of the man who gave birth to humanism.*

Friendship between men surely brings us closer to war than peace. Not only does humanism not exclude racism, it remains haunted by the call to murder. The division of vocabulary, the open origin of human language cannot repair difference, still visible in the name of the One, the Father, or God. Genet, who cannot believe in this hope-filled origin, does not recognize himself in this law.

On a manuscript page of his last book, Genet asked himself, as he noted down this reflection that seems an echo of the division of vocabulary that Erasmus saw: "All over the world and in every age, plays upon words, accents or even letters have often caused quite bitter conflict." After these words, "responsibility, authority, order," he writes for himself, "Responsible, of what in front of whom, reduced in front of whom, risking which punishment, given down by whom?" And then: "Authority? On what basis is built the hierarchy descending from a king?" Finally: "An order given? Who gives? What gift?" Responsibility, judgment, and witnessing will be the last words. Genet: "I've said this, I've written it."[26]

I hoped to offer the last Genet's story as a trip up the course of a river, toward its source. But there is no source (origin). If we could write this story with a needle on the inside of an eye, it would give thought to those who know how to think.

ENDNOTES

1 Erasmus, *The Correspondence of Erasmus: Letters 1252–1355 (1522–1523)* (Toronto: University of Toronto Press, 1989), 320.

2. Erasmus, *Collected Works of Erasmus: Literary and Educational Writings (ER)* (Toronto: University of Toronto Press, 1989), 5:296.

3. "For George Jackson"; *DE*, 66.

4. *Querelle of Brest* (London: Faber & Faber Press, 2001).

5. A. Godin; *ER*, CXLVII.

6. Erasmus, *Opera omnia*, Vol. 1, bk. 4, chap. 32 (Amsterdam, 1969), 621–622.

7. *ER*, 296.

8. Ibid., 295–296.

9. Ibid., 311.

10. Ibid., 314.

11. Erasmus, *Collected Works of Erasmus: Expositions of the Psalms, Volume 64* (Toronto: University of Toronto Press), 232. (*ER2*)

12. *ER*, 299.

13. Ibid., 300.

14. Ibid., 300–305.

15. Ibid., 303.

16. *ER*, 231.

17. Ibid., 238.

18. Ibid., 238–239.

19. Ibid., 231.

20. *ER*, 302.

21. Ibid., 314.

22. Ibid., 315.

23. Ibid.

24. Ibid., 316.

25. Ibid., 296–299.

26. Un captif amoureux. Manuscript, Gallimard Collection, 79; *CA*, 92.

Chronology Part 1

1517

Erasmus, *The Complaint of Peace Spurned*, or *Querela Pacis*.

1529

The Siege of Vienna by the Turks; the Christian world is threatened.

1910

Jean Genet is born in Paris, December 19. His mother is Camille Gabrielle Genet. He will never know the name of his father.

1917

The Balfour Declaration that foresees the creation of a national homeland for the Jewish people.

1930

Jean Genet's first sojourn in the Middle East: in Damascus, he serves in the French Army occupying Syria. His first occupation experience. Of it he will say, "I used to play cards with the Syrians in the little mosques."

1932

Henri Michaux publishes *A Barbarian in Asia*.

1933

The first meeting of the Muslim Brotherhood in Cairo.
Ezra Pound meets Mussolini.

1939–1945

World War II.

1942

The German occupation of France: Jean Genet is imprisoned in France, he fears the concentration camps, then is freed. Second occupation experience.

1943

Ezra Pound accused of treason, imprisoned in a cage north of Pisa.

1944

The beginning of the restitution of Alsace and Lorraine to France.
Genet: "If I'd had to be someone other than myself—a difficult choice—I'd have been a native of Alsace-Lorraine" (*PL*, 170).
Jean Genet, *Our Lady of the Flowers*, his first book, is published.

1945

The Holocaust: six million European Jews murdered.

1946

Creation of the Ligue française pour la Palestine libre (Jean-Paul
Sartre, Edgar Faure, and others).

1947

First Palestinian exile.

Antonin Artaud, *Pour en finir avec le jugement de Dieu*.

1948

Second Palestinian exile.

Creation of the State of Israel.

Third Palestinian exile: in all, some 726,000 Palestinians. Yasser
Arafat leaves university to take up arms: "Those who have no
homeland have no dignity, and those who have no dignity can learn
nothing."

Jean-Paul Sartre, *What Is Literature?*

1951

Abdallah, King of Jordan, is assassinated in front of the El Aksa
mosque in Jerusalem by a Palestinian, member of Firket el-Tadmir
("the legion of destruction").

1952

Franz Fanon, *Black Skin, White Masks*.

1954

Beginning of the Algerian insurrection.

1956

Tunisia and Morocco gain independence.

1957

Samuel Beckett, *Endgame*.

1959

On the banks of the Nile, Arafat launches the Palestinian Liberation
Movement, or *Fatah*.

1960

The Eichmann Trial in Jerusalem. Ben Gurion declares, "The Jewish
State is the sole heir of six million murdered Jews."

The George Jackson trial. He is imprisoned for a seventy dollar theft
and will never go free; he is eighteen years old.

The "Manifeste des 121" against the Algerian War.

Genet: "I approve of rebels whatever they do. And I'm the only writer in France who can't say it" (*Correspondance*, September 1960).

1961

Malcolm X, Harvard speech.

1962

Algerian independence.
Nelson Mandela arrested in South Africa.

1963

The first Black Arts festival in Algeria (Alioune Diop).

1964

Malcolm X breaks with the Black Muslims. Creation of the Afro-American Unity Organization. Pilgrimage to Mecca, speech in Paris.
The Civil Rights Act, abolition of racial discrimination.
The General Union of Palestinian Students, and Yasser Arafat in particular, meet in Gaza and create the Palestinian Liberation Organization (PLO).

1965

Malcolm X is assassinated in the Audubon Ballroom, Harlem.
Watts, Los Angeles Riots: thirty-four dead.
Fatah carries out its first attack against Israel.

1966

The first fedayee dies by Lebanese torture: Jamal Kaouache.
Stokely Carmichael launches Black Power.
Creation of the Black Panther Party in Oakland, California by three students excluded from college: Bobby Seale, Eldridge Cleaver, and Huey Newton.
Kateb Yacine, *Le Polygone étoilé*.
Henri Michaux, *The Major Ordeals of the Mind and the Countless Minor Ones*.

1967

Six Day War. Israel takes over Sinai, the West Bank, and the Golan Heights. De Gaulle speaks of a developing resistance against Israel, which he then calls terrorism.
Creation in Lebanon of the Popular Front for the Liberation of Palestine (PFLP) by Georges Habash, a Catholic.
The Black Panthers take over the chamber of the state senate of California, the Capitol Building.

Huey Newton arrested; beginning of the "Free Huey" campaign.

In Berlin, demonstrations against the Shah of Iran. The police kill Benno Ohnesorg.

Paul Celan meets Martin Heidegger.

In France, creation of a research and action group for the settling of the Palestinian problem (Maxime Rodinson, Jacques Berque, François Châtelet, and others).

Genet travels to Japan. In the airplane, he speaks of throwing off the thick, black Judeo-Christian moral code.

1965–1975

Vietnam War.

1968

The Battle of Karameh in Jordan; the Palestinians are victorious.

Attack on an El Al plane by the PFLP, forced landing in Algiers.

Tommie Smith and John Carlos raise the Black Power salute at the Mexico City Olympic Games.

The police murder Bobby Hutton, a seventeen-year-old Black Panther.

"Peace and Freedom": peace in Vietnam, freedom for black citizens.

Arson attacks against the Kauhoff and Schneider stores in Frankfurt. First arrest of Andreas Baader and Gudrun Ensslin.

Attack against Rudi Dutschke, a figure of the German student movement. Paul Celan writes the poem "Mapesbury Road" about the event.

The barricades in Paris (May 10 and 24, June 11).

Jean Genet travels to the United States for the first time, August 24–28. He writes, "A policeman's black leather visor intrudes between me and the world" (*DE*, 270).

1969

Yasser Arafat becomes PLO president. The Cairo Accord is brokered by Gamal Abdel Nasser between Emile Bustani and Arafat. Palestinian military autonomy in southern Lebanon.

Concert at Woodstock.

Bobby Seale's trial begins; he is gagged in the courtroom.

Chicago Seven trial after the Democratic Convention. Only Bobby Seale is kept in prison.

1970

Death of Nasser.

Conference of non-aligned nations.

Four airplanes hijacked simultaneously (Leila Khaled), landing in the desert of Zarka, Jordan.

Black September in Jordan, fourth Palestinian exile, into Lebanon.

George Jackson, John Clutchette, and Fleeta Drumgo—the Soledad Brothers—are accused of the murder of prison guard Mills. Jonathan Jackson is killed after an attempted hostage-taking to liberate the Brothers.

Guilty verdict against David Hilliard and Angela Davis, both Black Panthers.

Prison escape, Andreas Baader.

Paul Celan commits suicide in the Seine in Paris.

Tenement fire in Aubervilliers, suburbs of Paris: four workers from Mali and one from Mauritania die.

Jean Genet's second and last stay in the United States. From March to May, he attends Bobby Seale's trial. Second stay in the Middle East. Between October 1970 and April 1971, Genet is in Jordan, at the Irbid camp, in Hamza's house. Genet meets Arafat.

Bobby Seale publishes *Seize the Time: The Story of the Black Panther Party and Huey P. Newton.*

1971

Creation of the Front homosexuel d'action révolutionnaire.

George Jackson is killed in prison by police. Uprising at the Attica Prison, forty dead.

The police murder Petra Schelm and Georg von Rauch. Other members of the Red Army Faction arrested: Horst Mahler, Margrit Schiller.

Creation of the Groupe d'information sur les prisons (GIP, with Michel Foucault, Daniel Defert, and others). The group publishes a pamphlet, *Intolérable.*

The Red Army Faction, *On Armed Struggle in Western Europe.*

Jean Genet on George Jackson: "It is obvious that if he wrote his book—and he did write it—he was incapable of carrying out the assassination" (*DE,* 82).

1972

Election of Itzhak Shamir, Likud Party: fifteen years of right-wing rule in Israel.

Andreas Baader visits the PFLP base of Baddawi in Lebanon; Genet is in Jordan for the third time.

Palestinian attack against Israeli athletes in Munich.

Explosion at the European headquarters of the American Army in Heidelberg: "The computer that directed the bombing of Vietnam was hit," according to *Rouge*.

The second arrest of Andreas Baader, Ulrike Meinhof, Gudrun Ensslin, and Holger Meins. They are held in sensory deprivation chambers.

In Paris, Genet converses with seven Palestinian students.

Nabile Farès, *Le Champ des oliviers*.

Pierre Overney assassinated in front of the Renault factory, Paris.

Joseph Beuys. *Dürer, I will guide Baader + Meinhof through Dokumenta personally (Dürer, ich führe persönlich Baader + Meinhof durch die Dokumenta V)*. Two wood-fiber boards, two wood planks, paint, two carpet-slippers, fat, and rose stems.

1973

The Yom Kippur War: Israel's second occupation of Gaza, East Jerusalem, and the Golan.

Mossad operation in Beirut, Spring of Youth: three leading members of *Fatah* linked to the Munich attack are assassinated; 350,000 people attend their funeral.

Garbage collectors' strike in Paris; invitation to breakfast at the Élysée presidential palace. See Genet: "Mourir sous Giscard d'Estaing," *L'Humanité*, May 13, 1974.

Tahar Ben Jelloun, *Harrouda*.

Ahmed, *Une vie d'Algérien, est-ce que ça fait un livre que les gens vont lire?*

1974

Point 2 of the PLO's charter states that the movement will accept "any part of liberated territory"; end of the negation of Israel.

Death of Holger Meins, member of the RAF, after a hunger strike.

Valéry Giscard d'Estaing, president for seven years: thirty-five years of right-wing rule in France. A plan for a total halt to immigration into France. Jacques Chirac, Prime Minister, states, "The issue of low-cost housing has no importance in my eyes."

Jacques Derrida publishes *Glas*.

1975–1978

    War in Lebanon between Palestinians and Lebanese.

1975

    United Nations Resolution 3379: "Zionism is a form of racism and
       racial discrimination."

    The Baader-Meinhof law: restrictions to the rights of the defense.

    Trial of the Baader-Meinhof Gang begins.

    Prison reform in France and the invention of the Quartier de Haute
       Sécurité (QHS).

    Michel Foucault, *Surveiller et Punir* (English version 1977, *Discipline
       and Punish*).

    Genet: "Yes and no. My admiration for Hitler emptied out but the
       spot has not been occupied by anything else. It's a void."

1976

    Ulrike Meinhof commits suicide in her cell.

    Mahmoud Issa (Selim), *Je suis un fedayin*.

1977

    Congress in Upper Egypt of 4,000 religious associations,
       assassination of the Minister of Wafqs, attempt to establish *sharia*
       law.

    Kidnapping of Hans Martin Schleyer, industrialist and former Nazi,
       by the second generation of the RAF.

    The principle of *sanctuarisation* ("sanctuarization") that attempted
       to neutralize French territory and keep it free of terrorism. Abu
       Daoud, suspected of being one of the planners of the Munich
       attack, is expelled three days after his arrest in France.

    Massive unemployment in France. Minister Barre has 49,000 letters
       sent to the foreign unemployed offering a one-time payment if they
       leave the country.

    Michel Foucault, "The Lives of Infamous Men" (*Cahiers du chemin*)
       and "Va-t-on extrader Klaus Croissant?" (*Le Nouvel Observateur*).

    Tahar Ben Jelloun, *The Highest Solitude*.

    Textes des prisonniers de la Fraction Armée Rouge, preface by Jean
       Genet.

    Genet: "Violence and life are more or less synonymous."

1978

    Occupation of southern Lebanon: 25,000 Israeli soldiers, 285,000
       inhabitants leave the region.

Peace agreement between Egypt's Anwar Sadat and Israel's Menachem Begin.

Kateb Yacine presents his play about Palestine in Algeria, *La Guerre de deux mille ans.*

1979

Iranian Revolution against the Shah and Khomeini's victory. "Iran is our second home after Palestine," Arafat declares.

1980–1988

Iran-Iraq War.

1980

Israel adopts a law making Jerusalem the eternal capital of the nation.

Jean-Paul Sartre is buried.

1981

François Mitterrand is elected. Capital punishment is abolished as well as some anti-riot measures.

Roger Knobelspiess, *QHS.*

1982

The Falklands War.

The war in Lebanon and the occupation of the south: Israelis and Palestinians clash.

Operation "Peace in Galilee." The multinational force evacuates the city, Bechir Gemayel is assassinated, Jean Genet stands on the balcony in Beirut occupied by the Israeli army. Fourth stay in the Middle East and third and last occupation witnessed by Genet.

The Sabra and Shatila massacres. The Palestinians' fifth exodus, this time to Tunis.

The Kahan Report on Israeli responsibility: "We watched the camps as if we were in the first row of a theater."

Homosexuality is no longer a crime in France.

Genet: "The abolition of capital punishment in France makes absolutely no difference to me."

1983

Toumi Djadja is wounded by gunfire at Les Minguettes; demonstration by French-born Arabs.

Law recognizing the legitimacy of foreigners to live in France.

Bernard-Marie Koltès, *Black Battles with Dogs.*

Genet, interview in Vienna: "I submitted myself to the real world ...

and no longer to the grammatical world. I must describe a reality that isn't mine with words that are mine."

1984

Israeli civil and penal codes are extended to the occupied territories.
Genet's last visit to Jordan. On the anniversary of Abdallah's assassination in July 1951, Genet goes to the Irbid camp to see Hamza's house.

1985

Black Ramadan. The refugee camp war in Lebanon: the alliance of the PLO and Hezbollah against the Amal Shiites. Further massacres at Shatila.
Henri Michaux, posthumous publication of *Déplacements, Dégagements.*
Joint statement of the RAF and the French Action Directe: "For the Unity of the Revolutionaries in Western Europe."

1986

Death of Jean Genet.
Publication of *Un captif amoureux* (*Prisoner of Love*), his last book.
Genet: "The bursting forth out of shame was easy."
Action directe kills Renault Chairman of the Board Georges Besse in Paris.

1987–1993

The Intifada, demonstrations on the West Bank and Gaza to honor the massacres at Shatila, Palestinian uprising.

1987

Near Orléans, south of Paris, Action directe members Jann-Marc Rouillan, Nathalie Ménigon, Joëlle Aubron, and Georges Cipriani are arrested.

1988

PLO: proclamation of a Palestinian state and the recognition of UN Resolution 242 on the existence of Israel.
Gerhard Richter. *October 18, 1977* (*18. Oktober, 1977*). Fifteen paintings after the death of Andreas Baader, Gudrun Ensslin, Holger Meins, and Ulrike Meinhof at the high security prison in Stammheim, Germany.

1989

Yasser Arafat visits France.

The *fatwa* declared by Khomeini against Salman Rushdie, a year after
The Satanic Verses is published.

Death of Kateb Yacine.

1991

Abrogation of UN Resolution 3379 linking Zionism to racism.

1992

The Rodney King trial: riots in Los Angeles cause fifty-eight deaths.

1993

The PLO and Israel recognize each other in Washington.

1994

The end of apartheid in South Africa.

Beginning of Palestinian autonomy in Gaza and Jericho.

The first Palestinian prisoner dies in Palestinian custody in Gaza:
Farid Hachem Jarbou was twenty-eight years old.

1995

Assassination of Yitzhak Rabin.

1999

Ehud Barak—who in 1973 during the covert mission "Spring of
Youth" in Beirut was disguised as a woman in order to assassinate
members of the PLO—is elected prime minister of Israel.

Police kill Horst Ludwig Meyer in Vienna and arrest Andrea Klump.
Both were searched for proof of presumed membership in the RAF.

2000

Ariel Sharon's visit to the Haram al-Sharif (Temple Mount).

Second Intifada.

2001

Saeed Hotari (1980–2001) blows himself up at the entrance of the
Dolphinarium disco in Tel Aviv, leaving twenty-one people dead
and about sixty injured. Islamic Jihad says it carried out the attack.

Izz al-Din Shuheil al-Masri blows himself up in the Sbarro pizza
restaurant chain in Jerusalem, leaving fifteen people dead and about
ninety injured. Hamas says it carried out the attack.

On what is now referred to as simply "9/11," al-Qaeda terrorists
hijacked four commercial airliners; two of the planes destroyed
the World Trade Center "Twin Towers" in New York, a third
crashed into the Pentagon in Washington, and a fourth crashed
in a Pennsylvania field after passengers wrested control from the
hijackers. 2,995 people died in the coordinated attacks.

2002

Jean-Marie Le Pen reaches the second round of the French
presidential election ahead of Lionel Jospin and after Jacques
Chirac.

Abdel-Basset Odeh, a twenty-five-year-old Hamas member from
the West Bank town of Tulkarem, blows himself up in the Israeli
resort of Netanya at the Park Hotel, killing twenty-eight Israelis
celebrating Passover.

Israel begins a massive military assault on the West Bank. Yasser
Arafat's Ramallah headquarters are targeted and Palestinian
militants take refuge in the Church of the Nativity in Bethlehem.

Israel begins construction of its West Bank security barrier, a
440-mile-long structure designed to keep Palestinian suicide
bombers out of Israel.

2003

Death of Edward Saïd.

Jean Genet's father is identified by Albert Dichy who acquired access
to the writer's "Dossier de pupille" (student records) through the
Assistance publique de la Seine (welfare office), Côte D 5X42970.
On the form that records the questioning of Camille Gabrielle
Genet on March 10, 1911, the father's name is written "in a
different ink." His name is Frédéric Blanc.

2004

Israel assassinates Sheikh Ahmed Yassin, spiritual leader of Hamas, in
an air strike.

Death of Jacques Derrida.

Death of Yasser Arafat (in Paris).

2005

Mahmoud Abbas succeeds Yasser Arafat as chairman of the
Palestinian Authority.

2006

Death of Joëlle Aubron (Action directe).

After a stroke, Ariel Sharon is placed in an induced coma. He is
currently (2010) in a persistent vegetative state.

Jacques Derrida, *L'animal que donc je suis*. Paris: Éditions Galilée. (*The
Animal That Therefore I Am*. New York: Fordham University Press,
2008.) First posthumous book.

2008

Nathalie Ménigon is freed after twenty years in prison.

Barack Hussein Obama is elected President of the United States of America.

Death of Mahmoud Darwish.

2009

Verena Becker is arrested on the allegation of having participated in the 1977 attack on Federal Prosecutor Buback with the RAF.

2010

Centennial of Jean Genet's birth.

Chronology Part 2: Works by Jean Genet

1944

Notre-Dame-des-Fleurs. (English trans. *Our Lady of the Flowers*.
  Translated by Bernard Fretchman. New York: Grove Press, 1963.)

1946

Miracle de la rose. (*Miracle of the Rose*. Translated by Bernard
  Fretchman. New York: Grove Press, 1966.)

1947

Pompes funèbres (*Funeral Rites*. Translated by Bernard Fretchman.
  New York: Grove Press, 1969.); *Querelle de Brest* (*Querelle of Brest*.
  Translated by Gregory Streatham. London: Faber & Faber Press,
  2001.); *Haute Surveillance* (*Deathwatch: A Play*. Translated by
  Bernard Fretchman. London: Faber and Faber, 1961.); *Les Bonnes*
  (*The Maids: And Deathwatch, Two Plays*. Translated by Bernard
  Fretchman. New York: Grove Press, 1962.).

1948

Adame Miroir (in *Fragments of the Artwork*. Translated by Charlotte
  Mandell. Standford: Standford University Press, 2003.); *Poèmes*;
  L'enfant criminel.

1949

Journal du voleur. (*The Thief's Journal*. Translated by Bernard
  Fretchman. New York: Grove Press, 1964.)

1950

Un chant d'amour (film).

1951

Oeuvres completes. Paris: Gallimard, 1951–.

1955

"Conference de Stockholm." Broadcast on Swedish radio in
  November, Pierre-André-Benoît Museum-Library.

1956

Le Balcon. (*The Balcony: Le Balcon, a Play in Nine Scenes*. Translated by
  Bernard Fretchman. New York: Grove Press, 1960.)

1957

Le Funambule; L'Atelier d'Alberto Giacometti (in Fragments of the Artwork, Charlotte Mandell).

1958

Les Nègres. (The Blacks: A Clownshow. Translated by Bernard Fretchman. London: Faber, 1960.)

1960

"Je ne peux pas le dire." Letter to Bernard Fretchman. Published in part in Libération, April 7, 1988.

1961

Les Paravents. (The Screens: A Play in Seventeen Scenes. Translated by Bernard Fretchman. New York: Grove Press, 1962.)

1963

"To a Would Be Producer." Tulane Drama Review 7 (Spring): 80–81.

"What I Like About the English is That They Are Such Liars ..." Sunday Times Magazine, 11.

1964

Interview: "Jean Genet." Playboy, April, 44–55.*

1967

"Ce qui est resté d'un Rembrandt déchiré en petits carrés bien réguliers." Tel Quel, April.

1968

"Les maîtresses de Lénine." Le Nouvel Observateur, May 30.*

"Le bain de mai ..." Letter addressed in September to Carol Lange, personal collection.

"The Members of the Assembly." Esquire, November, 86–89.*

"A Salute to a Hundred Thousand Stars." Evergreen Review, December.*

1969

"Les pâtres du désordre." Pas à pas, March, VI–VII.*

"San Genet." Interview with José Monléon. Triunfo, November, 19–32.

1970

"Jean Genet cherche ou recherche ..." Tanger.*

"The Panthers and the Law." Newsweek, February 23, 1970.

---

* Texts republished in The Declared Enemy (translated by Jeff Fort. Stanford: Stanford University Press, 2004) are marked with an asterisk.

"Français, encore un effort." *L'Idiot international* 4 (March 1): 24.*

"Il me paraît indécent de parler de moi." MIT, Cambridge, March 10.*

Speech to City College of New York, quoted in *CCNY Observation Post*, March 13, 1970.

"Letter to American Intellectuals." Speech given March 18 at the University of Connecticut.*

"Bobby Seale, the Black Panthers and Us (White People)." *Black Panther Newspaper*, March 28, 7.*

"Introduction." In George Jackson, *Soledad Brother*. New York: Coward-McCann and Bentham, September. Extracts in *Le Monde*, April 2, 1971, published in the collection "Témoins." Paris: Gallimard, May 1971.*

"May Day Speech." New Haven, May 1.*

"Jean Genet chez les Panthères noires." Interview with Michèle Manceaux. *Le Nouvel Observateur*, May 25.*

"Here and now for Bobby Seale." *Ramparts* 8, no. 12 (June 1970): 30–31.

"Angela et ses frères." *Le Nouvel Observateur*, August 31, 19–22 (alternative title: "L'homme qui se croyait juge").*

"Un appel de M. Jean Genet en faveur des Noirs américains." *Le Monde*, October 15, 7.*

"Jean Genet chez les Panthères noires." Interview with F.-M. Banier. *Le Monde*, October 23, 3.

"Angela Davis est entre vos pattes." Read October 16, broadcast on "L'invité du dimanche," November 8.*

"Lettres sur Claudel." To Patrick Prado, January. Reprinted in *Itinéraires*, advertisement and brochure for the Arab World Institute, IMEC, 1992.

1971

"Jean Genet témoigne pour les Soledad Brothers." *La Nouvelle Critique* 45 (June).

"Pour George Jackson." ("For George Jackson.") Manifesto, July.*

"Après l'assassinat." Unpublished. August. ("After the Assassination.")*

"L'Amerique a peur." ("America is Afraid.") *Le Nouvel Observateur*, August 30, 33.*

"Les Palestiniens" (I). Commentary on ten photographs by B. Barbey. *Zoom*, August.*

"The Americans Kill Off the Blacks." *Black Panther Newspaper*, September 4.

"The Black and the Red." *Black Panther Newspaper*, September 11.*

"L'assassinat de George Jackson." *Intolérable*. GIP brochure. Paris: Gallimard, November 10. [BN impr 8-G (or 6) 19758 (3)].

1972

"Entretien." *Libre* 2 (Spanish), December 1971–January 1972.

"Un lettre de Jean Genet." *Les Lettres françaises* 1429, March 29, 14.*

"Faites connaissance aves les Guaranis." *Le Démocrate vernonnais*, June 2.*

"Conversation with Jean Genet." P. Demeron, Chicago. *Oui*, November.

1973

"Les Palisteniens" (II). In Arabic. *Shoun Falestine*, Beyrouth, 1973; in English, *Journal of Palestine Studies* 73 (Fall): 3–34; in French, *Genet à Shatila*, new edition. Arles, Actes Sud, "Babel" collection, 1994, pp. 99–169.

1974

"Sur deux ou trois livres dont personne n'a jamais parlé." "Reflexion faite," France-Culture, May 2, reprinted under the title "Jean Genet et la condition des immigrés." *L'Humanité*, May 3, 12.*

"Quand le pire est toujours sûr." Unpublished. May 7.*

"Mourir sous Giscard d'Estaing." *L'Humanité*, May 13.*

"Et pourquoi pas la sottise en bretelles?" *L'Humanité*, May 25.*

"Les femmes de Djebel Hussein." *Le Monde diplomatique*, July 1.*

"Un héros litteraire: le défunt volubile." *La Nouvelle Critique* 75, no. 256, new series (June–July): 15–16.

1975

"Entretien avec Angela Davis." By Jean Genet. *L'Unité*, May 23.

"Des esprits moins charitables que le mien pourraient croître déceler une piètre opération politique." *L'Humanité*, August 13.

"Les frères Karamazov." *La Nouvelle Revue française* 405 (October): 69–72.*

1976

"Interview with Hubert Fichte." *Die Zeit*, no. 8 (February 13): 35–37 (reprinted in the United States, England, Spain, and France: *Magazine littéraire*, no. 174, June 1981).*

La Nuit venue. Scenario written in collaboration with Mohammed El Katrani. IMEC manuscript.

1977

"La ténacité des Noirs américains." *L'Humanité*, April 16, 1.*

"Cathédrale de Chartres, vue cavalière" ("Chartres Cathedral"); alternative title, "Micro-traité d'une mini-politique." *L'Humanité*, June 30, 2.*

"Violence et brutalité." *Le Monde*, September 2. Preface to *Textes des prisonniers de la Fraction Armée rouge et Dernières Lettres d'Ulrike Meinhof*. Paris: Maspero, December.*

1979

"Près d'Ajloun." In *Per un Palestinese, Dediche a più voci a Waël Zouaiter*. Milan: G Mazzotta. (*For a Palestinian*. Under the direction of Janet Venn-Brown. London, Boston: Kegan Paul International, 1984.)*

"Entretien avec Jean Genet." T. Ben Jelloun. *Le Monde du dimanche*, November 11, 4.*

1981

Le Langage de la muraille. Historical fiction on the colony of Mettray. IMEC manuscript.

1982

"Entretien avec Antoine Bourseiller (I) / Bertrand Poirot-Delpech (II)." Video, "Témoins" collection, 1981 and January 25, 1982; extracts in *Le Nouvel Observateur*, October 20, 1982, and *Le Monde aujourd'hui*, April 20, 1986.*

1983

"Quatre heures à Shatila." ("Four Hours in Shatila.") *Revue d'études palestiniennes* 6 (January 1).*

"No. matricule 1155." "La rupture" exhibit catalogue, Le Creusot, March 1.*

"An Interview with E. de Grazia." *Cardozo Studies in Law and Literature* 5, no. 2 (Fall): 307–323.

1985

"Entretien avec Nigel Williams." BBC, Royaume-Uni, November 12.*

"Entretien: la mille et unième blessure de l'humanié." *Palestine al-*

thawra (Arabic) no. 560 (June): 46–48. ("The Thousand and First Injury of Human History," English translation based on French translation by Basma el Omari and Hadrien Laroche.)

1986

"Interview with Bertrand Poirot-Delpech." *Le Monde aujourd'hui*, April 20.*

"Une recontre avec Jean Genet." ("Interview with Wischenbart and Barrada.") *Revue d'études palestiniennes* 21 (Fall): 11.*

"Entretient avec Jean Genet." By Saadalah Wannous: "Saint Genet, Palestinien et poète." *L'Autre Journal* 18: 23–24.

Un captif amoreaux. Paris: Gallimard. Posthumous. (*Prisoner of Love.* Translated by Barbara Bray. New York: New York Review Books, 2003.)

1988

"Chère madame." Six letters to Anne Bloch, Merlin-Verlag.

Lettres à Olga et Marc Barbezat. Lyon: M. Barbezat, L'Arbalète.

1991

L'Ennemi déclaré. Paris: Gallimard. Posthumous. (*The Declared Enemy*, Jeff Fort).

1992

"Genet à Shatila." Paris: Solin. Posthumous. New edition, Arles: Actes Sud, "Babel" collection, 1994.

2000

Lettres au petit Franz (1943–1944). Paris: Le Promeneur.

2003

Théâtre complet. Edited by Michel Corbin and Albert Dichy. Paris: Gallimard, 2002.

Undated

Un captif amoureux, volume I, Souvenirs I, Souvenirs II. Manuscript. Gallimard Collection.

Bibliography

Abi Sa'ab, P. "Le contenu et la marge: une leçon qui s'appelle Jean Genet." *Al yom assabeh* 2 (Arabic.) (June 1986).

Abood, Edward. "Genet, an Underground Man." *Psychological Perspectives* 2 (Fall 1971): 113–125.

Adams, Stephen D. *The Homosexual as Hero in Contemporary Fiction.* New York: Vision Press, 1980.

Afnan El Kasm. "Entre Pound et Genet, la Palestine." *El Talia'a Arabia* (Arabic), July 21, 1986.

Ahmed. *Une vie d'Algérien, est-ce que ça fait un livre que les gens vont lire?* Paris: Seuil, 1973.

Ajchenbaum, Yves-Marc. "Une division SS islamiste en Bosnie." *Le Monde du dimanche*, November 14, 1993.

Applebaum, J. "Citizen Genet." *Berkeley Tribe Newspaper*, March 27, 1970.

A. Artaud, "Révélations" (December 1943), *Là Tour de feu*, no. 63–64 (June 1948): 32.

Attinelli, Lucio. "Genet et l'Italie." *Cahiers des saisons* 21 (January 15, 1960): 50–51.

Bacigalupo, Massimo. "Ezra Pound's Cantos 72 and 73: An Annotated Translation." *Paideuma* 20, no. 1–2 (1991): 9–41.

Baker, H. "Genet Pleads Cause of the Black Panthers." *MIT Tech Newspaper*, March 17, 1970.

Banier, François Marie. "Jean Genet et Angela Davis." *Le Monde*, October 23, 1970.

Bataille, Georges. *Visions of Excess: Selected Writings 1927–1939.* Translated by A. Stoekl, C.R. Lovitt and D.M. Leslie Jr. Manchester: Manchester University Press, 1985.

Becker, Jillian. *Hitler's Children: Story of the Baader-Meinhof Terrorist Gang.* Philadelphia: Lippincott, 1977.

Bell, J. Bowyer. "Arafat's Man in the Mirror: The Myth of the Fedayeen." *New Middle East* 19 (April 1970): 19–24.

Bella, Moshe. *The World of Jabotinsky* (Hebrew). Jerusalem, 1984.

Ben Jelloun, Tahar. *Harrouda.* Paris: Éditions du Seuil, 1973.

———. "Un entretien avec J. Genet sur les immigrés." *Le Monde*, November 11, 1974.

———. "Pour Jean Genet." *Le Monde*, September 24, 1977.

———. "Jean Genet avec les Palestiniens." *Le Monde diplomatique*, July 1979.

———. "Le mal-pensant et la féministe." Following a testimony from Amidou (actor in *Paravents*). *Jeune Afrique*, May 7, 1986.

Bergen, Veronique. *Jean Genet: entre mythe et réalité*. Preface by M. Surya. De Boeck Université, 1993.

Bergson, Henri. *The Two Sources of Morality and Religion*. Translated by R.A. Audra and C. Brereton, with W.H. Carter. New York: Henry Holt and Company, 1935.

Berque, Jacques. *L'Islam au défi*. Paris: Gallimard, 1980.

Berrada. "Jean Genet seul dans sa chambre." *Al yom assabeh* 28 (Arabic) (April 1986): 39.

Bersani, Leo. *A Future for Astyanax: Character and Desire in Literature*. Boston: Little, Brown and Co., 1976.

Berzen, A. "Orientalism and After: An Interview with Edward Said." *Radical Philosophy* 63 (Spring 1993): 22–32.

Bigsby, C.W.E. "The Public Self: The Black Autobiography." *Zeitschrift für Literaturwissenschaft und Linguistik* 9, no. 35 (1979): 27–42.

Birch, Thomas H. "The Incarceration of Wildness: Wilderness Areas as Prisons." *Environmental Ethics*, 1990, no. 12: 3–26.

Black Panther Newspaper, January 26, 1968.

Blumenfeld, Samuel. "Antisionisme et antisémitisme de Jean Genet: analyse critique d'*Un captif amoureux*." *Pardès* 6 (1987): 117–125.

Boguiml, S. "Poésie et violence: Dorst, Müller, Genet." *Revue de la Société d'histoire du théâtre* 38 (1986): 20–38.

Boisdeffre, Pierre de. "L'expérience de la révolte: Leiris, Genet." In *Où va le roman?* Paris: Del Duca, 1972.

———. "Réponse à Jean Genet: comment faire face à la violence?" *Le Monde*, September 17, 1977.

Bonis, J. de and C. Glucksmann. "Jean Genet témoigne pour les Soledad Brothers." *La Nouvelle Critique* 5 (June 1971): 54–63.

Boudjedra, Rachid. *Journal palestinien* (1972). French translation, Paris, 1982.

Bougon, Patrice. "Un captif amoureux." *L'Infini* 22 (Summer 1988): 109–126.

Breton, André. *Œuvres complètes*. Paris: Gallimard, Pléiade, 1992.

Brigouleix, B. "La presse allemande accuse *Le Monde* d'antigermanisme." *Le Monde*, September 14, 1977.

Brynen, Rex. *Sanctuary and Survival: The PLO in Lebanon*. Boulder: Westview Press, 1990.

Bülow, Catherine von and Fazia Ben Ali. *La Goutte-d'Or ou le Mal des racines*. Paris: Grasset, 1979.

Burroughs, William. "Eccentric View." *Time*, September 6, 1968.

———. "The Coming of the Purple Better One." *Esquire*, November 1978, 89–91.

Butler, Judith. "Desire and Recognition in Sartre's *Saint Genet* and *The Family Idiot*." *International Philosophy Quarterly* 26, no. 4 (1986): 359–374.

Carpenter, Humphrey. *A Serious Character: The Life of Ezra Pound*. Boston: Houghton Mifflin, 1988.

Carré, O. "Arafat vingt ans après: 'Cent ans de solitude ...'" *Maghreb-Machrek* 104 (June 1984): 51–65.

Celan, Paul. *Paul Celan: Poems*. Translated by Michael Hamburger. New York: Persea Books, 1980.

Chaliand, Gerard. *The Palestinian Resistance*. Translated by Michael Perl. New York: Penguin, 1972.

Chester, Alfred. *Looking for Genet: Literary Essays and Reviews*. Santa Rosa: Black Sparrow Press, 1992.

Chevaly, Maurice. *Genet*. Marseille: Le Temps parallèle, "Rencontes" collection, 1989.

Choukri, Mohamed. "L'homme que Genet n'a pas giflé," interview. *Jeune Afrique*, August 6, 1986, 50–51.

———. *Jean Genet et Tennessee Williams à Tanger*. Paris: Quai Voltaire, 1993.

———. *Jean Genet in Tangier*. Translated by Paul Bowles. New York: Ecco Press, 1974.

Clark, Kenneth B. *The Negro protest: James Baldwin, Malcolm X, Martin Luther King talk with Kenneth B. Clark*. Boston: Beacon Press, 1963.

Cleaver, Eldridge. "Three Notes from Exile." *Ramparts*, September 1969.

Cleaver, Kathleen. "On Eldridge Cleaver." *Ramparts*, June 1969, 4–11.

Clerc, Michel. "Quand Jean Genet vient boire à la Sorbonne le petit lait de la révolution." *L'Aurore*, May 31, 1968.

Cocteau, Jean. *Le Passé défini*. Paris, 1983.

Coe, Richard N. "Les anarchistes de droite. Ionesco, Beckett, Genet, Arrabal." *Cahiers de la Compagnie Renaud-Barrault* 67 (September 1968): 99–125.

————. "Jean Genet: A Check-List of his Works in French, English and German." *Australian Journal of French Studies* 6, no. 1 (1969).

————. *The Theater of Jean Genet, A Case-Book.* New York: Grove Press, 1970.

Cohn-Bendit, Daniel. "Entretien." *Le Nouvel Observateur*, November 24, 1977.

Colle, Jean-Louis. *Le Sacré dans l'œuvre de Jean Genet.* Doctorate thesis. Paris-IV, 1990.

Colomes, F. "La Fraction Armée Rouge." *Le Point*, October 24, 1977.

Committee on Internal Security. *The Black Panther Party: Its Origin and Development as Reflected in its Official Weekly Newspaper "The Black Panther Black Community News Service."* Washington: US Government Printing, 1970.

Critchley, Simon. "Writing the Revolution: The Politics of Truth in Genet's *Prisoner of Love." Radical Philosophy* 56 (Fall 1990): 25–34.

Dachy, Marc. *Dada & les Dadaïsmes.* Paris: Gallimard, "Essay Folio" collection, 1994.

Dagher, C. "Sur la tombe de Jean Genet." *Al Hayat* (Arabic), August 1992.

Daney, Serge. "Un chant d'amour." *Cahiers du cinéma* 264 (February 1976): 60.

Darnton, John. "Genet Emerges as an Idol of Panthers." *New York Times*, May 1, 1970.

Darwish, Mahmoud. *Memory for Forgetfulness: August, Beirut, 1982.* Translated by I. Muhawi. Berkeley and Los Angeles: University of California Press, 1995.

Dattas, Lydie. *La chaste vie de Jean Genet.* Paris: Gallimard, 2006.

Dauga, Jean. "Le monde de Jean Genet." *La Revue universelle* 36 (October 1977): 80–82.

Davis, A. "Journées Jean Genet." Paris, Théâtre de l'Odéon, May 1991.

Davis, Colin. *"Un captif amoureux* and the Commitment of Jean Genet." *French Studies Bulletin, A Quarterly Supplement*, Summer 1987, no. 23: 16–18.

Deguy, Michel. "Genet, Saint John Perse, Zanzotto." *Sud* 78–79 (1988): 16–21.

Deleuze, Gilles. "La honte et la gloire: T.E. Lawrence." In *Critique et Clinique*, 143–157. Paris: Minuit, 1993.

De Quincey, Thomas. "On Murder Considered as One of the Fine Arts." In

Selected Writings. Edited by P. Van Doren Stern. London: The Nonesuch Press; New York: Random House, 1939.

Derrida, Jacques. *Glas* (1974). Paris: Denoël/Gonthier, 1981.

———. "Autour de 'Quartre heures à Shatila.'" (Debate at Gennevilliers Theatre.) March 21, 1992.

Detrez, Conrad. "Une lecture de *Notre-Dame-des-Fleurs*. Jean Genet, écrivain religieux." *Masques* 12 (Winter 1981–82): 54–57.

Dichy, Albert. Critical edition of *L'Ennemi Déclaré* (see Jean Genet, 1991).

Dichy, Albert. *Jean Genet, essai de chronologie*. Paris: Gallimard, 2010.

Dichy, Albert and Pascal Fouché. *Jean Genet: essai de chronologie 1910–1944*. Paris, 1988.

Dieckhoff, Alain. *The Invention of a Nation: Zionist Thought and the Making of Modern Israel*. Translated by Jonathan Derrick. New York: Columbia University Press, 2003.

Duault, Nicole. "A la Sorbonne: 'Ma supériorité sur vous, c'est que je suis inculte,' déclare le poète Jean Genet." *France-Soir*, May 31, 1968.

Dubois, Claude. "Genet duplice?" *Études* 337 (July 1972): 64–73.

Duverger, Maurice. "Le fascisme rouge." *Le Monde*, September 11–12, 1977.

Eddé, Dominique. *Le crime de Jean Genet*. Paris: Seuil, 2007.

Ellul, Jacques. "La violence c'est la violence." *Le Monde*, September 8, 1977.

Epps, Brad. "Thievish Subjectivity: Self-Writing in Jean Genet and Juan Goytisolo." *Revista de estudios hispanicos* 26 (1992): 163–181.

Erasmus. *Opera omnia*, Vol. 1, bk. 4. Amsterdam, 1969.

———. *Collected Works of Erasmus: Literary and Educational Writings (ER)*. Toronto: University of Toronto Press, 1989.

———. *Collected Works of Erasmus: Expositions of the Psalms, Volume 64 (ER2)*. Toronto: University of Toronto Press.

———. *The Correspondence of Erasmus: Letters 1252–1355 (1522–1523)*. Toronto: University of Toronto Press, 1989.

Eribon, Didier. *Michel Foucault*. Translated by Betsy Wing. Cambridge: Harvard University Press, 1991.

———. *Une morale du minoritaire: variations sur un thème de Jean Genet*. Paris: Fayard, 2001.

Fay, M. and O. Sol Dourdin. "Genet tel qu'en lui-même." *Lamalif* (Morocco), June 1986, 58–59.

FBI files: Hampton, *The National Observer*, September 2, 1968.

Feal, Gisèle. "*Le Balcon* de Genet ou le culte matriarchal." *The French Review* 48, no. 5 (April 1975): 897–907.

Feinstein, M. "Genet Calls Black Panthers Camarades." *CCNY Observation Post Newspaper,* April 10, 1970.

Ferro, Marc. *Colonization: a Global History.* Translated by K.D. Prithipaul. London: Routledge, 1997.

Fioupou, Christiane. "Wole Soyinka / Jean Genet. Images et reflets du pouvoir: une Danse des Géants ou la métamorphose des Triplés." *Nouvelles du Sud* 5 (1987): 29–61.

———. "Le pouvoir sur scène: contorsions politiques dans le théâtre de Soyinka." *Cahiers d'études africaines* (Paris) 29 (1989): 419–445.

Foner, Philip S. *Black Panthers Speak.* Cambridge, MA: Da Capo Press, 2002.

Foucault, Michel. "Va-t-on aider Klaus Croissant?" *Le Nouvel Observateur,* November 14–20, 1977.

———. "Lettre à quelques leaders de la gauche." *Le Nouvel Observateur,* November 28–December 4, 1977.

———. "Wir fühlten uns als schmutzige Spezies." *Der Spiegel.* December 19, 1977.

———. "Alain Peyrefitte s'explique … et M. Foucault lui répond." *Le Nouvel Observateur,* January 23, 1978.

———. *Power, Truth, Strategy.* Sydney: Feral Publications, 1979.

———. In *Libération,* June 30, 1984.

———. *Dits et Écrits.* Paris: Gallimard, 1994.

———. "The Lives of Infamous Men." In *The Essential Works of Foucault 1954–1984,* Volume 3, 157–175. New York: The New Press, 2000.

Foucher, Michel. "Israël-Palestine: quelles frontières? Géographie physique et humaine de la Cisjourdanie." *Hérodote* 29–30 (September 1983).

Frechtman, Bernard. "Gesprek met Jean Genet." *Litterair paspoort,* May–June 1953, 142–143.

Frechtman file. The Moraly Collection.

Fredette, Nathalie. "A propos de la fiction autobiographique." *Études françaises* (Montréal) 26, no. 1 (Spring 1990): 131–145.

Gadda, Carlo Emilio. "Il faut d'abord être coupable sur Genet." *Change* 39 (1980): 8–18.

Gaitet, Pascale. "Jean Genet's American Dream: The Black Panthers." *Literature and History* 1 (1992): 48–63.

Geertz, Clifford. "Genet's Last Stand: *Prisoner of Love.*" *New York Review of Books* 39, no. 19 (November 19, 1992): 3–7.

Giles, Jane. *Le Cinéma de Jean Genet.* Paris: Macula, 1993.

Givet, Jacques. *La Gauche contre Israël? Essai sur le néo-antisémitisme.* Paris: Pauvert, 1968.

Goldschmidt, Georges-Arthur. "'La bande à Baader' et le phénomène de la totalisation." *Allemagne d'aujourd'hui* 58 (May–June 1977).

Goytisolo, Juan. *Les Royaumes déchirés.* Translated by J. Lacor. Paris, 1988.

———. "Le poète enterré à Larache." *Revue d'études palestiniennes* 45 (Fall 1992).

Grazia, Edward de. "An Interview with Jean Genet." *Cardozo Studies in Law and Literature* 5, no. 2 (Fall 1993): 307–324.

Greilsamer, Laurent. "Jacques Vergès, un maître iconoclaste." *Le Monde,* May 11, 1987.

Grimblat, "La communauté chiite libanaise et le mouvement national palestinien 1967–1986." *Guerres mondiales et Conflits contemporains* 151 (July 1988): 71–91.

Guattari, Félix. "Genet retrouvé." *Revue d'études palestiniennes* 21 (Fall 1986).

Guyon, Marc. "La politesse de Jean Genet." *La Nouvelle Revue française* 465 (October 1991): 61–65.

Guyotat, R. "Genet à Mettray." *Le Monde,* October 3, 1992.

Hanrez, Marc. "Un rituel érotico-guerrier: *Pompes funèbres.*" *Kentucky Romance Quarterly* (Lexington) 15 (1968): 387–393.

Harding, Vincent. "The Religion of Black Power." In *The World Year Book of Religions.* London: Evans Brothers, 1969.

Harris, Frederick J. "Linguistic Reality–Historical Reality: Genet, Céline, Grass." *Neohelicon* 14 (Acta Comparationis Litterarum Universum) (1987): 8–16.

Hassan, Ihab. *The Dismemberment of Orpheus.* New York: Oxford University Press, 1971.

Henric, Jacques. "Monsieur Jean Genet, nouveau patriote." *Libération,* September 21, 1977.

———. "Aux couleurs de la France." *Art Press International* 11 (October 1977): 5.

———. "Merci Jean Genet, vous au moins vous dîtes vrai." *Art Press International,* December 1977, 2.

Héron, Pierre-Marie. "Jean Genet et Fontevrault: une mythologie à usage privé." Fontevrault: Histoire-archéologie, 1992.

———. "Sur un biographie attendue de Genet: la vérité de la littérature." Université Paul-Valéry/Montpellier-III (letter to author), 1994.

————. *Esthétique et Morale dans les œuvres de Marcel Jouhandeau et Jean Genet*. Thesis. Paris-III, 1995.

Hervic, Elisabeth. "L'espace des *Paravents*, espace d'un mystère." *Revue d'histoire du théâtre* 2 (1983): 251–266.

Hilliard, David. "The Ideology of the Black Panther Party." *Black Panther Newspaper*, November 8, 1969.

Hilliard, David and Lewis Cole. *This Side of Glory: The Autobiography of David Hilliard and the Story of the Black Panther Party*. Boston: Back Bay Books, 1993.

Israel, Abigail. "The Aesthetic of Violence: Rimbaud and Genet." *Yale French Studies* 46 (1971): 157–160.

Issa, Mahmoud (Selim). *Je suis un fedayin*. Paris, 1976.

Jablonka, Ivan. *Les vérités inavouables de Jean Genet*. Paris: Seuil, 2004.

Jackson, George. *Blood in my Eye*. New York: Random House, 1972.

Jasem, F. "Genet et de Beauvoir: mais qu'est-ce qu'il y a derrière cette contradiction?" *El Talia'a Arabia* 157 (Arabic) (May 12, 1986).

Jehad. *Al yom assabeh*, April 20, 1987. Translated by B. El Omari and Hadrien Laroche.

Jones, Charles E. "The Political Repression of the Black Panther Party 1966–1971: The Case of the Oakland Bay Area." *Journal of Black Studies* 18, no. 4 (1988): 415–434.

Josselin, Jean-Francois. "Pas de purgatoire pour Jean Genet." *Le Nouvel Observateur*, November 21, 1977.

Jouffroy, Alain. "Rimbaud, T.E. Lawrence, Genet et les marais occidentaux." *Revue des deux mondes*, June 1991, 135–143.

Kadra, H. *Aspects politiques du "Journal du Voleur."* Master's thesis. Paris-VII, 1991.

Kapeliouk, Amnon. *Sabra and Shatila: Inquiry into a Massacre*. London: Five Leaves, 1984.

Kandell, J. "Genet on Terrorism." *New York Times*, September 7, 1977.

Kasm, Afnan el. "Between Pound and Genet, Palestine." In *El Talia'a Arabia* ["Arab avant-garde"] (July 21, 1986).

Kassir, Samir and Farouk Mardam-Bey. *Itinéraires de Paris à Jerusalem: la France et le conflit israélo-arabe*. Book 2, 1958–1991. Paris: Les livres de la *Revue d'études palestiniennes*, 1993.

Kazen, J. "L'adorateur des Palistiniens." *Al yom assabeh* (Arabic), April 20, 1987, 38–39.

Kerouani, O. and C. Ben Achour. "Jean Genet et les Arabes." IMA press kit. Paris, 1992.

Khatibi, Abdelkébir. *Vomito Blanco: le sionisme et la conscience malheureuse.* "10/18" collection. Paris: Bourgois, 1974.

———. *Figures de l'étranger dans la littérature française.* Paris: Denoël, 1987. See especially pp. 160–167.

Khun, Reinhard. "Genet: Prisoner of Society." In *Fiction, Form, Experience: The French Novel from Naturalism to the Present.* Montréal: Éditions France-Québec, 1976. Also in J.E. Flowers, *Writers and Politics in Modern France (1909–1961),* 160–167. London, 1977.

Klausmann-Molter, Birgit. *Außenseiter Frau, zur Darstellung der Frau in den Werken von Jean Genet.* Germany: Peter Lang, 1986.

Kleffner, Heike. "The Black Panthers: Interviews with Geronimo ji Jaga Pratt and Mumia Abu Jamal." *Race and Class* 35, no. 1 (July–September 1993): 14, 24.

Kramer, Martin. "Arab Nationalism: Mistaken Identity." *Daedalus* 122, no. 3 (Summer 1993): 171–207. See especially p. 196.

Krivine, Alain. "La Fraction Armée Rouge." *Rouge,* September 7, 1977.

Lange, Monique. *Les Cahiers déchirés.* Paris: Nil, 1994.

Laquer, Walter and Barry Rubin, eds. *The Israel-Arab Reader: A Documentary History of the Middle East Conflict.* New York: Penguin, 2008.

Laroche, Hadrien. "Le terrorisme de l'amour et de la langue." *Kanal magazine* 35–36 (Spring 1988).

———. "Le dernier Genet." *L'immature, littérature* 3 (1993): 80–82.

———. "Gulliver: politique de Genet." *Les Inrockuptibles* 51 (December 1993): 74–80.

———. "Actualité de Jean Genet." *Universalia,* Annual supplement to *l'Encyclopædia Universalis.* 1994, 449.

———. "Les doigts pleins de spectres: Genet auprès des Palestiniens." *Revue d'études palestiniennes* 57, no. 5 (September 1995): 60–73.

———. *Le Dernier Genet,* new paperback edition. Paris: Champs-Flammarion, 2010.

Latner, Teishan. *The Quotable Rebel: Political Quotations for Dangerous Times.* Monroe: Common Courage Press, 2005.

Lautrette, Laurence. *Pour Jean Genet.* Paris: Éditions Hors Commerce, 1994.

Lawrence, T.E. *The Seven Pillars of Wisdom.* Fordingbridge: J. and N. Wilson, 1992.

Lebouleux, Jean. "Genet: Non aux idoles, oui à l'homme." *Combat*, May 31, 1968, 13.

Le Monde, October 10, 1970.

Lévy, Bernard-Henri. *Les Aventures de la liberté*. Paris, 1991.

Lewis, Bernard. *Islam in History: Ideas, Men and Events in the Middle East*. London: Alcove Press, 1973.

Libération, November 23, 1993.

Liégeois, J.-P. *Angela Davis et Jean Genet, gens de liberté*. Paris, 1978.

Lloyd, David. "Genet's Genealogy: European Minorities and the Ends of the Canon." In *The Nature and Context of Minority Discourse*, edited by D. Lloyd and A. Jan Mohamed. Oxford: Oxford University Press, 1990.

Luttmann, Stephen. "Narrators, Narrated Realities and the Nature of Artwork in Jean Genet's Novel *Querelle de Brest* and Rainer Werner Fassbinder's Film *Querelle*." *Kodikas, Code-Ars semiotica* 14 (1991): 9–35.

Lyotard, Jean-François and Jean-Loup Thébaud. *Just Gaming*. Translated by Wlad Godzich. Minneapolis: University of Minnesota Press, 1985.

Magazine littéraire 174 (June 1981), *Jean Genet par lui-même*.

Malcolm X. *The Speeches at Harvard*. New York: W. Morrow, 1968.

———. *Malcolm X Talks to Young People: Speeches in the US, Britain, and Africa*. New York: Pathfinder Press, 1991.

———. *Malcolm X Speaks: Selected Speeches and Statements*. Edited by G. Breitman. New York: Grove Press, 1994.

Malcolm X and A. Haley. *The Autobiography of Malcolm X: As Told to Alex Haley*. New York: Ballantine, 1992.

Marcus, Yoel. "The War Is Inevitable." *Ha'Haretz*, March 26, 1982.

Martin, Graham Dunstan. "Racism in Genet's *Les Nègres*." *Modern Language Review* 70 (1975): 517–525.

Marty, Éric. *Bref séjour à Jérusalem*. Paris: Gallimard, 2003.

———. *Jean Genet, post-scriptum*. Lagrasse: Verdier, 2006.

Mauriac, Claude. "Les espaces imaginires." In *Le Temps immobile*. Paris, 1975.

Meinhof, Ulrike. *Textes de prisonniers de la Fraction Armée rouge et dernières lettres D'Ulrike Meinhof*. Paris: Maspero, 1977.

———. *Everybody is Talking About the Weather – We Don't: The Writings of Ulrike Meinhof*. Edited by K. Bauer. New York: Seven Stories Press, 2008.

Meitinger, Serge. "L'irréel de jouissance dans *Le Journal du voleur* de Genet." *Poétique* 62 (May 1986): 65–74.

Ménager, Serge Dominique. "Disparaître: de l'invisibilité comme technique de survie chez Jean Genet." *University of Natal journal,* n.d.: 67–75.

Ménager, Serge Dominique and Vanessa Samways. "Remembrance of Genet's Passing. Jean Genet's Tomb." *Journal of Studies in the Arts, Humanities and Social Sciences, Literature,* May 1986, no. 62: 65–74.

Mickolus, Edward F. *Transnational Terrorism: A Chronology of Events, 1968–1979.* London: Aldwich Press, 1980.

Milianti, Alain. "Le fils de la honte: notes sur l'engagement politique de Jean Genet." *Revue d'études palestiniennes* 4 (Winter 1992): 205–212.

Milstein, Tom. "A Perspective on the Panthers." *Commentary,* September 1970.

Moraly, Jean-Bernard Yehouda. "Les cinq vies de Jean Genet." *Revue d'histoire du théâtre* 3 (1986): 219–245.

———. "La critique selon Jean Genet." *Le Français dans le monde,* February–March 1988, 104–109.

———. "Claude le fou, Genet le sage." *Revue d'histoire du théâtre* 40 (October–December 1988): 311–329.

Nachman, Larry David. "Violence in the Court: The Political Meaning of Chicago." *The Nation,* March 23, 1970.

Naïm, M. "Les massacres de Sabra et Shatila." *Le Monde,* September 13–14 1992, section entitled "Il y a dix ans."

Nerval, Gérard de. *Voyage en Orient.* Volume 2, Chapter 1 in *Oeuvres complètes.* Paris: Gallimard, Pléiade edition, 1984.

Newton, Huey P., Bobby Seale, and Eldridge Cleaver. *Black Panther Leaders Speak.* Edited by G. Louis Heath. Metuchen: Scarecrow Press, 1976.

No. Matricule 1155. Exhibit catalogue, "La Rupture." Le Creusot, March 1, 1983.

Nora, Pierre. *Les Lieux de mémoire,* tome 2: *La Nation.* Paris: Gallimard, 1986.

Obstfeld, Renee. "Idealization, Transformation, and Disillusion in the Art of a Cross-addicted Transsexual." *American Journal of Art Therapy* 32, no. 1 (1993): 12–21.

O'Donnell, Thomas J. "T.E. Lawrence and the Confessional Tradition: Either Angel or Beast." *Genre* 9, no. 2 (Summer 1976): 135–151.

Olender, Maurice. *The Languages of Paradise: Race, Religion, and Philology in the Nineteenth Century.* Translated by Arthur Goldhammer. Cambridge: Harvard University Press, 2008.

Oswald, Laura R. *Jean Genet and the Semiotics of Performance.* Bloomington: Indiana University Press, 1989.

———. "Middle East voices: *Un captif amoureux* et 'Quatres heures à Shatila.'" *Diacritics,* Spring 1991, 46–62.

Pasolini, Pier Paolo. *Petrolio.* Translated by A. Goldstein. New York: Pantheon, 1997.

———. *Qui je suis* (1966). Paris: Arléa, 1994.

Paxton, Robert O. "The Five Stages of Fascism." The Journal of Modern History 70, no. 1 (March 1998): 1–23.

Perlmutter, Amos. "The Crisis of the PLO: Dilemmas of an Absolutist Movement." *Encounter,* February 1988, 27.

Picaudou, Nadine. "Genèse des élites politiques palestiniennes: 1948–1982." *Revue française de sciences politiques* 34, no. 2 (April 1984): 324–351.

Pinguet, Catherine. "Mourir en un temps bref ou chanter pour l'éternité (Jean Genet et la résistance palestinienne)." *Lignes* 19 (May 1993): 98–110.

Piper, Adrien. *Out of the Corner.* Installation at the Whitney Museum of American Art, New York, October 1990.

"Point: L'UNRWA." *Le Monde,* January 14, 1994.

Polli, G. "Un captif amoureaux." *Francofonia* 8, no. 14 (1998–1989).

Poulet, R. "Jean Genet ou l'ennemi." In *Aveux spontanés,* 109–114. Paris, 1963.

Pound, Ezra. *The Cantos of Ezra Pound.* New York: New Directions, 1996.

R.V. "L'Allemagne démocratique en proie au terrorisme." *Rivarol,* September 8, 1977.

Rabate, Jean-Michel. *La Beauté amère. Fragments d'esthétique.* Paris, 1986.

Redonnet, Marie. *Jean Genet, le poète travesti: portrait d'une œuvre.* Paris: B. Grasset, 2000.

Regnault, François. *La Famille des orties: esquisses et croquis autour des 'Paravents' de Jean Genet.* Nanterre/Amandiers, 1983.

Revel, Jean-François. *Le Terrorisme contre la démocratie.* Paris, 1987. See especially pp. 13–17.

Rodinson, Maxime. *The Arabs.* Translated by Arthur Goldhammer. Chicago: University of Chicago Press, 1981.

Roudinesco, Élisabeth. *Retour sur la question juive.* Paris: Albin Michel, 2009.

"Rubin Says the Old Put Young on Trial." *CCNY Observation Post Newspaper,* March 13, 1970.

Rushdie, Salman. *Satanic Verses.* New York: Viking, 1989.

————. *Imaginary Homelands: Essays and Criticism 1981–1991*. London: Granta Books, 1991.

Saïd, Edward. "On Jean Genet's Late Work." *Grand Street* 9 (1990): 27–42.

————. "Les derniers écrits de Jean Genet." *Revue d'études palestiniennes* 39 (Spring 1991).

————. "Reflections on Twenty Years of Palestinian History." *Journal of Palestine Studies* 20, no. 4 (Summer 1991): 5–22.

————. "*Orientalism* and After: An Interview with Edward Said." *Radical Philosophy* 63 (spring 1993): 22–32.

Sanbar, Elias. *Les Palestiniens dans le siècle*. Paris: Gallimard, 1994.

Sandarg, Robert Morrison. *Jean Genet: Thirty Years of Criticism in France, England and America*. Thesis. Chapel Hill: University of North Carolina; *Dissertation Abstract* 36, no. 12 (December 1975–76): 3702 A.

————. "Greco-Roman Mythology in Genet's Novels." *Romance Notes* 20 (1979–80): 163–166.

————. "Jean Genet in America." *French-American Review* 1 (1976): 47–53.

————. "The Politics of Jean Genet." *Research Studies* 50, no. 3 (1982): 111–118.

————. "Jean Genet and the Black Panther Party." *Journal of Black Studies* 16, no. 3 (March 1986).

————. "Genet in Chicago." *Romance Quarterly* 38 (Lexington) (1991): 39–47.

Sartre, Jean-Paul. *Saint Genet comédien et martyr*. Paris, 1952.

Savona, Jeannette Laillou "Théâtre et univers carcéral: Jean Genet et Michel Foucault." *French Forum* 10, no. 2 (May 1985): 201–214.

Scherer, René. "Deux saints tutélaires: Genet, Pasolini." Chapter 8 in *Zeus hospitalier*. Paris: Armand Colin, 1993.

Seale, Bobby. *Seize the Time*. New York: Random House, 1970.

Sellin, Eric. "The Oriental Influence in Modern Western Drama." *France-Asie-Asia* 187 (Fall 1966): 85–92.

Segev, Tom. *The Seventh Million: the Israelis and the Holocaust*. Translated by H. Watzman. New York: Holt Paperbacks, 2000.

Sharabi, Hisham. "Un captif amoureux." *Journal of Palestine Studies* 16, no. 4 (Winter 1987): 129–132.

Simont, Juliette. "Bel effet d'où jaillissent les roses: à propos du *Saint Genet* de Sartre et du *Glas* de Derrida." *Les Temps modernes* 44, no. 510 (January 1989): 113–139.

Sivanandan, A. "Race: The Politics of Existence." *Politics and Society* 1, no. 2 (January 1971): 225-233.

Sohlich, W.F. "Genet's *The Blacks* and *The Screens*: Dialectic of Refusal and Revolutionary Consciousness." *Comparative Drama* 10, no. 3 (Fall 1976): 216-235.

Sollers, Phillippe. "Physique de Jean Genet." In *La Guerre du goût*. Paris: Gallimard, 1994.

Stanciu, V.V. "La victime et le tyran." *Le Monde*, September 10, 1977.

Steiner, Anne and Loïc Debray. *La Fraction Armée rouge: guérilla urbaine en Europe occidentale*. Paris: Méridiens-Klincksieck, 1987.

Stewart, Harry E. "Jean Genet's Favorite Murderers." *The French Reveiew* 60, no. 5 (April 1987): 635-643.

———. "Jean Genet's *mentalité douteuse*." *Romance Quarterly* 39 (1992): 299-310.

———. "Jean Genet from Fascism to Nihilism." Lang, *Romance Language and Literature* 205, American Universities Studies (1993).

Sward, S. "Genet Urges Whites to Support Panthers." *UCLA Daily Bruin*, April 28, 1970.

Taguieff, Pierre-André. *Les Protocoles des Sages de Sion: introduction à l'étude des "Protocoles," un faux et ses usages dans le siècle*." Paris: Berg International, 1992. See especially p. 356.

Thomasseau, Jean-Marie. "Genet et l'anthroponymie maghrébine, les noms propres féminins dans 'Les Paravents.'" *Poétique* 54 (April 1983): 213-232.

Van Zele, M. "Jean Genet: le brûlot." Presentation of a documentary project for France 3, a Cinétévé production. Paris, October 1994.

Vannouvong, Agnès. *Jean Genet: les revers du genre*. Dijon: Les presses du réel, 2010.

Varaut, Jean-Marc. *Poètes en prison: de Charles d'Orléans à Jean Genet*. Paris, 1989.

Vesper, Bernward. *Die Reise: Romanessay*. Jossa, 1983.

Viderman, S. "L'écriture ambiguë de Genet." *Revue française de psychanalyse* 38, no. 1 (January 1974): 137-151.

Walker, David H. "Revolution and Revisions in Genet's *Le Balcon*." *Modern Language Review* 79, no. 4 (October 1984): 817-831.

Walter, Eric. "La prison-poème ou les disciplines perverties. Jalons pour relire Genet à la lumière de Michel Foucault." In *Jean Genet aujourd'hui*, 5-33. Maison de la culture d'Amiens, December 1976.

Warner, Keith Q. "*Les Nègres*: A Look at Genet's Excursion into Black

Consciousness." *College Language Association Journal* 26, no. 4 (June 1983): 397–414.

Watts, Philip. "Political Discourse and Poetic Register in Jean Genet's *Pompes funèbres.*" *French Forum* 17 (1992): 191–203.

Weatherby, W.J. "After the Panthers—What Next?" *New Society*, August 1970.

Webb, Richard C. *File on Genet*. London, 1992.

Weil, Patrick. *La France et ses étrangers*. Paris: Gallimard, 1991.

Weiler, Gershon. *Jewish Theocracy*. Leiden: Brill, 1988.

Weinstein, H.E. "Conversation with Cleaver." *The Nation*, January 20, 1969.

White, Edmund. *Genet: A Biography*. New York, Knopf, 1993.

Wilcocks, Robert. "Genet's Preoccupation with Language." *Modern Language Review* 65 (1970): 785–792.

Witt, Mary Ann Frese. "Mothers and Stories, Female Presence-Power in Genet." *French Forum* 34 (Lexington) (1989): 173–186.

Filmography

Algérie, année zéro. 40′. Directed by Marceline Loridan and Jean-Pierre Sergent. France: Capi Films, 1963–64.

Anou Banou, les filles de l'utopie. Directed by Edna Politi. Israel/RFA: Citevox, 1982.

Attica. Directed by Cinda Firestone. USA, France, 1974.

Avoir vingt ans dans les Aurès. Directed by René Vautier. France: UPCB, 1972.

Berlin-Jérusalem. DVD. Directed by Amos Gitaï. France, 1989; Chicago: Facets Video, 2003.

Biram pour toujours. Directed by Ibrahim Khill. France, 1993.

Circoncision. Directed by Jean Rouch. France, 1949.

Le Conte des trois joyaux perdus (Hikayatul jawahiri thalath). VHS. Directed by Michel Khleifi. BBC/Arte, 1995; Arab Film Distribution, 2003.

Couvre-feu. Directed by Rashid Masharawi. Palestine/Pays-Bas: Argus Film Produktie, 1993.

Eldridge Cleaver. Directed by William Klein. USA: O.N.C.I.C., 1970.

Les Enfants du feu. Directed by Mai Masri. Palestine, 1990.

Et la paix alors? Directed by Ibrahim Khill. France, 1990.

Le fond de l'air est rouge. Directed by Chris Marker. France, 1977.

Le Joli Mai. Directed by Chris Marker. France: Dovidis, 1962.

Ici et ailleurs (Jusqu'à la victoire). VHS. Directed by Jean-Luc Godard, Jean-Pierre Gorin, and Anne-Marie Miéville. France: Gaumont, 1970, 1974; Chicago: Facets Video, 2000.

Lawrence of Arabia. DVD. Directed by David Lean. UK: Horizon Pictures, 1962; Culver City, CA: Columbia Tristar Home Entertainment, 2002.

Liberté, la nuit. Directed by Philippe Garrel. France: Institut National de la Communication Audiovisuelle, 1983.

Liberty belle. Directed by Pascal Kané. France: Les Films du Losange, 1983.

Loin du Vietnam. Directed by Jean-Luc Godard, Joris Ivens, William Klein, Chris Marker, Claude Lelouch, Alain Resnais, Agnès Varda. France/USA: Societé pour le Lancement des Oeuvres Nouvelles, 1966.

Maîtres fous. Directed by Jean Rouch. France: Les Films de la Pléiade, 1968.

The Fertile Memory (Al Dhakira al Khasba). DVD. Directed by Michel Khleifi. Palestine/Belgium, 1980; New York: Kino Video, 2004.

Mourir à trente ans. Directed by Romain Goupil. France: MK2 Productions, 1982.

Muriel ou le Temps d'un retour. DVD. Directed by Alain Resnais. France: Alpha Productions, 1963; London: Eureka, 2009.

Wedding in Galilee (Urs al-jalil). DVD. Directed by Michel Khleifi. London/ RFA/Belgium/France: Marisa Films, 1987; New York: Kino Video, 2004.

Octobre à Paris. Directed by Groupe Vérité-Liberté (Jacques Panijel). France, 1962.

Les Oliviers de la justice. Directed by James Blue. Algeria/France: Societé Algerienne, 1962.

Sympathy for the Devil (One plus one). DVD. Directed by Jean-Luc Godard. UK: Cupid Productions, 1968; Abkco, 2003.

Le Petit Soldat. DVD. Directed by Jean-Luc Godard. France: Les Productions Georges de Beauregard, 1960–63; New York: Fox Lorber, 2001.

Pour constat: Rudy Dutschke. Directed by Günter Gauss. Germany, 1967.

Les Réfugiés. Directed by Cécile Decugis. France, 1958.

Le Rendez-vous des quais. Directed by Paul Carpita. France: Films du Soleil, 1953–94.

Les Sacrifiés. Directed by Okacha Touita. Algeria, 1982.

La Seconda Volta. VHS. Directed by Mimmo Calopresti. Italy, 1996.

Die dritte Generation (The Third Generation). DVD. Directed by Rainer W. Fassbinder. West Germany: Filmverlag der Autoren, 1979; Escondido, CA: Tango Entertainment, 2006.

Tsahal. Directed by Claude Lanzmann. France: Bavaria Film, 1994; why not productions, 2008.

Ulrike Marie Meinhof. 16 mm. Directed by Timon Koulmasis. Germany: ARTE, 1994.

Rih al awras (The Winds of the Aures). Directed by Mohammed Lakhdar Hamina. Algeria: O.N.C.I.C., 1967.

Ha-Chayim Al-Pi Agfa (Life According to Agfa). Directed by Assi Dayan. Israel: Mecklberg Media Group, 1992.

In the Year of the Pig. Directed by Emile de Antonio. USA: Emile de Antonio Productions, 1968.

ACKNOWLEDGMENTS

I would like to thank all those who helped the English translation of this book become a reality.

Robert Ballantyne and Brian Lam, my publishers at Arsenal Pulp Press, believed in the relevance of this book in today's world and had the utmost faith in my work. It has been a pleasure being associated with people of such generosity.

David Homel, my English translator, who witnessed some of the events described herein as a young man in Chicago, was able to create a style from Genet's times that remains true to today's reader. I am grateful to him and his friendship.

Thanks also to all those who supported me during the translation process: Serge Belet, Colin Browne, Sima Godfrey, Serge Guilbault, Ralph Sarkonak, Juanita Odin, and Ian Wallace.

For the French edition of this book, my appreciation goes to Laurent Boyer, Michel Deguy, René de Ceccatty, Albert Dichy, Denis Roche, Elias Sanbar, as well as Jean-Bernard Yehouda Moraly (the Frechtman archive) and Christine Schwarz (the FBI archives), to Editions Gallimard and the staff of these libraries: the Institut Mémoires et Editions contemporaines (IMEC), the Institut des Sciences politiques (Sciences Po in Paris), the Bibliothèque nationale (Paris), the Institut du Monde Arabe (IMA, Paris), the Institut universitaire européen in Florence (Italy), and the Universities of Cairo (Egypt), Jerusalem (Israel), and New York (USA).

Thanks also to Elise, my wife, who, though she was not yet my wife, was there during my research for what would become *Le Dernier Genet* and who today, with the publication of *The Last Genet*, is still with me.

I want to end by honoring my debt to Jacques Derrida for this book.

Hadrien Laroche

INDEX